IN THE PINES

IN THE PINES

A LYNCHING, A LIE, A RECKONING

Grace Elizabeth Hale

Little, Brown and Company

New York   Boston   London

Little, Brown and Company
Hachette Book Group
1290 Avenue of the Americas, New York, NY 10104
littlebrown.com

First Edition: November 2023

Little, Brown and Company is a division of Hachette Book Group, Inc. The Little, Brown name and logo are trademarks of Hachette Book Group, Inc.

The publisher is not responsible for websites (or their content) that are not owned by the publisher.

The Hachette Speakers Bureau provides a wide range of authors for speaking events. To find out more, go to hachettespeakersbureau.com or email hachettespeakers@hbgusa.com.

Little, Brown and Company books may be purchased in bulk for business, educational, or promotional use. For information, please contact your local bookseller or the Hachette Book Group Special Markets Department at special.markets@hbgusa.com.

Maps by James Fenelon

ISBN 9780316564748
LCCN 2023935282

Printing 1, 2023

LSC-C

Printed in the United States of America

for the people who have died at the hands of the law

CONTENTS

Maps	*viii–ix*
Foreword by John Grisham	*xi*
Author's Note	*xv*
Prologue: Two Tales	xvii
Introduction: Splinters and Silence	xxvii
Part I: The Road to the Lipsey Farm	
1: In the Pines	3
2: A Gamble	18
3: A Separate World	26
4: Black Boy	44
Part II: "Quiet and Orderly"	
5: The Law	65
6: Gone Underground	90
7: A Lie	116
8: The Cost	133
Epilogue: Unwritten History	160
Acknowledgments	*167*
A Note on Sources	*171*
Notes	*175*
Illustration Credits	*201*
Index	*203*

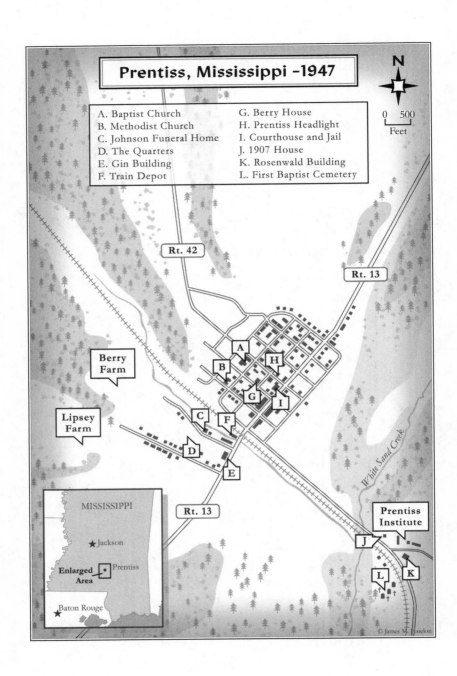

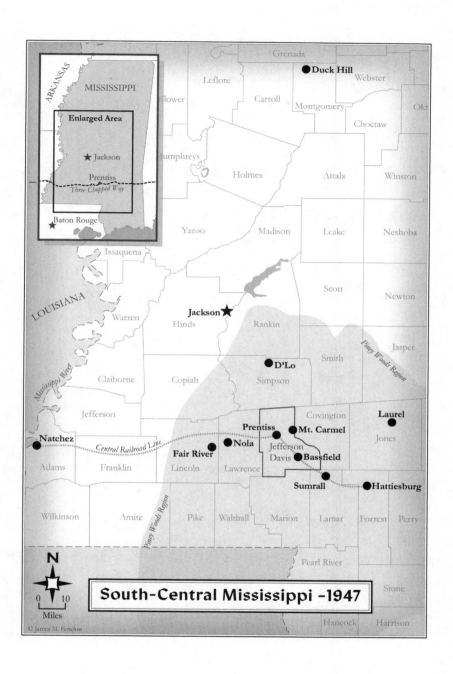

FOREWORD

In 2018, the Equal Justice Initiative opened the National Lynching Museum, as it is informally known, in downtown Montgomery, Alabama. It is an open-air structure, and under its roof are 805 steel rectangular boxes, hanging from the ceiling. Each box represents a county, virtually all in the South, in which a black person was lynched by a white mob. The names of the victims are cut into the steel in neat block letters, along with the dates of the lynchings. There are 4,400 names, all of individuals murdered between 1877 and 1950. Each killing was documented by the EJI, and it is widely believed that many more were never reported.

My home state of Mississippi has the highest number, at 659. DeSoto County, the place where I grew up, has 11 names. My ancestors are from Prentiss County, and it has only one name. Out of 82 counties, only a handful have no record of lynchings.

The first time my wife, Renee, and I visited the museum we were stunned by the sheer number of killings. We knew something of the history; however, the real history of slavery in all its horrors has been sanitized and kept away from impressionable young minds. Remarkably, some school boards now want to whitewash it even more.

Walking through the hanging monuments is a sobering experience. The museum is much quieter than most, the air filled with the solemnity of respect for the dead but also the sheer disbelief that the slaughter was so widespread.

When we found the steel box that represented DeSoto County and read the eleven names, we found a seat nearby and struggled with our emotions. It is easy to be whipsawed between guilt and remorse on the one hand, and the images of the violence on the other. It is easy to be overwhelmed.

Virtually all lynchings were mob killings, some carefully orchestrated, even advertised, others spur-of-the-moment snatchings while someone found a rope. They were spectacles to be enjoyed by white citizens, but some were more gruesome than others. Some of the victims were tortured. Some were burned before and after they were dead. Some were women and children. The mobs were people, otherwise law-abiding white folks who voted and believed in justice and went to church on Sunday. Merchants, farmers, laborers, even sheriffs, came together for one purpose and did the killing. And they did so with complete impunity because they were white and thought that they were superior, and because justice by their definition called for a lynching.

We asked ourselves: Who were these people? And how were they capable of such inhumanity? Could they really be our ancestors?

Were they us in a different era?

The answers are still elusive, still troubling.

For most white southerners of an age, the questions are easier to ignore. Most of us know a family with a grandfather or a dead uncle who wore robes and burned crosses. Virtually all of us have heard stories of beatings and lynchings. I know a man in DeSoto County whose father killed three black men eighty years ago. He was never arrested. I have a college friend whose grandfather was a Klansman.

For other reasons, my parents never encouraged their children to dig too deep around the family tree. I've dug enough to believe that my ancestors were not the ones who joined mobs. They were, however, part of the culture that looked the other way as their friends and neighbors did so. We did not live in DeSoto County until the late 1960s and could not have known the victims. But did we know the descendants of the people who lynched them?

In the Pines is the remarkable story of one white southerner's courage in asking the questions and searching for the answers. It is beautifully written by Grace Elizabeth Hale, a professor and scholar who studies, teaches, and writes about culture and race in America. In 1947, her grandfather, a man she adored, was the sheriff of Jeff Davis County in southern Mississippi. He was a widely respected leader in the county, who, as the elected sheriff, wielded enormous power.

A pregnant white woman cried rape and pointed the finger at Versie Johnson.

The sheriff arrested the black man and locked him in jail. When a mob showed up, Dr. Hale's grandfather bravely confronted the vigilantes, blocked the door, and saved Versie's life.

Or something like that, according to the family legend.

Over time, though, the legend began to crack. When she heard other versions of the story, Dr. Hale plunged into history and investigated not only her family's past, but Versie Johnson's as well. Due to a dearth of record keeping and a veil of distortions, the research was slow and tedious and often ran into dead ends, but her dogged search for the truth, regardless of how painful, brings the story to life.

Along with her family's narrative, Dr. Hale deftly captures the racial terror of the Jim Crow South. For those of us who remember it and now look back in disbelief, it is hard to digest.

This book reminded me of walking through the lynching museum, staring at the names, and asking, "What kind of society allowed this to happen?"

John Grisham
Charlottesville, Virginia
August 1, 2023

AUTHOR'S NOTE

There have been many books on the use of the N-word and its racist origins. I have chosen to replace all but its first and last letters with asterisks when I quote white people using the word, because of their weaponization of the term. Black people have repurposed the word, so I have chosen to spell it out in full when I quote Black people using it, except in situations where these sources are themselves quoting white people's racist usage. I have also spelled out the word in reference to a creek in Jefferson Davis County, because that is the way the waterway is identified in official documents—like the large, multicolored soil map produced by the US Department of Agriculture in 1915 and now housed at the Mississippi Department of Archives and History (MDAH).

TWO TALES

People are trapped in history and history is trapped
in them.

—James Baldwin, *Notes of a Native Son*

I was in college and home for a visit when my mom first shared a tale
straight out of *To Kill a Mockingbird*. We were in the kitchen in our
house in suburban Atlanta, and our conversation turned to my grandfather, who had died a few years earlier. All these decades later, I still
remember how the afternoon light made the red counters glow as she told
me a story that I had never heard before but would never after that day
forget.

The events my mom described occurred during her childhood, when
her father, Oury Berry, was serving his first term as sheriff of rural Jefferson
Davis County, Mississippi. One summer day, someone their family knew
found a pregnant and injured white woman walking along a country road
in the heat and gave her a ride into Prentiss, the county seat. At the courthouse, the woman reported that early that same morning, her husband
had left their house—which was located on a nearby farm—to work in
town. After he was gone, a Black man had come to the door and asked for
a drink of water. When she returned with a glass, he attacked her, dragged
her into the woods, and raped her.

My grandfather and his deputies, my mother told me, used this information to find the man whom the injured woman had accused. They arrested the suspect and placed him in the jail next to the courthouse.

By evening, a crowd had gathered outside my grandfather's office in the courthouse. Carrying his pistol, my grandfather walked outside to speak to the armed and sweating men. "I've known most of you all my life, and I sure am going to hate to have to shoot you," he said, just like Gregory Peck playing Atticus Finch, "but no one is taking a man out of my jail."

Willing to uphold the law even against the people who voted him into office, my grandfather prevented a lynching, my mother told me. He was a hero.

The tragedy, as my mother described it, happened the next morning, after her father went home to get some sleep. In his absence, his deputies and a highway patrolman took the alleged rapist to the scene of the crime, the woods on the edge of a farm just outside Prentiss, so he could explain what happened. There, the Black man attempted to escape, grabbing the patrolman's improperly holstered gun. The officers had no alternative but to shoot.

My grandfather was upset at the patrolman's negligence, according to my mom. But he also believed that the accused man had chosen to die this way rather than be lynched or executed in Mississippi's mobile electric chair. The way she remembered it, her father the sheriff understood what happened as the man's decision.

A few years later, in graduate school, I learned another version of this story.

Growing up, I had loved my grandfather deeply, but my mom's story had made me proud of him as well. It had also inspired me to research lynching. As I was finishing my dissertation, I went to visit my grandmother in Prentiss. It would be the last time I saw her in the hundred-year-old house at the corner of Second Street and Pearl where, in my memory, she had always lived. Unlike my grandfather, she did not like to talk about the past, so I spent a day at the office of the *Prentiss Headlight* reading bound volumes of old editions of the newspaper to try to find out more about what my mom had told me. I wanted to see what the local newspaper reported about my grandfather's act of bravery in preventing a lynching.

Many Americans have a limited and narrow understanding of lynchings as hangings conducted by vigilantes. Schooled by my research in the writings of Black journalist and activist Ida B. Wells, who pioneered the study of this violence in the 1890s, as well as by my studies of investigative reports on these killings compiled by the National Association for the Advancement of Colored People (NAACP), I knew that lynchings took a variety of forms: not just hanging but also burning, shooting, torture, and other kinds of violence. According to Wells, lynchings were crimes committed by communities rather than individuals. In the early twentieth century, sociologist James Elbert Cutler agreed: "Popular justification" was the essential characteristic of the practice, he wrote. The Dyer Anti-Lynching Bill, passed by the House in early 1922 but defeated in the Senate by a filibuster, extended this understanding.

By the 1930s, as increasing numbers of white southerners turned against the practice, anti-lynching activists fought over how to expand the definition to take in acts of lethal vigilante violence not sanctioned by broad community approval. By 1940, three characteristics were usually required for anti-lynching activists to label an act of violence a lynching: the victim had to die, three or in some cases two or more people had to participate in the murder, and the killers had to operate under the pretext of delivering justice or upholding tradition. This definition would become crucial to the alternate version of my mom's story that I would learn at the newspaper office.

Reading the *Prentiss Headlight,* I learned details that my mom had not remembered: August 1, 1947, the date of the shooting; the Lipsey farm, the scene of the alleged crime; and Versie Johnson, the name of the man who was killed.

But it was the difference between the newspaper's account and my mom's story that shocked me. Thanks to my research, I also had learned how to interpret descriptions of racial violence in white southern news-papers and how to spot the stories that white southerners used to hide the truth. As I skimmed the articles in those old *Headlights,* I found one of these narratives right there on the brittle, brown page.

According to the front-page story in the August 7, 1947, edition, although there had been a crowd in front of the jail, no *Mockingbird*-type standoff had occurred. Instead, the reporter wrote, Versie Johnson "told the sheriff he wanted to return to the scene of the crime to talk to him about what had happened." In the paper's account, my grandfather was not only present, but he was in charge. With the aid of two highway patrolmen, Spencer Puckett and Andy Hopkins (rather than as my mom had described, one state officer plus several sheriff's deputies), he took Johnson out to those woods on the edge of the Lipsey farm. There, the three white men claimed, Johnson confessed to the crime and showed them exactly where the rape had occurred. And there, according to the paper, Johnson tried to escape: "As Patrolman Puckett stooped to make an investigation, the negro grabbed him around the waist and threw him to the ground and had a hold on his pistol when the officers fired upon the negro." Three shots rang out, "two in the chest and one in the neck," and Johnson fell dead.

If Versie Johnson had blocked Puckett's access to his gun, the shooters must have been the other two officers: Berry and Hopkins. If my beloved grandfather Oury Berry did not kill Johnson, he had certainly tried.

Yet the *Prentiss Headlight* story was also confusing. Sitting at a small table beside the big plate glass window at the newspaper office, I struggled desperately to make sense of the words. The paper called the crowd gathered at the jail "large but orderly," which begged the question of why it was necessary to quote my grandfather Sheriff Berry insisting that "at no time was the situation out of control." The *Headlight* article also constructed an impossibly compressed timeline. Somehow, the journalist alleged, a long list of actions had taken place between nine in the morning and sometime the same afternoon: the rape, the injured pregnant woman's walk into town in the heat to locate her husband, the couple's trip together to the courthouse to speak to my grandfather, the manhunt to find Johnson, some unexplained process in which the woman confirmed her attacker's identity, Johnson's jailing, his decision to ask the sheriff to take him back to the Lipsey farm, the highway patrolmen coming to Prentiss to help, and the drive back out to the scene of the crime.

What worried me the most, however, was the newspaper's claim that Johnson, a Black man accused of raping a white woman in prime lynching territory, had asked to be taken out of the jail, through that crowd, and out into the countryside.

The *Headlight*'s account of Versie Johnson's death upended what I thought I knew about my grandfather and left me with a feeling of cold horror. But it was clear that neither my mother nor the *Headlight* had described what really happened to Versie Johnson.

On shaking legs I walked the block and a half from the newspaper office back to my grandmother's house. I showed her the photocopy of the *Headlight* article, repeated my mom's version of the story, and asked her what she knew.

My grandmother said she did not remember anything about Johnson's killing.

Even then, I understood that her answer was a lie.

Over the next few years, I turned my dissertation into a prizewinning book about the history of southern segregation, lynching, and white supremacy and took a job as a professor at the University of Virginia. I taught southern history, even as I ran away from my own family's past. But I never forgot that *Prentiss Headlight* article.

My reluctance to dig into my mom's cherished story, and the things that I discovered when I finally did, taught me a great deal: about my grandparents, about the world that produced them, and about the deep and still often unacknowledged history of white supremacy in America— a legacy with which, as my own family shows, we are only just beginning to engage.

Except for a stint in the navy, my grandfather Guy Oury Berry, my mother's father, spent his whole life in Jefferson Davis County in south-central Mississippi. I am from a different South, metropolitan Atlanta. In my childhood, the old city, its more established neighborhoods, and a band of new suburbs sat inside a rough circle created by I-285. Outside this perimeter highway, sprawl had just started to eat the farms and turn a far ring of small towns into bedroom communities. Jonesboro, where I grew up, fit this pattern. My parents built our home on a new winding road that hugged the shore of a man-made lake. Behind our backyard, pine saplings sprouted between the peach trees of an abandoned orchard. Over the next decade and a half, new subdivisions and strip malls steadily filled in a landscape of rolling red clay hills unremarkable except for its role as the location of Tara, the fictional plantation belonging to Scarlett O'Hara's family in *Gone with the Wind*.

For many southerners, these new suburbs seemed like the promised land. My dad had left his home in the cotton lands along the Mississippi River in northeast Arkansas and my mom had moved away from the Piney Woods of south-central Mississippi in search of greater opportunity and better jobs—but also a broader culture. Separately, they ended up in Atlanta, working in that city's most modern industry, the airlines. Thrilled to be out of their tiny hometowns and living in the wider world, they rarely looked back as they met and married and started a family.

My hometown had integrated schools and new shopping centers, but traces of an older regional history remained. At the northwest end of Jonesboro's Main Street, a Confederate cemetery held the bodies of men who had died nearby when the Union army marched on Atlanta. Lee Park, named after the fabled commander of the Confederate army, sat in the center of the historic downtown. A local restaurant called Butch's, where we ate Truett Cathy's original Chick-fil-A sandwiches long before he started his chain, hosted meetings of the local KKK as matter-of-factly as another place might have housed the Lions Club. But my parents were not interested in history. What mattered to them was what was ahead.

Even as a child, I somehow understood my grandparents as the past. Like many other migrant southerners, my mom sent me and my siblings "back home" in the summers. I loved everything about these Mississippi visits with Pa and Monk, as we called my mom's parents. The time I spent with them had a profound influence on the adult I would become.

When I visited Oury and Grace Berry growing up, they still lived in the home that they had bought in 1951 after selling their farm just northwest of town near the railroad tracks. A single-story Victorian with a tall roof to trap the heat, the house sat on a double corner lot in the downtown section of Prentiss. Fans—features that were, at the time, as rare in suburbia as Victrolas with horns—spun in the center of the high ceilings. A few window air-conditioning units produced more noise than cool air. In the kitchen, an old-fashioned sink with a wide, porcelain sideboard splayed out under a sunny window. In the den, a picture of a rooster made out of dried beans and seeds crowed over a newish brown couch. In the bathroom, a seemingly giant claw-foot tub invited me in for a bubbly swim. Everything about the place seemed interesting and special, and somehow more real than what we had at home.

The town, too, radiated an exotic, old-time aura. Most noticeable to a kid, Prentiss had different businesses than the Atlanta suburbs, strange grocery chains called Jitney Jungle and Sunflower and homegrown places like Walker's, a dollar store, and Garraway's, a shop that spread through several buildings and sold everything from food and farm supplies to clothes. Instead of fast-food franchises like McDonald's or Burger King, the town had a drive-up diner called the Triangle that sold burgers, shakes, and fries. My grandparents lived one block from the brick main street, Columbia Avenue, and unlike at home, I could walk almost everywhere— to the post office, my grandparents' church, and most of the stores. I went to the public library across the street from my grandparents' house at least once a day and read every book on its shelves about horses, girls, and dogs.

On hot summer afternoons, my grandmother showed me how to crochet, piece quilts, and do needlepoint and a kind of embroidery called crewel. She also taught me to cook. At five, I could make biscuits, although my grandmother handled the scary part, pulling the hot sheet pan dotted with baked rounds of buttery dough out of the wide white range. Though the house was old and they were careful with their money, my grandfather always wanted my grandmother to have modern appliances. A white chest freezer full of corn, beans, and peas from their garden, and quail that my grandfather had shot shared part of one wall with a regular refrigerator.

The first microwave I ever saw, a metal box that looked like something astronauts would use, sat on the Formica counter. After supper—"dinner" in Prentiss was the meal that we called "lunch" in Atlanta—I would tag along as my grandmother took long walks with her friends. When her minister's wife started an exercise class in the church fellowship hall, I joined that, too. Walking back home afterward, we would laugh about the woman who never missed a session but barely moved her arms and legs, too much of a "lady" to sweat.

The very best thing about my Mississippi visits, though, was my grand-father. Because my grandmother worked half days then at the chancery clerk's office, I spent a lot of time on these trips wandering the countryside with Pa. Most days, we stopped at country stores and bought Cokes and candy bars. More than once, we listened to the sing-song twang of auction-eers and bid on cows we never intended to buy. And always, as he drove, he talked. Pa's stories transformed the buggy pastures and swampy woods of Jefferson Davis County into a dense and magical landscape layered with traces of the people, buildings, and relationships that had come before. Driving the back roads, he would point out the open window of his GMC truck to a spot where the jonquils bloomed in a line in an empty field and conjure the now-vanished Brady farm or Mt. Carmel settlement with his words. Or he would stop suddenly on the weedy shoulder of a dirt road and say, "I think this is it." Bushwhacking back through tangles of blackberry bushes, he would uncover a choked spring that he remembered from his youth. Miraculously, to this suburban girl at least, we would kneel and drink the clear and cool and delicious water straight from that muddy ground.

Besides being a child's best possible companion, the grandfather I knew was respected by family, friends, and neighbors. His grandparents on both sides had owned farms, but he had grown up hard because his own father was an alcoholic, a serious problem for a person to have in a state that held on to prohibition until 1966. As a boy, he worked so much he missed a lot of school. Against his own family's wishes, he married my grandmother, who came from a very poor family and was considered an "old maid" at age twenty-three, and he loved her fiercely until the day he died. As an adult, he helped his seven siblings when necessary, especially a sister who never married and a brother who lived with a disability.

I was a teenager who could drive, and Pa was dead, by the time Lorraine Lockhart—a Black woman who operated a little country store near a piece of property he had owned—moved into her new place. But "Miss Lorraine" (as I was taught to call her) gave me a tour of her new home and told me that my grandfather had helped her with the paperwork for the federal government program, probably a Farmers Home Administration loan, that had enabled her to build a brick house with her first indoor plumbing.

My grandfather taught me to love history. In the slow, wet heat of those Mississippi summers, I got tangled up in the very past that my parents were trying to leave behind. When I was a child, that world often felt more like home to me than the Atlanta suburb where I actually lived. But love is not the same thing as knowledge. It would take decades for me to realize how little I understood about my grandfather and the history that he had helped to make.

SPLINTERS AND SILENCE

From the Jackson airport now named for murdered NAACP leader Medgar Evers, the route to the place many locals call Jeff Davis County follows I-20 west for a bit before heading south on Highway 49. For a few miles, the road pushes through a snarl of traffic lights, strip malls, and fast-food franchises. Orange and white barricades squeeze the lanes where a widening project has stalled. In the middle of this construction, a large electronic billboard blinks cheerful words of therapy that flash and then are gone: "Life is a work of art. If you don't like what you see, paint over it." A smaller, portable sign pushes another kind of comfort, the legalization of marijuana. More traditional remedies, southern food and faith, also appear, sometimes at the same spot, like the giant white cross towering over the barn-shaped building that houses Berry's Seafood and Catfish Restaurant.

The first time I drive this route in a quarter of a century, the clouds look like someone has plowed them, and the morning sun turns the furrows into ditches of light. Nothing seems familiar. All the way to the Piney Woods Farm School, a Black institution founded in 1909 and the first landmark I recognize, I worry that I am lost.

About halfway to Prentiss, before a town called Mendenhall, the route turns right onto Highway 13. Mixed forests and farmed pines grow right up to the road, and then suddenly ravaged scenes from an unreported conflict appear, acres clear-cut and not replanted. Cut trunks sticky with sap sit stacked beside the road or chained to metal poles on the open backs of trucks. Occasionally I pass a farm, often an older, wood-frame house sharing space with a red-brick ranch and a smattering of barns and other ramshackle outbuildings in varying degrees of disrepair. Sweaty cows swat flies in emerald fields fenced with barbed wire.

The end of the smooth asphalt and another clear-cut announce the Jeff Davis County line. Neat red chicken houses line up perpendicular to the road and fill my car with a hint of their noxious smell. Old gas wells sit on bare dirt lots bristling with rusty pipes, tanks, gauges, and gates. Single- and double-wide trailers, more brick ranches, and a farmhouse or two stand scattered among plots of scraggly pines or older oak trees and pecans. On the outskirts of Prentiss, three white wooden crosses guard a pond filled with scum in a pasture gone to scrub.

Prentiss, the county seat of Jeff Davis, has been dying for more than half a century. Downtown, where old Highway 13 becomes Columbia Avenue, the town has paved over the brick main street I remember from my childhood. But the bones of a once-thriving place remain. Old, mostly empty store buildings fill the blocks between First and Third Streets. Palace Drugs survives on the corner of Second and Columbia by filling prescriptions for elderly residents. A taller brick building, a former movie theater, stands abandoned. A senior center occupies one old storefront, and a junk store that never seems to be open fills another. The *Prentiss Headlight*'s little building still stands on Third, across from a county annex that once housed the offices of the sheriff and the chancery clerk, where at various times my grandfather and grandmother, respectively, worked. Near the railroad tracks, a different bank operates in the old columned, two-story Bank of Prentiss building on the corner. Just outside downtown, the Triangle, the drive-through diner that I remember from my youth, stands empty.

On the town's edges, some newer businesses operate. Near where the original Highway 13 intersects the original Highway 84 bypass, an outlet of a small, regional fast-food chain called Ward's sells burgers and fries. Across the street sits a Dollar General. Closer to downtown, a tiny modern Pizza Hut offers takeout. Nearby, a patch of green park, a small pavilion, and some picnic tables mark the entrance to a rail-to-trails project called the Longleaf Trace that follows the route of the old Mississippi Central Railroad all the way to Hattiesburg. A sign welcomes runners, cyclists, and riders, but in all my visits I have never seen a single person on it, much less a horse.

Jeff Davis County's grim statistics match this landscape of decline. The town of Prentiss has been overwhelmingly white throughout its history, and today, an aging white majority hangs on with about 52 percent of the population, as the number of Black residents steadily climbs. In contrast, the county has always had a Black majority, and currently about 60 percent of Jeff Davis residents are Black. Elderly white folks on Social Security and other retirement payments skew the numbers a bit, masking the economic precarity of younger and non-white residents. Overall, the poverty rate is about 25 percent. Only about 14 percent of Jeff Davis residents hold a four-year college degree, and 15 percent lack health insurance. In 2021, the county issued zero building permits.

To prepare for my research trips to Prentiss, I dig into federal, state, and organizational archives. At the Mississippi Department of Archives and History in Jackson, I examine materials on the county collected by the Works Progress Administration (WPA), church histories, and other relevant documents. I study the digital records of the NAACP and discover the organization's 1958 voting rights case *Darby v. Daniel*, which accused Jeff Davis County's circuit clerk of systematically rejecting Black residents trying to register to vote. The NAACP lost that case, but Black residents of Jeff Davis County kept fighting and persuaded the Justice Department to investigate. At the southeast branch of the National Archives outside Atlanta, I dig through the boxes of court transcripts, subpoenas, and rejected voter applications generated by this federal agency's examination of ongoing discrimination against Black would-be voters in Jeff Davis

County, a lawsuit that was not resolved until the passage of the 1965 Voting Rights Act.

I learn a lot during these preparatory research sessions, including the fact that many Black residents of Jeff Davis voted for years until purged from the rolls in the aftermath of the 1954 Supreme Court decision *Brown v. Board of Education* outlawing segregation. Yet there is so much I cannot know without going back to Jeff Davis County itself. Only when I do will I finally figure out what I have been thinking about and also fearing for all these years.

In Prentiss, I work long weeks at the chancery clerk's office in the back room full of filing cabinets and oversize maps and long, waist-high racks of ledgers. I read the weekly issues of the county's only paper and the minutes of the meetings of the Board of Supervisors. I scour the tax assessment rolls, the large red binders filled with land deeds, and the circuit court records. The first time I encounter my grandmother's looping cursive sprawling across a page listing title transfers, I cry.

My grandfather was in and out of the sheriff's office because by law he could not hold the job two terms in a row. He began his last term when I was in kindergarten. Even after he retired, he knew all the local leaders, elected officials, ministers, and businesspeople in Prentiss. He drank coffee with some of them. Their wives knew my grandmother and asked about my uncle and my mom. When I visited as a child, I even met some of these people myself. My grandmother and Mrs. Ruth Parker, the editor of the *Headlight,* were as close as Baptists and Methodists could be in a small southern town where their lives revolved around different churches.

As I read editorials in the *Headlight* calling civil rights leaders hatemongers and federal intervention in the region the end of Christian civilization, I imagine Mrs. Parker's face. I remember the taste of her famous dinner rolls and pies. I think about the copy of her book *Down Home Cookin'* that she signed and gave me when I was a teenager and how it sits today on a shelf in my own century-old home, its broken spine and battered pages attesting to years of use.

White records, voices, and memories fill these early days of research in

Prentiss. Little of what I learn yields much insight into the lives of Black people in Jeff Davis County during the Jim Crow era. Black residents who did not commit crimes rarely appeared in the *Headlight,* for example, outside of an occasional short column called "News of Interest to Colored Readers," notices about events like a Black agricultural fair or a school graduation, and segregated lists of people who had been hospitalized or inducted into the military. Published county and school budgets demonstrate vast inequalities in salaries, school facilities, and other distributions of resources, yet leave faceless and nameless the people whose lives were shaped by those disparities.

To fill in these gaps, I reach out to the alumni group of a now-shuttered Black high school and college called the Prentiss Institute; to leaders of the local NAACP chapter; to the owners of the Johnson Funeral Home, a business operated in Prentiss by the same family since 1940; and to anyone else who I think might be willing to speak with me. And when I find people who do agree to talk, they narrate a history I never heard my grandparents share.

In this way I learn the story of how, beginning during Reconstruction, Black residents of what is today Jeff Davis County not only built the country churches whose sanctuaries and cemeteries still sit along rural roads across the county but also bought hundreds of acres of farmland and founded and funded their own high school and college. On the mostly abandoned campus, I tour the Prentiss Institute's original building, a small structure called the 1907 House, as well as the large and meticulously restored Rosenwald Building, which houses a small museum in one of its former classrooms. With names in hand, I trace Black landowners through the county deed books. A man who grew up on the edge of the Prentiss Institute campus helps me connect those family names to specific churches.

As I meet more of them, current and former Black residents of Jeff Davis County describe a once-flourishing rural community. As one man explained, "Most restaurants and cafés were segregated and you had to use the back door so we ate at home. But we did not care. We had our own world."

Not surprisingly, white and Black residents of Jeff Davis County remember the last decades of Jim Crow differently. Multiple acts of violence, including the near-lynching of two Black men who allegedly killed a former Prentiss constable in 1940 and the 1947 shooting of Versie Johnson, shaped Black life in the area for years. No one I knew growing up ever talked about this violence, or the fact that the NAACP, the FBI, and the Justice Department all conducted civil rights investigations here in the 1950s and 1960s.

Everyone I speak with is wary. But one person leads to another, and finally I find myself interviewing a lifelong Jeff Davis County resident, Mitchell Gamblin, who remembers the act of violence that I am investigating—a killing that unfolded so differently in my mother's memory and in the pages of the *Prentiss Headlight*. Putting Gamblin's account together with written records and reporting by Black newspapers, I uncover a third, and very different, story of what happened to Versie Johnson.

The past does not have to be ancient to be made of splinters and silence. In the 1940s, white southerners learned to hide from newspapers and state and federal courts the acts of violence that enforced what they called "the southern way of life"; they learned to bury their brutality rather than brag about it.

Earlier in the century, lynch mobs had committed their violence openly. Photographers made and sold images of participants and spectators. Railroads ran special excursion trains to carry spectators. Newspapers and radio programs advertised these grisly murders. In the face of growing anti-lynching activism in the 1930s and 1940s, however, some white southerners learned that they needed to manage the news. As the NAACP argued in a report published in1940, lynching was "entering a new and altogether dangerous phase." Instead of aiding and exonerating participants in public lynch mobs, local officials increasingly arranged and often participated in quieter murders. While the number of lynchings seemed to be decreasing, in reality the practice had, in the NAACP phrase, "gone underground." The boundaries between legal executions, killings committed by law enforcement officials and other white citizens, and publicly recognized lynchings blurred.

This change did not mean that the violence was invisible. Rather, it simply meant that white leaders conspired to keep what had happened out of the press. Because nothing had officially occurred, there was nothing for outsiders like FBI agents or undercover NAACP activists to investigate. But local people still talked, and they still knew. Sometimes, Black residents managed to pass along reports to Black papers published in places like Baltimore and Chicago. Otherwise, these acts of violence in tiny, Deep South places like Prentiss left little trace in the records, and they are often left out of lynching tallies.

Most Americans today do not understand that Jim Crow survived into the late 1960s in large part because of this wave of "underground" white supremacist violence. This ignorance is part of the broader problem of how many Americans have remembered, and reckoned with, white supremacy—that is, the persistent belief that people defined as white are somehow better than and more deserving of resources and power than people who are not and the systems that create and maintain these inequalities. Denial about the centrality of white violence in American history remains so powerful that the Equal Justice Initiative (EJI), an Alabama nonprofit that provides free legal representation to people facing the death penalty, has identified a false understanding of this past as one of the major obstacles preventing their clients from receiving justice. EJI built the National Memorial for Peace and Justice, a monument to the victims of what the organization calls "racial terror lynchings," to create a space to confront this history and to grieve these lost lives.

This lynching memorial is one answer to the question of how to push all Americans to reckon more fully with the legacy of white supremacy. The story I tell here of my grandfather, Oury Berry, and Versie Johnson offers another.

Over the last four decades, historians have done a brilliant job of narrating the history of the long struggle for civil rights in the South, from the Reconstruction era through the 1960s. In persuasive detail, they have described individual and collective acts of protest; legal challenges to segregation; the politics of fighting Jim Crow at the national, state, and local levels; the work of civil rights organizations; the role of national and grassroots civil rights leaders; and the stories of Black communities living through and participating in periods of sweeping change. Yet one unintended consequence of this deep and rich body of scholarship is that its cumulative power overwhelms a sense of historical contingency. Looking back, Americans can see an upward march of triumph, from the trail of NAACP legal victories in the 1940s and 1950s and the Montgomery bus boycott to the sit-in movement, the Freedom Rides, and the nonviolent mass protests that pushed elected officials to pass the Civil Rights and Voting Rights Acts. A comparatively much smaller group of historians have written about the history of organized white resistance to Black rights, the long segregationist movement that has stopped progress toward equality again and again throughout American history.

Because not as much research has been conducted into opposition to the civil rights movement, it is easy to miss how hard many white southerners fought to preserve white supremacy anchored in Jim Crow segregation—a set of laws and conventions created to control how and where Black people worked, studied, lived, shopped, traveled, and accessed the ballot box. Many Americans do not know that presidents from FDR to Nixon deferred to the congressional power of white southern Democrats, or that the country's fabled "postwar consensus"—a now-celebrated age of relative bipartisanship in American politics—rested on widespread white acceptance of Black exclusion. Even fewer understand the local implications of this uneven "consensus." To cite just one powerful example, thirty-three Mississippi school districts—including Jeff Davis County—ran separate Black schools through the summer of 1970, sixteen years after the *Brown* decision.

In the mid-twentieth century, segregationists had reasons to believe they would be able to preserve their Jim Crow world for another generation. Black Americans and their allies had reasons to fear that these white southerners might succeed. In Mississippi in particular, Black and white residents living through this period would not have recognized the sense now shared by many contemporary Americans that the victory over Jim Crow was inevitable.

On that August afternoon in 1947, the personal histories of these two men—my grandfather the sheriff, and the accused man whom he had taken into custody—collided. But local, regional, and national histories were also at play. Postwar Black demands for equal citizenship met a wall of white backlash, especially in places with a Black majority like Jeff Davis County. And expanding opposition to lynching and other forms of vigilante violence among many Americans ran headlong into some white southerners' determination to continue taking the law into their own hands.

When Oury Berry and Versie Johnson confronted each other in a field at the Lipsey farm just outside Prentiss, what happened next was not only about them. It was also about the history of the territory that became Jeff Davis County. It was about all that had occurred in the South since Reconstruction. It was about the questions at the heart of the nation: Who exactly gets to have life and liberty, much less happiness? Who gets to be a full American?

For too long, too many white Americans have had too much faith in the patriotic myth of history as progress. This way of thinking superficially celebrates particular historical moments while grossly underestimating the cumulative power of the past—not just as myth but also as the consequences of human decisions—in shaping the present. By selectively remembering history, many white Americans have spared themselves the discomfort of dealing with its legacy.

The irony of this story is that I grew up to be a historian because I am one of these white Americans—because I am part of this tradition of choosing what parts of history to acknowledge and what to ignore. If my parents had not fled their small-town, segregated southern origins and turned their backs on their past, I would not have grown up thinking about the differences between the worlds in which they were raised and the place in which I spent my own childhood. And if I had not followed the pattern my own parents set and fled my own upbringing in the New South's white-flight suburbs, I would not have been in a position to do this research and write this book.

Being able to live relatively free of the bonds of history has been one of white Americans' greatest privileges. I have come to see this particular entitlement as foundational, the one that supports all the rest. The process has taken most of my adult life, but I have finally learned that taking responsibility for the past is, for me at least, both an intellectual project and a personal one.

In the course of my research, many people have asked me why I am telling this story. Some of them are my relatives. Others are former or current white residents of Jeff Davis County. And some are people who wonder if the granddaughter of a sheriff is ever the right person to write a history of a Black man who died in that particular white man's custody. My answer—that as a historian who has long researched racial inequality, I have the skills to investigate a story that will otherwise remain buried— cannot satisfy all of these divergent critics.

To be clear, I do not believe the issues raised by these different groups are equally valid. Like most people, I care a lot about what my family thinks; personally, I also worry a great deal about the objections of people with whom I share a commitment to the political project of dismantling white supremacy. On the other hand, I reject the argument (whether explicit or implicit) that this painful history ought to stay buried because it causes discomfort to white readers or the white residents of the place where Versie Johnson died.

My own commitment to telling this story has been motivated by a somewhat different question, one that I have been asking myself since that day in the mid-1990s when I first read the account of Versie Johnson's killing in the *Prentiss Headlight*. Why am I, a historian, a person whose job is teaching, researching, and writing about the past, not telling this story? Is it not my obligation to name names and expose lies?

History, in its highest form, is not a dry and abstract account of external forces, nor is it a mythic tale of heroes and villains. Rather, it is personal and intimate, the story of each and every one of us and our ancestors. Yet the best history is not based on people's feelings or memories alone. It must also be built upon facts—on material traces of past lives mined from documents, archives, and landscapes. This principle has guided me in writing this book. In telling the true story of what happened to Versie Johnson on August 1, 1947, I have done my best to view this personal tale through the lens of a historical investigator. I have tried to place my own family within the flow of history, rather than leaving it within the misty precincts of my own imagination.

If being able to understand yourself as living free of the past is a foundational part of white supremacy, then putting your own family inside the stream of history is a part of the project of dismantling it. This kind of research can lay the groundwork for repair, for acknowledgment and apology but also for reparations—material compensation for past injury of the sort that is long overdue to Black Americans. Because white violence did not stop with Emancipation, a commitment to repair cannot be limited to the age of slavery.

Opponents of reparations often argue that the logistics are impossible, that for wrongs suffered so long ago there is no way to determine who is owed and how much they should be paid. Who is not at issue. Americans who can trace their ancestry back to Black people listed in the 1870 census should all be eligible for reparations for slavery, because few Africans or people in the African diaspora migrated to America voluntarily before that date, and most Black people outside the South also had enslaved ancestors. Standard amounts could easily be set based on estimations of average profits generated by each enslaved person. The same methods of identification and estimation could be used to determine reparations for the descendants of Black people who lived in the Jim Crow South. In cases of particular acts of violence, scholars can conduct more specific research. This story is proof that we have the tools to transform history from something symbolic and abstract into something palpable and real—and therefore redressable.

In addition to viewing my own family's history as an extension of the history that I have studied as a scholar, I also have attempted to place Versie Johnson himself at the center of this particular historical tale. Generations of Black families and historians have worked to counteract the way white supremacy erases evidence of past Black lives, and I draw on their research and the archives they have created here to offer an account not just of Versie Johnson's death but also of his life. I reconstruct the story of how, in the grim context of Jim Crow Mississippi, the part of the Piney Woods that became Jeff Davis County was something of a refuge for many Black people, among them Versie Johnson and members of his family. Without an understanding of this Black flourishing, of the separate Black world some Black people were able to build in Jeff Davis County, it is impossible to know what was lost when Versie Johnson died.

PART I

The Road to the Lipsey Farm

IN THE PINES

By the time my grandfather shot Versie Johnson, it was hard for most people to remember that the place where it all happened had once been considered a kind of paradise by some earlier inhabitants. Unlike the forests of fairy tales, the old-growth woods that had long covered southern Mississippi were full of light. Longleaf pines soared straight up as high as 130 feet, their blackened trunks mostly bare of branches below high crowns. Together with other pines, loblolly and slash and shortleaf, they formed an evergreen landscape that stretched over one hundred miles inland from the coastal plains. Travelers and the few white farmers who settled there in the early nineteenth century called this majestic forest the Piney Woods. What started as a description became a name.

Like other longleaf pine forests that once stretched from Virginia to Texas, the Mississippi Piney Woods depended on fire. For centuries, lightning strikes and Choctaws started the blazes that cleared away competing shrubs and saplings. Regular burnings created an open landscape of widely spaced trees rolling up and down ridges. High grass and cane grew in the sunshine that reached the forest floor. Quail, deer, and wild turkey foraged. Springs seeped out of shallow folds and trickled into clear creeks full of bass, catfish, and crappie. Sometimes, other trees claimed a spot, bald and pond cypresses in the wetter bottoms or sweet gums, water oaks, and hickories on the banks of waterways where the land was more fertile and the fires did not reach. But the pine trees ruled. Their sharp smell filled the air. Their green hue tinted the light. Their fallen needles muffled the clomp of hooves and feet on what white people called Old Choctaw or McClarey's, paths that passed for roads.

In the light between the pines, people who looked could see what was coming. Forced by the federal government to leave, Choctaws walked out of groves where their families had lived and hunted for centuries, leaving their homes and their sacred sites behind. Federal land surveyors stopped at springs to water weary horses. New settlers like my own ancestors rode in wagons or floated in canoes or flatboats down rivers like the Leaf or the Chickasawhay or the Pearl, surrounded by their lashed-down belongings. Enslaved people traveled on foot or by water, forced to move with the white men and women who claimed to own them or the traders who bought, chained, and sold them. Among them were at least some of Versie Johnson's great-grandparents.

Across much of the nineteenth century, white Piney Woods settlers who could stand the isolation lived in a bountiful land. They chopped down trees and used the logs or boards made from them with hand tools or at small, water-powered sawmills to build cabins. Mostly, they kept livestock more than farmed, allowing their cattle and the pigs they called Piney Woods rooters to forage in the grass between the pines. They also hunted and fished. Boundary lines meant little. Livestock roamed free. People did not consider taking timber from public lands a crime.

To grow a few vegetables and a little corn to grind for bread, inhabitants of the pine forests chopped down more trees. Sometimes, they built furniture, buildings, or fences out of the heartwood or cut trunks into cords for their fireplaces. Then they burned whatever was left and planted small crops directly in the ash. The thin, sandy soil wore out quickly. Every few years, people who stayed had to make a new garden patch. In 1853, Edwin Ruffin, a Virginia planter and later ardent Confederate who helped invent the study of soil chemistry, called these inhabitants of the southern pine forests "land killers."

After the Civil War, Piney Woods people found new markets for the one thing they possessed in abundance, old trees. When the water was high, men cut down pines and other trees and dragged them with mules and oxen to rivers and creeks. There, they carved their names in what they called the "butt cut," lashed the trimmed trunks into rafts, and floated mats of logs downstream. Selling timber this way to mills on larger rivers or at ports on the coast offered a rare source of cash. Other settlers took up turpentine and pitch production, wrecking less-perfect trees near navigable waterways.

Though these practices affected relatively few of the trees southerners called yellow pines, the forest mostly failed to regenerate. Without the Choctaws, fires burned the woods less frequently. Fewer longleaf saplings sprouted. Those that did struggled in the crowded scrub. Feral hogs dug up and ate the starchy roots of others before they had a chance to bolt for the sky.

But the Piney Woods were lucky. Back from the coast and away from the banks of rivers, the old-growth forest survived well into the early twentieth century. When the Mississippi legislature carved Jefferson Davis out of neighboring Lawrence and Covington Counties in 1906, pine trees covered much of the new county. Locals did not imagine then that only a few tracts would still be standing in the late 1930s. In any time and place, even in a forest full of light, people saw some things and they refused to see others. Like land killing and longleaf pines, not-looking had deep roots.

The first Black people who lived in the Piney Woods did not choose this land. Some traveled to the area with the people who enslaved them. The rest came with slave traders, walking hundreds of miles in shackles along primitive roads or chained in ships that sailed out of eastern ports like Charleston and Norfolk bound for slave markets in places like New Orleans. Forced to move west, they left behind everybody and everything they loved. The journey battered their souls. The work they had to do when they arrived—building log shelters and cutting fields out of forests— wrecked their bodies. Many did not survive.

The way white people told it, the first Black death in the Piney Woods was an accident. Someone drowned in one of the many creeks that curved through the tall woods. Maybe that was right. A woman lost her footing trying to wade across while carrying a load of firewood. A man fell in while trying to cut down a tree growing on the bank. White folks then and in the years since did not want to think about the alternative, that a human being might choose death over bondage. After a rainstorm, it would have been easy enough to step out from the muddy bank in a deep spot where the sandy floor dropped away. In the water between the pines, a person might just stop fighting and seek release. Afterward, white people who lived nearby marked this tragedy by naming the stream Nigger Creek.

In the antebellum era, the Black population of the Piney Woods remained small. White men and women wealthy enough to be enslavers usually settled elsewhere. Many kept moving west on the Three Chopped Way—a path named for the three slashes on trees used to mark the route—until they reached the deep soil of the area near Natchez. Enslavers that did settle in the Piney Woods often left in the 1830s as Choctaws and other Native Americans were forced out of more fertile lands in central Mississippi. Some Piney Woods farmers used enslaved people to grow cotton and other crops on more fertile bottomland along waterways like the Pearl. Enslaved people also worked at small, water-powered mills used to saw timber or grind corn for the local market.

After Emancipation, some formerly enslaved people began to see this region as a place of promise. Unlike in plantation districts, land in the Piney Woods was cheap or, in cases where the government still owned it, free. Some Black families acquired property by homesteading, working the five years required by the 1866 Southern Homestead Act to wrench farms out of the forest in order to earn title to public lands. Others bought. In 1870, a Black man named Ira Warren Lucas led a group of freed people into the flatlands between White Sand and Silver Creeks where they formed an all-Black settlement they named Lucas. There and elsewhere, newcomers mixed with established Black families—Williamses and Holloways and Fortenberrys, Polks and Johnsons and Magees.

As white men used violence to attack Black political rights during and after Reconstruction, landownership provided some small measure of security. On their own place, Black men could decide what and when to plant. Black women could avoid close interactions with white men. Black parents could protect their children.

For a while, some Black farmers prospered alongside their white neighbors, growing, making, and hunting most of what they needed and raising cotton or cutting timber to sell so they could pay for the rest. But when the timber companies came, everything began to change.

In the 1890s, men who had made their money cutting trees in places like Pennsylvania and Michigan discovered Mississippi. Unlike remaining old-growth forests in other places, Mississippi's pines grew on gentle hills. Winters were mild. Wooded land, shunned by local farmers who knew firsthand the labor involved in clearing new fields, went for as little as $1.25 an acre. Great tracts of trees in the Piney Woods ended up for sale as Mississippi's public colleges and railroads like the Gulf and Ship Island sold many of the thousands of acres they received through federal and state land grants. As timber companies bought them, they started pushing north from the Gulf Coast and inland from the Pearl and Pascagoula Rivers and their tributaries.

When large-scale lumbering arrived in the area, longleaf pines still grew where the original square-mile grid of downtown Prentiss would stand. Clusters of white and Black farm families worked the richer lands near creeks like White Sand, and trees covered the rest. Small settlements like Mt. Carmel and Blountville grew up around churches, schools, and stores. No real towns existed. People lived in the country.

Some folks liked that life. Others wanted a more modern existence, indoor plumbing, electric lights, stores and churches close by, a school that was more than one room with one teacher, easy access to a telegraph office and maybe even telephones, more possibilities for entertainment, mail every day, including packages from catalogs like Sears, Roebuck, new things to own and to do and to see. In a few churches, members opposed modern conveniences. At Bethany Baptist, founded in May 1819 and one of the oldest churches in the area, the congregation divided bitterly over wiring the sanctuary for electric light in 1940. For everyone else, it was not a sin to want new things.

P. W. "Prent" Berry, first cousin of my great-great-grandfather Albert Berry, knew a railroad was coming. J. J. Newman Lumber Company had opened huge sawmills in the new towns of Hattiesburg and Sumrall. To bring the pine logs in and ship lumber out, Newman Lumber began building their own line, the Pearl and Leaf Rivers Railroad. As the company cut over lands along their route, they kept extending their tracks westward. Old communities reached by the tracks prospered. New settlements sprang up overnight. Sawmill towns boomed.

Prent Berry owned the store at Blountville with two of his brothers and a large farm north of that settlement. The day the engineers planning the route came by the store, a storm flooded the flatlands there near Whitesand Creek. Berry suggested an alternate route. Instead of running through Blountville, maybe they should build the tracks across the hills farther north. So he made a deal with the railroad to lay the line through his farm. On a rainy Christmas Eve in 1902, workers shared a "bucket" of spirits to ward off the wet cold as they pushed to finish the route. Berry held a pine torch high for light as they hammered the last spike.

In return for building what was then the end of the line on his land, Prent Berry deeded every other block of the square-mile town of numbered streets and avenues named Leaf, Pearl, and Columbia to the railroad. The railroad built the depot. The lumber company cut the longleaf pines and shipped the logs to their sawmill in Sumrall to be made into lumber. Then Berry and the company sold the lots. A few businesses moved "over the ditch" from Blountville. Some of them built new buildings on Columbia Avenue, the main street that ran by the depot perpendicular to the tracks. Others used sledges, poles, and mules to relocate their buildings. Better-off white families in Mt. Carmel bought property and built Victorian and Craftsman-style houses. Named for its founder, Prentiss started as a business venture.

In 1903, when the state legislature awarded the settlement of about three hundred a village charter, Prentiss was a work in progress, a grid of dirt streets and construction sites beside a railroad depot. Already on Columbia Avenue, the Bank of Blountville welcomed savers and borrowers, and the Berry Mercantile served customers. On Leaf Avenue, Prentiss Baptist Church, built on land donated by Prent Berry, welcomed worshippers. A block over, what would become Prentiss Methodist Church was under construction. Across town on Third Street, a new school had opened.

In Prentiss, the new residential areas were for white people only. Later, a few Black people lived in small houses next to the cotton gins, the small sawmills, and the warehouses used to store lumber and cotton. Locals called the area Sawmill Quarters, Stamps Quarters, or just the Quarters.

The railroad made the town. For people who lived and shopped and worshipped and went to school in Prentiss, the railroad offered something new, a chance for locals to participate in modern life. For the pine forests, the railroad meant the beginning of the end.

While people had always cut the trees, big timber companies like Newman Lumber brought a new, mechanized form of logging to the Piney Woods. Unlike in the past, when loggers often felled select trees and left others standing, the new companies cut down everything. They built temporary "dummy" railroad lines deep into the old pine forests. They also used steam skidders, huge engines with mile-long cables for dragging logs from where they were cut to the railroad cars. Logs pulled in this way ravaged the land, cutting trenches in the ground and killing every small tree and sapling in their path. For Newman and other companies, time equaled money. They came in fast, clear-cut the trees, and then moved on to the next tract. When all the pines in the region were gone, the big companies shut down the huge sawmills, abandoned entire towns and villages, sold off their main railroad lines, and left the state to start the process again in another old-growth forest. In their wake, they left thousands of acres of bare and muddy ground.

The longleaf forests shaped how people settled this place, who decided to stay, and how they made a living there, even after most of the original pines were gone.

Family trees are metaphors. They share with pines both a basic structure and a tendency to flourish only when conditions are right. Online genealogical sites are not very helpful if some lasting authority like a church or a state has not created and preserved documents like birth, death, and marriage records. Some American families fill holes in repositories of official records because they have ancestors who saved stories about the past, papers, or other artifacts and passed down an interest in history to their descendants. Yet most people do not have access to these kinds of family archives.

Paradoxically, many white Americans have been able to ignore the past while also, if they desire, using government documents to research their ancestry. Despite my parents' and grandparents' lack of interest in family history, I can trace my own genealogy back for generations through census and other records. These documents reveal two waves of migration from Virginia through the Carolinas and later on to Mississippi. Without knowing it, when I moved to Charlottesville, I completed a circle, ending up about fourteen miles from White Hall, Virginia, where the Berry family migration began before the American Revolution.

By the standards of the colonial era, people like my ancestors could travel relatively easily along the fall line on the Great Valley Road. Unlike most overland trails, this route had actually been widened to handle wheels, and travelers could walk or ride horseback or even drive a wagon from Philadelphia down through the Shenandoah Valley of Virginia and across the Carolinas to Georgia. There were challenges. Wagons got stuck in the mud up to their axles. Horses went lame. Thieves stole coins and other easily carried valuables. People died and were buried along the route. In winter, ice and snow made the footing treacherous. In summer, mosquitoes and flies attacked the sweaty skin of horses and humans alike. Sometimes, travelers waited days at a ford for the water to drop, drove on in the rain, and then waited days again at the next crossing. In other places, alternate paths skirted mud or high water, but it was not always easy to know which fork to choose.

My ancestors almost certainly took this route south. Around 1765, John and Susannah Berry, my great-great-great-great-great-grandparents, were living in Virginia, where they had a son they named John. Five years later, they had a daughter they called Jemima. That same year they left the state, most likely taking a narrow track west, crossing the Blue Ridge Mountains at Rockfish Gap, and meeting the Great Wagon Road at Staunton, a distance of about thirty miles. During the family's journey through North Carolina, Susannah gave birth to another son, and she and John named him German. Near the border between the Carolinas, the young family probably took the Great Wagon Road's eastern fork toward Camden. Eventually they settled farther east in the Cheraws district.

For the four Berry siblings—John, Jemima, German, and David, born soon after the family arrived in South Carolina—that part of the district later called Chesterfield County became home. Over half a century they grew up, married people from South Carolina and just across the nearby border in North Carolina, and had lots of children. Longleaf pine forest covered most of Chesterfield, part of a landscape now called the Carolina Sandhills, just like it did the Berrys' future home in the Mississippi Piney Woods. Before 1800 settlers there lived in a similar way, taking most of what they needed from the forest and growing the rest around the stumps of felled trees.

But the invention of the cotton gin in the late eighteenth century transformed how people lived in that area and also changed my family's fortunes. Planters had been growing long staple cotton, a version of the commodity prized for its long fibers, on the Carolina coast for decades. Short staple cotton could be grown in a variety of locations where land was much cheaper, but it had another drawback: its sticky green seeds were very hard to separate from its short fibers. After Eli Whitney built a machine that would do that work, short staple cotton spread across upland South Carolina like fire in the pines. Farmers turned into planters, growing the white fiber rather than food in those fields cut from the forests. In the early years of the nineteenth century, the crop proved profitable almost everywhere in the state, but the boom did not last because the new crop stripped the sandy soil fast. A few years of cotton and then of corn, and yields often fell too low to make a profit. Planters responded by abandoning their worn acres and cutting trees to create fresh fields. Slavery had spread along with cotton production, but labor proved more valuable than land. When cotton or corn crops failed or planters simply wanted money, they sold people. By 1810, some of the Berrys had made enough money to join the enslaver class. Jemima's husband, John Shivers, enslaved one person, David Berry enslaved two.

Sometime after 1810, all four Berry siblings left Chesterfield, joining a growing stream of Americans moving westward. Traveling overland to Mississippi in the decade after 1810 was probably more difficult than the journey south had been half a century before. The Great Wagon Road carried travelers only as far as Augusta. A bad but passable track then crossed Georgia to the state capital at Milledgeville. There, migrants picked up a trail the US Army began constructing out of Creek and Choctaw paths in 1807. The Three Chopped Way eventually ran from Milledgeville all the way west to Natchez on the Mississippi River, connecting the settled east to the future states of Alabama and Mississippi. By the middle of the 1810s, a ferry carried travelers over the Alabama River, and causeways made of felled trees crossed bogs and smaller waterways. Wagons could pass from Milledgeville as far as Fort St. Stephens on the Tombigbee River, an improved section of the Three Chopped renamed the Federal Road. West of there, the Berry families had to transfer their belongings to pack horses and either walk or ride the route from the Tombigbee River west to the Pearl.

Whether or not they traveled all those hard miles together, by 1820 John, German, and David Berry and their sister and brother-in-law, Jemima and John Shivers, lived scattered across the new state of Mississippi. German enslaved four people, and David enslaved eight. Living apart, the Berry siblings might have realized how much they wanted to be close. Or perhaps the plan all along had been to spread out and find a place where everyone could buy land together. The rolling ridges of giant trees in the Piney Woods must have reminded them of their Chesterfield home.

Maybe, when they saw the old forests still standing, they felt like they had traveled in a loop back to their Carolina childhoods. Maybe, after all the hard miles, that feeling was enough.

However the siblings made their decision, by the mid-1820s my ancestors had settled in the well-watered country along Bowie and Silver Creeks about eight miles west of the Pearl River and between ten and twenty miles north of the Three Chopped Way, on either side of what was then the border between Simpson and Lawrence Counties. Their timing was right. Recent changes in federal law prevented people from buying land on installment but also dropped the price to $1.25 an acre and the minimum purchase to eighty acres. The wealthiest of my Berry ancestors, enslavers David and German Berry, began filing patents, how individuals bought what had been Native American land from the federal government, in 1825.

A few years later, in 1830, President Andrew Jackson led a sharply divided Congress to pass the Indian Removal Act. Soon afterward, the State of Mississippi used the new law to negotiate the Treaty of Dancing Rabbit Creek with the Choctaws, forcing most members to give up their land there in exchange for territory out west in what would become Oklahoma. The removal of other nations living in Mississippi, including the Chickasaws, followed, opening up land for white settlement across the state. Especially in the rich river deltas and bottomlands, many of the new settlers were enslavers. In Mississippi, the expansion of slavery and the theft of Native American land went hand in hand. By 1840, relatives of the original four Berry siblings owned hundreds of acres, mostly in a band stretching from west of Shivers, a Simpson County community named after Jemima's husband, John, or their descendants to east of the Berry Cemetery in what would later become Jefferson Davis County.

This pine forest family reunion did not last. Jemima Shivers died soon after she arrived, sometime before 1827. John Berry and his wife, Edith Ann Polk Berry, built a log cabin on a branch of Silver Creek sometime in the mid-1820s, but my great-great-great-great-grandparents died within a decade. Their son Henry Berry, called Harry, and his wife, Zilla

Huckaby Berry, my great-great-great-grandparents, moved into the cabin and purchased the surrounding land with a patent registered in 1840.

Like the longleaf pines that grew across their land, the next generation of our family sank their roots deep. Harry and Zilla's son Albert Gallatin Berry, my great-great-grandfather and Oury Berry's grandfather, lived his whole life in this part of Mississippi, except the years he served in the Confederate army. He lost an eye at Antietam. After the war, he married Lucy Mullins in a ceremony witnessed by his first cousin and fellow Confederate veteran Abner Wilkes Berry, the older brother of P. W. Berry, founder of Prentiss. Albert and Lucy Berry's oldest son, Henry Jackson Berry, born in 1874, was my great-grandfather and Oury Berry's father. He died twelve years before I was born.

Everyone has ancestors, but family trees, genealogies filled with relatives' names and the dates when they were born and died, depend on archives. And official repositories of documents in turn depend on a society's ideas about who matters. What people with power think is important gets recorded and saved. Other information is often lost.

In this way, white supremacy does not just shape the course of human affairs. It does not just kill and injure people. It also destroys evidence. It makes it difficult and even at times impossible for Americans to know the truth about their history. Without official documents or family papers and oral histories, family trees can be as stunted as pine saplings deprived of space and light.

For Black Americans with enslaved ancestors, official records produced before Emancipation offer little information. In 1850 and 1860, the US Census produced "slave schedules," forms which listed enslaved people by age and gender and race, either Black or "mulatto," a term used then to refer to biracial or mixed Black and white ancestry, under the name of their master or mistress. But these documents rarely included these individuals' names. The US Census, the once-a-decade count of the nation's population, did not provide anything close to a full accounting of Black people by name until 1870.

As a result, it is difficult to trace Versie Johnson's ancestors in official documents back before 1870. His great-great-grandparents Jack and Rachel Baggett lived in Lawrence County then in a section surveyed as Township 6 North, Range 11 West, a rural area just west of the Pearl River and not that far from the future Lawrence–Jeff Davis County border. Rachel, about forty-five, and Jack, about fifty, worked as farm laborers. Before Emancipation, they had likely been enslaved by William Pickens Baggett, a Lawrence County resident living in an area that would become southwestern Jeff Davis County. Thirty people are listed by age and gender under Baggett's name in the 1860 "slave census," including a Black man age forty, a Black woman age thirty-four, and two Black girls, ages nine and five, likely Jack and Rachel and their two daughters, Anna and Clara. Jack died between 1870 and 1880. After losing her husband, Rachel moved in with her daughter Clara Baggett Cooper, whose occupation was "keeping house"; her son-in-law James Cooper, a farmer; and her five-year-old granddaughter, Anna, named after one of Rachel's other daughters. Their household was in Beat 1 of Lawrence County (beats are political precincts). Census takers in 1880 described Rachel, age sixty, as having no occupation. In actuality, she was retired.

Like most people in bondage in Mississippi, Versie Johnson's great-great-grandmother Rachel Baggett ended up in the state as part of what scholars called the second Middle Passage, a domestic slave trade that sent approximately one million men, women, and children west from eastern states like Virginia. However difficult the overland journey was for white settlers, enslaved people traveled all those hard miles on foot or in wagons or boats carrying a burden of unimaginable loss. Because Rachel lived long enough to be counted in the 1880 census, which collected each person's birthplace as well as the birthplaces of their mother and father, she left a partial map of her forced journey. Like the Berry siblings, her mother and father were both born in Virginia. Her grandparents and great-grandparents might have been born at any of the points along the winding routes of the transatlantic slave trade, a nation or empire in the central or western regions of Africa like the Asante Empire, a colonial outpost in the Caribbean like Barbados, or a plantation along the James River in Virginia or in the Low Country of South Carolina. At some point in her youth, Rachel's mother was forced to move. When she gave birth to Rachel around 1820 in North Carolina, she might already have been on the road to Mississippi. Alternately, those who claimed to own her might have migrated south to North Carolina before selling Rachel to traders or taking her with them as they migrated again, this time to Mississippi.

Emancipation gave Clara and James Cooper, Versie Johnson's grandparents, the opportunity to stay in one area on land they rented or sharecropped in Lawrence County near the Fair River community, a rural settlement that would fall on either side of a new boundary line when Lincoln County was formed in 1870. Their daughter Lizzie Cooper, Versie Johnson's mother, was born there in June 1880, likely right after the census taker recorded the names of her grandmother, parents, and sister.

Lizzie grew up in Fair River, taking advantage of her freedom to go to school and learn to read and write, an opportunity her parents and grandmother had been denied. On December 23, 1898, she married William Johnson in Lincoln County.

Because Johnson is a common last name in Mississippi and William often gets shortened to Will, Willie, or Bill, the genealogy of Versie Johnson's father remains a mystery. Versie's birth certificate lists his parents as Bill Johnson and Lizzie Cooper Johnson of Nola, Mississippi, a small settlement just north of Fair River. His death certificate states his father, Willie Johnson, was born in Rankin County. The 1880 census included no Black boys the right age in Rankin County, but two lived in Hinds, the next county west. Either could be Versie Johnson's father, but it was also possible Willie's family moved to another part of the state or even to another state after he was born. Without this paternal genealogy, Versie Johnson's family tree is missing half its branches.

People from elsewhere tend to think of Mississippi as somehow outside of time, stuck in the past and isolated, a place where nothing ever changes. South Mississippi, like many places in this mostly rural state and in other parts of rural America, defies this stereotype. In the Piney Woods, radical change has shaped the lives of people in every generation: Choctaws and white people fighting over the land, the Civil War and Reconstruction, a late nineteenth-century economic depression, waves of lynching and other acts of racial violence, the clear-cutting of the old forests between the 1890s and the 1930s, the Great Depression, World War II, and the civil rights movement. People who live there differ radically from one another in the degree to which they have been the perpetrators or the victims of the violence that often accompanied these transformations. Yet they do share one thing. Since the early nineteenth century, there has never been enough peace in this place to establish something as static as "a way of life."

Oury Berry was born in Jeff Davis County in 1907. Versie Johnson was born eight years later, about twenty-five miles west of Prentiss in Lawrence County. Maybe in their separate childhoods, the two boys had a chance to run in the open green light of the giant pines, hunt quail in the grass between the trees, fish in a creek, or nap on the long, sweet needles. Maybe they caught a glimpse of what their world had been. Whether they experienced the beauty or not, they certainly saw the carnage—miles of stumps, rotting piles of slash, red clay gullies, silted-up streams, idle saw-mills, lumber camps full of abandoned "cut-to-pattern" houses, railroad spurs sprouting weeds, gaunt cities, and lean towns. They spent their lives in the ruins.

2.

A GAMBLE

In 1906, before Oury Berry and Versie Johnson were born, before Jeff Davis County had even held an election or built a courthouse, a Black man named Wood Ambrose—or more likely Ambrose Wood—was lynched in Prentiss.

The trouble started with a game. Playing craps in a circle of swept dirt in the yard of a mill was a dangerous way to make a dollar. Wood must have known this when he joined the bettors on a June Sunday. He brought his gun. But just living was a gamble. Why not make a bet and roll?

Nothing Wood could do was actually safe. He might have been employed at the place where he played craps. Whether it processed logs or ground corn or both for locals, Watkins mill, about a mile west of Prentiss, was a small operation. But the big timber companies busy turning the old longleaf pine forests into lumber needed so many men that they had driven up pay across the Piney Woods. Laborers, some of them Black men, were making as much as $1.50 or even $2.00 for a twelve-hour day at the large sawmills. The problem was the risk. Human limbs got caught in the whizzing belts and blades. Boilers blew. Cables snapped. Rough logs as well as finished boards fell. Men died. Injured men who survived often had to find different jobs if they could work at all.

Other jobs wrecked Black lives in other ways. In the Piney Woods, timber companies built their own railroads. Ambrose Wood might have graded routes or laid track. He could have worked on a timber crew, running a saw through the thick-sapped pines, trimming off the branches, and loading the trunks onto railroad cars. Whatever other jobs he held, at some point he probably spent time on a farm. Some landowners hired hands, though wages were low, around 50 cents a day. Sharecropping, more common, was another kind of gamble. If Wood had a wife and kids, the family would work all year, planting and chopping and picking cotton, hostage to the whims of weather, markets, and merchants, waiting on an annual payout that rarely came. The few jobs outside timber and agriculture had their own problems. Feeding raw cotton into a gin only lasted the length of the picking season. Loading supplies into white men's wagons outside a store required bowing and scraping and yes-sir-ing in a humiliating performance of subservience.

Wood's other option was rambling, making a living on the road. If he played an instrument, he could earn food and drink and a few dollars playing at informal venues called juke joints, barrelhouses, or blind tigers. In these kinds of places, Black musicians were inventing the blues. Other men on the move worked as professional gamblers, winning locals' money at logging and railroad camps and mill settlements through skill and trickery.

Wood was probably not a local, because no one with a name anything like his appeared in southern Mississippi in the 1900 census. Wherever he moved from, if he worked at the mill he likely lived nearby, possibly in housing supplied by his boss. If he lived on the road, he probably showed up at Watkins mill Saturday night, just as men who earned cash wages were being paid. Maybe he played cards, too, or ran the craps game himself. One newspaper report said he used the alias Bud Maston. That was not the kind of detail white papers usually lied about. He must have had a reason to hide his real name. Mill owners and foremen tried to keep known gamblers out of their camps. Most men had knives. Many had guns. Men would lose their money and get mad. Someone might get killed. Someone often did.

If the fighting at Watkins mill that Sunday summer evening had just been between Black people, nobody with any authority would have cared. But white men were there, too. In theory, in this Jim Crow world, an illegal gambling party should have been segregated. In practice, white men went where they wanted. On Sundays, the only thing officially open in the Piney Woods was church. At the mill, Black men and possibly women were having a ball betting and drinking. On the edge of the crowd, someone probably played a guitar and sang. Some white men, likely timber or mill workers or young farmers, decided to go, knowing no Black person could stop them. H. J. Berry, Oury Berry's father and my great-grandfather, could well have been one of the white men there that afternoon. He worked in the timber industry and lived west of Prentiss in the direction of Watkins mill. He also drank. Whether or not he gambled, the liquor might have drawn him.

Somehow, the craps game turned violent. One newspaper described Wood shooting into a mixed-race crowd and also firing at John Williams, a white man, six times without hitting him. Other newspapers reported that Wood killed a white man, often unnamed but sometimes referred to as Sullivan. Wood might have been running a rigged game, and a white man who felt he was cheated got mad. It was also possible that someone else was running a crooked game and that Wood was the player who felt he had been taken. Or the game might have been fair, and Wood simply "lost his money and temper," as one newspaper reported, or Wood won, and a white man did not like it.

Any of these things could have happened. What was clear was that white and Black men were gambling and drinking, and someone started shooting. Newspapers reported that Wood fired and then fled.

It was possible that vigilantes had killed Black people in this area before 1906, when the land was part of Covington and Lawrence Counties. The Equal Justice Initiative found no lynchings in Covington, but it did record six in Lawrence, and no exact location survived for three of them, one in 1886 and two in 1890 carried out as part of whites' violent reassertion of white supremacy in the late 1880s and early 1890s. It was also possible that other, unreported lynchings of Black people occurred in this territory—both before and after Ambrose Wood was killed.

But because Wood's murder became the first recorded lynching in the new county, it established a pattern for Versie Johnson's death four decades later. The Mississippi legislature had created the county that spring, and residents had just chosen the three-year-old railroad town of Prentiss as the county seat. When vigilantes aided by local law enforcement officials killed Ambrose Wood, everything there was new except white people's determination to assert white supremacy.

Appointed officials Constable T. E. Davidson and Marshal R. R. Berry, a future sheriff and my grandfather Oury Berry's distant cousin, told a paper they tried to arrest Wood in Prentiss, the only place they would have had jurisdiction. They claimed he drew his pistol, and in response, they shot him in the leg. Still, Wood managed to run. What other option did he have? The two officers chased him a mile before they caught him. Then they placed Wood in whatever structure passed for a jail in the new town.

As they worked to capture Wood, the two officers probably had some help from local white citizens. Like many of their counterparts across the South, Piney Woods white men had always taken the law into their own hands. Rather than an abstract set of rules and principles, the law was whatever respectable white men did to preserve their vision of the local order. The law was their collective authority to act. And their collective actions—their hands—were the law. Most of the time, white men delegated their authority to people they voted for, like sheriffs and constables. These men then became the hands of the law. But this delegation was always contingent. Government officials, even local men they knew, never held a monopoly on the right to threaten or use force. When those officials could not or would not act for them and even sometimes when they would, many white men believed they retained the collective authority to act for themselves. A mob, as the Jackson *Clarion-Ledger* declared in 1889, "may almost be termed a jury of the whole people." Thirty years later, the *Meridian Star* argued, "The men who do the lynchings are not the men who flout the law, but the men who sincerely believe they have the best interest of their fellow men and women at heart." In this way of thinking, white men were not vigilantes opposed to the rule of law. They were the citizens who embodied and created it. Their collective authority made abstract law live in the world.

While there were always some whites in the region who openly criticized other whites for taking the law into their own hands, many understood lynching and other acts of vigilante violence as community policing. This practice had deep roots in slave patrols, loosely organized groups of white men who threatened, assaulted, and killed Black men and women in the antebellum era. Sometimes, these patrols branched out into collective violence targeted at other white people, too. In the 1840s, a Piney Woods white man named Gallendee ran up to a traveler "shouting murder." "Judge Lynch"—a self-appointed group of white men who lived nearby—had accused him of stealing hogs and whipped him so harshly that his shirt hung in tatters. Half a century later, a mob accused another Piney Woods white man named Virgil Keene of raping a young white woman in Fair River near the border of Lincoln and Lawrence Counties. Keene was Oury Berry's father-in-law and another of my great-grandfathers. He survived because the woman took back her accusation. Other white men were not so lucky. The year a white mob killed Wood, several Mississippi white men lynched another white man after an argument about the treatment of a dog.

These exceptions notwithstanding, most of the victims of this kind of community law enforcement were Black. Before Emancipation, enslaved people who ran away or refused to work or did something else their owners or local law enforcement considered a crime could simply be sold. Freedom eliminated this check on white violence. Vigilante behavior exploded during Reconstruction, and in an era when Black men were still able to vote, whites in places with large Black majorities were often quicker to resort to violence. Between 1865 and 1877, white southerners lynched almost two thousand Black people.

In the late nineteenth century, violence again increased across the South as Black people struggled to hang on to their citizenship rights and white voters divided into factions that fought one another for control. Formerly enslaved people played a pivotal role in a variety of local and state-level political organizations in this period, creating alliances with white voters to form new branches of the Republican Party as well as new parties, and more rarely, to run alternative slates of Democratic candidates. They were opposed by members of the Democratic Party establishment and other white people working to reinstate white supremacy and elite control, an act they called by the euphemism "redemption." In the Piney Woods of Mississippi, a region with many more small farmers than planters, white and Black residents created branches of the Republican Party that successfully ran candidates. Local Republicans in Lawrence and Covington Counties remained competitive and elected local officials through the 1890s. In this period, it was not yet clear who would control the post-Reconstruction South. But as "redeemers" resorted to force to break up the political alliances that opposed them, lynchings and other acts of violence surged across the South. Between 1883 and 1905, lynchers in Mississippi murdered at least 379 Black people.

Sometimes, white men created more organized groups to do this work. During Reconstruction, terrorist militias like the KKK and less well-known groups like the Society of the White Rose, the Seventy-Six Association, and other white "protective" leagues killed around three hundred white and Black people in Mississippi and assaulted and threatened many more in an ultimately successful effort to disfranchise Black voters and their white allies and reassert racist rule. In the late nineteenth and early twentieth century, white residents of the Piney Woods organized armed militias called Whitecaps, a new version of the outlawed KKK with its white hoods. All around the territory that would become Jeff Davis County, these groups beat Black residents and fired shots into and burned their homes. They also attacked white merchants they accused of being foreigners and Jews. Three years before a mob killed Wood, members of a Lincoln County militia lynched two Black men who owned farms.

As this kind of political violence decreased in the twentieth century, lynching gradually took on a more specific meaning. Rather than any act of violence in which vigilantes killed someone, lynching became a racialized crime in which groups of white men who understood their own actions as delivering justice or upholding tradition killed Black people they accused of violating the law. The key characteristic was not how the victims died. Hangings and shootings and burnings could all be lynchings. What made a murder a lynching was not the manner of death but the intentions of the killers and the fact that they acted as a group. And these groups were bigger than they might have seemed at first glance; beyond the ranks of the direct participants always stood other white people who either condoned the violence or refused to hold the perpetrators accountable. Lynching became a more communal affair.

While many white men self-servingly perceived lynching and other kinds of collective violence as virtuous, Black southerners understood these acts as terrorism. And the practice was rampant in Mississippi. Calculated as a rate—the number of Black lynchings per 100,000 Black people— Mississippi ranked among the top four or five among eleven southern states. But in terms of raw numbers, Mississippi, with its large Black population, led the region. The Equal Justice Initiative has documented 656 lynchings of Black people in Mississippi between 1877 and 1950, the largest count for any state in the nation.

Wood may not have known all the specifics of this history, but what it meant for him would have been crystal clear. Given this context, he could not have been surprised when, after midnight, a mob of white men formed outside the jail.

Some of the white men who gathered that night were likely related to my grandfather Oury Berry, whose many ancestors lived in and all around the new town. Berrys had probably participated in vigilante violence in the past, before Jeff Davis County had even been incorporated. But this night marked the shocking inception of this kind of violence in the new county, a history in which Berry men would play an outsize role.

A Black Chicago paper offered a blunt report: "A mob of Christian gentlemen last Sunday busted in the jail at Prentiss, Mississippi and lynched a Negro by the name of Wood Ambrose, who had been charged with wounding a white man." White papers softened the story. In one account, "unknown" persons "overpowered" the jailer and tried to take Wood, but he fought back so ferociously that they killed him there, in the cell, firing over one hundred bullets into his body. In another account, this mysterious crowd shot through a barred window and killed Wood in his cell. Then they broke into the jail, stole Wood's body, and strung it up on a post nearby. Residents woke up the next morning to find what was left of Wood "dangling" there, a gruesome trophy for a half-finished town. Before Jeff Davis had even started building its courthouse, the new county had its first lynching.

In the aftermath of Wood's murder, a handful of unreliable details remained as a testament to his life, a few sentences sent out on the Associated Press wire and published in newspapers across the country and a few more substantial newspaper articles. If Wood's relatives remember him, they have kept their memories private. For everyone else, he has become Jeff Davis's only official entry in the lynching lists, the solitary name chiseled in the pair of rusting steel boxes that represent the county at the lynching monument in Montgomery, Alabama, the National Memorial for Peace and Justice. But just because there were no other recorded lynchings in Jeff Davis did not mean that no other lynchings occurred.

Wood's death was notable in another way, too. It helped establish a pattern for the use of vigilante violence in a new and modernizing county—a model that, over time, varied in only one respect. Back then, at the start of the twentieth century, many whites still bragged about killing or injuring Black people, though they did not always take care to get the details right. The lying would come later.

3 .

A SEPARATE WORLD

W hen white people attacked Black people in the South, they did not just kill individuals. They took aim at entire communities. Yet despite this violence and other forms of white supremacy and as a form of resistance to it, Black residents built their own separate world in the light between the pines. South-central Mississippi, where Versie Johnson lived, was not just a place of Black death. It was also, first and foremost, a place of Black life.

No one had gotten all the way to southern Mississippi without generations of violence and trauma: the Middle Passage, enslavement in the Caribbean and in older slave states like Virginia or South Carolina, the internal slave trade, the children sold away, the couples parted, parents and grandparents and siblings lost, and the murders that continued after Emancipation—all the rips in the fabric of family, the holes where loved ones were supposed to be. For a while, it looked like the pine woods and creek bottoms of the area that would become Jeff Davis County might be a refuge where Black folks could build what white Americans had denied them, the rich layers of deeply rooted lives: grandparents and parents and children baptized and married at the same church, land and houses shared across generations, and peach and apple trees planted so grandchildren could eat the fruit.

The four decades between Ambrose Wood's lynching and Johnson's killing were relatively peaceful years in Jeff Davis County compared to other parts of Mississippi and the rest of the Deep South. Though lynching statistics are widely agreed to be an undercount, no evidence of any other lynchings or other suspicious killings of Black people in Jeff Davis County survives in newspaper databases or the weekly *Prentiss Headlight*. When white Americans across the country joined a new version of the Ku Klux Klan in the aftermath of World War I, white residents of Jeff Davis County did not seem to form a chapter. Until 1940, the county had never even conducted a legal execution.

As the county grew, Black residents built their own rural world, a place where they could live relatively separate from white people. Black landowners had started buying land and homesteading in the area that would become Jeff Davis during Reconstruction. Paradoxically, the destruction of the longleaf forests made it possible for even more families to acquire property. Timber companies like J. J. Newman harvested the old pines and put cutover tracts up for sale at bargain prices. Poor men and women bought these ruined acres, often with money the men earned working at sawmills or on timber harvesting or railroad construction crews. Whole families went to work burning the slash, pulling out the stumps, and smoothing out the ruts left by steam loaders and temporary railroad tracks. Muscle and will, a dream of a homeplace, they believed, could make a farm. Sometimes they were right.

As Black southerners gained a measure of hard-won social, cultural, and even economic autonomy, white southerners worked to limit their political rights. Mississippi led this backlash. The state's 1890 constitution pioneered understanding clauses and poll taxes, new techniques for disfranchising Black citizens without mentioning race that quickly spread to other states. In theory, Black southerners retained the citizenship rights guaranteed by the Reconstruction era constitutional amendments: the Thirteenth, which abolished slavery; the Fourteenth, which established equal protection under the law; and the Fifteenth, which guaranteed the right to vote. In practice, Black voting disappeared, along with Black postmasters and politicians. Undermining the law while pretending to uphold it—a form of government-sanctioned lying—became an essential feature of the Jim Crow South. In the new century, it was hard to remember that such wonders as the first two Black senators to serve in Congress, Mississippi's own Hiram Revels and Blanche K. Bruce, had ever existed.

In this context, economic independence increasingly seemed like the only possible form of safety. Landownership meant families could feed and house themselves and separate their interests from white people. Freedom required property.

By the time Versie Johnson was born in neighboring Lawrence County in 1914, Black families with names like Polk, Hall, Griffith, and Johnson owned land all over Jeff Davis. The farms they built anchored communities connected by churches and the small primary schools they often housed, country stores, and a secondary school and college called the Prentiss Institute. Separation kept many of the daily humiliations of Jim Crow at bay. People could pray and learn and live with one another without having to answer to white folks. In the 1930s, Black sociologist Charles Johnson found that most Black farmers went into southern towns, where they had to navigate segregation laws and conventions and deal with white people, about once a month; the rest of the time, they stayed in their own, separate spaces. Around the same time, researchers working for the New Deal's WPA counted six hundred Black farm owners compared to nine hundred Black renters and sharecroppers in Jeff Davis County, an astonishingly high rate of property ownership for Black southerners and possibly a decline from an earlier, pre-Depression peak. In fact, some Black renters and sharecroppers worked land owned by other Black families, often relatives.

Well before Versie Johnson's birth and while he was growing up elsewhere in Mississippi, Black people in Jeff Davis had a great deal of success creating their own separate Black world. Other, most likely unrelated Johnsons—the educators Jonas Edward and Bertha Johnson and the farmer and business owner Estus Johnson—played important roles in making the county a place where a not-insignificant number of Black people flourished despite Jim Crow segregation.

Yet this thriving Black community was built on a foundation more precarious than it seemed when Versie Johnson moved into a house near Prentiss in the mid-1930s. The events of his death would have a profound impact not only on his own relatives but on Black people across the county.

Today, not much of this mostly rural and separate Black world has survived. By the time I made my first childhood visits to Prentiss, Jeff Davis County had already entered a period of economic decline and out-migration that would still be unfolding half a century later when I set out to write this book. Today, the county's half dozen country churches welcome dwindling congregations and are sustained as much by members who have moved away as by those who have stayed. Scattered homeplaces shelter former migrants who have come back to the family land to retire after working for decades in Atlanta, Chicago, or Oakland. The rest is fragments: the collective memories of scattered Black families, a handful of written memoirs, Black cemeteries, the mostly ruined campus of the Prentiss Institute, a slim file of historical photographs, occasional references in old copies of white newspapers, and the land deeds filed in the big red ledgers in the Jeff Davis chancery clerk's office. It's not enough, really, to conjure the enormity of what local people lost in the years after Versie Johnson died.

It took one kind of courage for a Black man with a gun to gamble with white men. It took an altogether different kind for a Black man with a college degree to ask a white man he hardly knew for money.

On an April day in 1907, less than a year after white men lynched Ambrose Wood, Jonas Edward Johnson must have made his way through Prentiss with care, stepping lightly between the mud and the manure, trying to keep his shoes neat. Maybe he walked in from a nearby farm. More likely, the family he was staying with hitched up a mule or a horse to a wagon and gave him a ride into Prentiss. They probably dropped him out past the Pearl and Leaf depot near Prentiss mayor J. S. Bozeman's cotton gin in the tiny Black part of town called the Quarters. From there, it would have been a short walk up Columbia Avenue, then more of a farmyard than a road with its wide expanse of rutted dirt and low well for watering stock. Along the way, Johnson would have passed businesses like J. H. Williams and Sons, a store that carried everything from coffee and corsets to coffins, and Palace Drugs, with medicine for sale on the first floor and doctors' offices on the second. Though Johnson was from Pike County, about fifty miles southwest of Jeff Davis, it would not have been hard for him to find his destination. After the brand-new courthouse, the Bank of Blountville was the second most impressive building in town.

A group of relatively prosperous local Black farmers, many of them landowners, had a bold vision of an independent Black future in Jeff Davis County, and they invited Johnson to Prentiss to build one pillar of this plan. At the time, two small Black schools already operated in the county. The oldest, Mt. Zion, opened in 1870 to educate the freed people. Around the time of Wood's lynching, local families organized a second school at Mt. Carmel, an old settlement taken over by Black folks after white residents abandoned it to move to the new railroad town of Prentiss. But farmers who lived near the county seat needed a school close enough that students would be able to walk to classes after finishing morning chores.

They could not count on any help from the state. Across America, only about one third of Black children ages five to fourteen attended school in 1900. In Mississippi, the situation was likely worse. Not only had Governor James K. Vardaman, who served from 1904 to 1908, condoned lynching and other forms of vigilante violence, but he had also called openly for the closing of public schools for Black residents and the repeal of the Fourteenth and Fifteenth Amendments guaranteeing Black citizenship rights. "Education," the governor argued, was "ruining our Negroes." If Black families wanted more educational opportunities, they would have to build their own institutions.

Five years earlier, Johnson had graduated from Alcorn, a public Mississippi college founded during Reconstruction to educate the descendants of enslaved people. His wife, Bertha LaBranche Johnson, also from Pike County, earned her degree from Tuskegee Institute in Alabama, where she

30

had met Booker T. Washington, the college's founder and president. In the Piney Woods region where college degrees were extremely rare, J. E. and Bertha stood out.

Because of the Johnsons' qualifications, Black farmers in the Prentiss area offered them an opportunity. If the couple would agree to move to the brand-new county and found a school, local people promised to help acquire the necessary land. Johnson had gone to Prentiss that day to inquire about a loan.

At the bank, Johnson would have faced the public humiliations of segregation. He had to enter through a side door. After he stated his business, a clerk whisked him to a back room away from the lobby to wait. Johnson must have been nervous, standing there in the suit that Bertha had probably wiped and pressed, as sweat began to dampen his best collar. At some point, a clerk appeared again to take him to the office of Leon Tyrone, the head of the bank.

Like Ambrose Wood, Johnson played his own dangerous game of chance. Black people in the Jim Crow South took a risk whenever they talked to white strangers. Just as many Black men worked hard to avoid ever having to speak to white women they did not already know because white men were so quick to make accusations of attempted rape, direct conversations with unknown white men could also be dangerous. As one of the new county's leading citizens, Leon Tyrone was probably secure enough not to take easy offense at Johnson's presence, but Johnson could not have been sure. Well-educated, well-spoken, and well-dressed Black people made it clear to many white people that their vaunted supremacy was a lie, and yet here was Johnson with his college degree and his suit asking for money. Somehow, he had to convey deference. His gestures had to be assuring, easy, even flattering. If Tyrone told a joke, even a racist one, Johnson had to laugh. Yet the educator also had to project competence. Eye contact, always risky when a Black man met a white stranger, was probably necessary.

Whatever Johnson said to the banker, he walked out that day with both his life and a loan, so he must have been convincing. The days when the state government of Mississippi had been interested in founding public colleges for Black residents had long passed. Alcorn was not a viable model. Instead, Johnson laid out a vision based on his wife's alma mater, that thriving Black school in rural Alabama called Tuskegee.

By 1907, Booker T. Washington had become a nationally known leader. White politicians sought his advice. Wealthy white philanthropists and business leaders gave him money. President Theodore Roosevelt invited him to dine at the White House. But both Washington and the school he had run since its founding had humble beginnings, an 1881 grant from the Alabama legislature for $2,000 and a one-room cabin owned by a Black church. Over a quarter century in which white southerners killed and assaulted Black folks with impunity and white supremacist politicians took over local and state governments across the region, Washington built one of the nation's most important Black educational institutions right in the middle of all that violence. He performed that miracle by persuading some wealthy white Americans to value a form of Black education that would teach students to be "useful" and "productive" citizens. While white Tuskegee supporters believed that meant Black subservience, rural southern Black people understood what Tuskegee offered as Black self-determination.

In Jeff Davis County, Black residents wanted to build their own Little Tuskegee, as the Prentiss Institute and two other Mississippi schools would one day be called. They recruited Jonas Edward Johnson to make their dream a reality.

Johnson had grown up "country" in a large, hardworking farm family in rural Pike County. At Alcorn, he had focused on science. But his future success suggested he also learned something watching Alcorn administrators and professors keep their school going even as radical white supremacists dominated Mississippi's state government. By the time he arrived in Jeff Davis County, Johnson already knew how to get along with Mississippi's white people by carefully attending to their anxieties and desires. In Prentiss, he frequently described himself as "plain as an old shoe." He also referred to himself and Bertha—who were more educated and cultured than most people in the county, Black or white—as just "home folks." In Johnson, locals found an educator who would not engage in risky talk or behavior that their white neighbors might interpret as advocating equality. He would keep his institution open.

Johnson and his Black backers also had the fortune of good timing. White Jeff Davis leaders imagined their new county as forward-thinking, a New South in contrast to the old, a dynamic place of prosperous farms organized around a cultured county seat. In the eastern half of the county, the booming timber industry was beginning to cut mile after mile of the old longleaf pines, opening up what white leaders imagined as vast tracts of cheap farmland for men who understood the new fertilizers and other "book" farming practices. It was not much of a stretch for Tyrone and other local white elites to see how a Tuskegee-type school with an agricultural program could be part of this vision.

With Black landowners providing security, Prentiss banker Leon Tyrone had agreed on that April day in 1907 to give Johnson a loan for $600. In two transactions that June and October, the Prentiss Institute acquired its original tract just southeast of Prentiss along the old Three Chopped Way.

The future campus had once been the Magee Plantation. When the Johnsons acquired the property in 1907, one building still stood there. Enslaved people had constructed the modest, four-room house out of hand-sawed boards around 1820, with two additional rooms in a rear lean-to added later. Tobias Magee lived there until he became wealthy enough to build a larger dwelling, a more traditional plantation "Big House." The tract also contained a semicircle of ruined cabins once occupied by enslaved people about fifty feet north of the cottage and the Magee family cemetery, still surrounded by the iron fence that in an earlier era kept out the free-roaming cows and pigs. J. E. and Bertha Johnson and their Black supporters gambled that they could turn this former site of bondage into a place of learning.

Prospects looked good that first fall when about forty students of all ages showed up for the opening session of what locals at first called the Johnson

School. Some were girls and boys starting their education in the regular course of their lives. Others were adults of different ages: young people strong from farmwork and eager to study now that there was a school close by, gray-haired grandparents who had grown up before the Civil War when it was illegal for enslaved people to learn, frazzled mothers with toddlers in tow, and farm men who milked and mucked at night during lay-by time so they could attend. All were drawn by the same promise: to get an education in order to build a life for themselves and their families free from white control.

That little house must have been bursting at the seams. Bertha and J. E. and their children lived there along with about four or five boarding students. Classes met in the front rooms and, when possible, outside under the trees. Most students had no money. Instead, they paid what they could in live chickens and smoked hams, baskets of eggs and meal, and bushels of corn and peas. Rosie Hawthorne's mother gave her a rooster to pay tuition for her and her brother, and she carried that bird four miles, the route she walked every day from her home to the school. More than once over those first few years, the Johnsons had to go house to house asking for donations so they could make the loan payments. A few well-off white families like the Dales and the Tyrones, banker Leon Tyrone and other members of his family, also contributed support.

The categories of public and private did not quite capture how schools operated in the early twentieth century in many areas of the rural South. In one sense, most schools were "private," meaning they were organized and run by the families that sent students and provided a building and other resources. In another sense, they were almost all public, as most got some funding—for Black schools it could be a pittance—from public revenues, including property taxes and, in the case of states like Alabama and Mississippi, revenues generated by publicly owned sixteenth-section lands. Counties often covered the low salaries of rural teachers and occasionally other expenses. In Jeff Davis, this blurred boundary between public and private schools lasted into the civil rights era.

In its early years, the Prentiss Institute served as an eight-month community school, instructing everyone who showed up in basic subjects like reading, writing, and math. Over the first decade, the Johnsons built this part of the institution into a more traditional primary school for nearby kids. But unlike most schools that served rural Black folks, the Prentiss Institute also offered more advanced courses for students who had mastered what was available at local one-room institutions. In 1909, the State of Mississippi recognized this work by issuing a charter allowing the Prentiss Institute to operate as a high school. Eight years later, the two-year high school program became four. Then the school expanded its agricultural department and won state approval for its normal school, or teacher training curriculum, and its junior college program, which also included vocational courses. In partnership with Mississippi Baptist Seminary, a statewide organization founded by Black leaders meeting at the Johnsons' home, it also provided Bible classes and other training for rural ministers. As it grew, the school changed its name to the Prentiss Normal and Industrial Institute. After World War II, it expanded again, and 150 veterans used their G.I. Bill benefits to take courses in shoe repair, dry cleaning and pressing, brick masonry, photography, and auto mechanics as well as more academic subjects. Over the course of its eighty-year history, the Prentiss Institute offered the programming of at least seven different kinds of educational institutions.

In the South, Black families paid property taxes that supported education for white children even as they often also paid public school fees or private school tuition—whether in cash or crops—to educate their own kids. By the 1920s, Jeff Davis officials began appropriating funds for the Prentiss Institute in recognition of the fact that the Johnsons were running the county's largest Black primary school as well as its only Black high school. In 1944, the Board of Supervisors borrowed $1,500 to pay "school carriers" transporting kids from across the county to the institute's campus. Six years later, instead of building a public high school for Black residents, Jeff Davis imposed county-wide special property tax levies to cover costs at the private institution.

In 1928, a white newspaper in the big sawmill and railroad city of Hattiesburg reported the story of an eighty-year-old man who went to school in the Rosenwald Building at the Prentiss Institute: "'Uncle' Joshua Johnson, ex-slave, African and proud of it, genuine connoisseur of all realms and varieties of garden sass, Plenipotentiary to all roasting ear patches, gardens, even cotton fields, has added another notch to his entitlements. He has learned to read." Thrilled with his accomplishments, the newly literate Johnson exclaimed, "Gwinter git one of dem Ph. D's, if dey don't watch out." Casting the older Black man's speech in a demeaning dialect, the paper urged its readers to laugh at his presumptions even as they celebrated his achievement.

Yet maybe Joshua Johnson meant what he said, and the white journalist used his own assumptions to twist the older man's remarks. The 1920 census reported that at age seventy-two, Joshua Johnson already knew how to read and write and that he and his wife, Margurette Johnson, lived with a son who was a landowner. At the Prentiss Institute, it was possible for a man who had grown up in bondage to go to school as a grandpa.

Given their shared surname, it was possible Versie Johnson and Joshua Johnson and even the Prentiss Institute's founder J. E. Johnson had a distant connection, common ancestors enslaved in southern Mississippi by a white man with the last name Johnson. But whether or not all these Johnsons were actually related, their lives intersected in a community powerfully shaped by something most Black people in the rural South could only dream of: an independent, Black-run educational institution with course offerings at multiple levels, including college. With its forward-looking motto "See no hills," the school J. E. and Bertha Johnson and local Black farmers built "sparked a bloodless educational revolution," in the words of a newspaper from a nearby county. By the time Versie Johnson moved to Prentiss between 1930 and 1935, the Prentiss Institute had helped nurture a local Black middle class—members of the school's faculty and staff as well as hundreds of Black farm owners, many of them alums or parents of alums.

Versie Johnson was not part of this educated and landowning class. Since he only went to school through the fourth grade and was at least fourteen when he arrived in the area, he probably never attended the Prentiss Institute. His life and death would demonstrate the limits of a vision that imagined Black education as the best way to defeat white supremacy. Yet even before he arrived in Jeff Davis County, other examples of these limits abounded.

In Jeff Davis County, as elsewhere, Black people's separate rural world did not keep all its inhabitants safe. What white men and boys wanted in Jim Crow Mississippi they often took. As far as many white southerners were concerned, Black women did not say no and Black girls were not really children. In reality, many Black women and girls and some men and boys, too, were assaulted and raped. Others could not say no because family members needed to eat or work or keep their home. Some knew that whatever they said, white men would have their way. Others reasoned that a connection to a powerful white man, a patron, might help a Black family buy land or get some measure of justice in an encounter with "the law."

The story of Delphia, a nineteenth-century Black teenager who grew up in the area that would one day become Prentiss, offers a glimpse of the snarled roots of Black and white families in the region. Her son would connect yet another family of Black Johnsons to the Berrys. This connection, too, would be defined by violence—but violence of a different kind.

What chance did Delphia have to dream? Her mother, Amanda, seventeen years old and enslaved when she gave birth, might not have even been allowed to pick out her daughter's name. In 1870 and 1880, Delphia lived with her mother, her stepfather, Sandy Johnson, and her half siblings on land they farmed but did not own and that would one day be Prentiss. She attended school occasionally but did not learn to read and write. At age thirteen, she should still have been in the classroom. Instead, she worked on the farm and nursed her baby daughter, Orah. At sixteen, she had a son she named Estus. A year later, she had another son, Joseph. All three bore the last name she got from her stepfather, Johnson. While it was possible Orah and Joseph had the same father, Estus was different. His father was white.

Black women with so-called mulatto children—offspring who, like

Delphia's son Estus Johnson, had white ancestors as well as Black ones—were not rare in that part of Mississippi in 1880. Alice Hartzogg, Delphia's closest neighbor, had a Black husband, Bill Hartzogg, and a five-year-old biracial daughter named Charlotte from before her marriage. Her husband's father, also Bill Hartzogg, lived next door with his second wife, two daughters, a stepdaughter, and his daughters' infants, one of them a three-month-old biracial grandson, Joseph Hartzogg.

More rarely, a household might include adults of more than one race—a reflection of the fact that outside of Mississippi's towns, residential segregation could be haphazard. Next to Bill Hartzogg Sr., for example, a white doctor and dentist named J. J. Packer lived in a household headed by a Black woman named Hannah Barnes.

Like in many rural southern communities, white and Black families sometimes shared the same surnames because enslaved people had been given their master's last name. White Hartzoggs old enough to have been enslavers lived close to Black Hartzoggs old enough to have been formerly enslaved. My grandfather Oury Berry had a great-great-uncle named Richard Talley Berry who, along with his wife, Martha, and their three youngest surviving children, lived between the Black and white Hartzoggs, not far from Delphia and her family. In rural Jeff Davis County, Black people created a separate world while sometimes actually living, by rural standards, close to white people.

My family also seems to have interacted with their Black neighbors in other, more brutal ways. Delphia must have confided in someone, because later relatives linked her middle child, Estus—so fair he could pass for white—to Richard Talley Berry's youngest son, Prentiss Webb Berry. Some of Estus Johnson's descendants believed that "Prent" Berry, namesake of the yet-to-be-founded town of Prentiss, was Estus's father.

Around fourteen or fifteen when Estus was born, Prent—who was also a first cousin of my great-great-grandfather—lived close enough to Delphia to walk to her house. His older brother John L. Berry, also living at home, would have been about seventeen. It was not at all unheard-of for teenage white boys to rape teenage Black girls, to use physical force or to otherwise pressure them into having sex, a practice established during slavery that did not die out after Emancipation. Alice Hartzogg was fifteen when she had her biracial daughter, Charlotte. Delphia, a stepdaughter in a family of Black farm laborers, would have been particularly vulnerable to the kind of sexual violence that might have befallen Alice. A person who lacked the freedom to say no also lacked the freedom to say yes. If Prent Berry, founding father of Prentiss, was Estus's father, then he was also a rapist.

Delphia Johnson's son Estus knew what it meant to chop other people's cotton, an endless task that involved using a hoe to thin and weed the young plants. His stepgrandfather and his grandmother were sharecroppers or possibly renters, a step up on the farm hierarchy that meant a family had resources, like their own plows and mules, and in return got to keep more of whatever they raised. His mother lived in their household, at least while her children were small. Estus studied for a while, probably at the school in the Mt. Zion community, though it would have been about a six-mile walk one way. But as the oldest son, he had to cut his education short to help support his mom and siblings. Mostly, what he did was work. He also fell in love. He and Rosie Mosson were married when he was about twenty.

After Rosie got pregnant, Estus left home for Hattiesburg, where he could make a dollar a day laying track for one of the railroads that would eventually come to Jeff Davis County. After Rosie gave birth to their first child, a daughter they named Doretha, Estus walked the forty-five miles home. In his pocket, he carried twenty-eight of the thirty dollars he had earned. If he had been able to stay longer, he might have made enough to buy a farm. But Estus understood what it meant for a young mother to have a baby without the father present. As much as he longed to own land, he also wanted to be home with his wife and his child. It was, he believed, his duty and responsibility as a Christian husband and father. He would have to find another way.

It was not easy for a Black man in rural Mississippi to ask a white man for something. With his hat perhaps in his hand, Estus would have knocked on the back door of the thirty-seven-year-old white landowner's home and asked the Black cook or maid if he could speak to the boss. Maybe Prent Berry and Estus Johnson talked there, on that back porch. If it was cold, they probably went into the kitchen, where Prent would have sat while Estus stood.

Maybe the young Black man and the white man who was probably his father spoke of their kinship. More likely, it saturated the air like humidity, adding weight to whatever they did actually say. Both men would go on to be leading citizens, Prent as the founder of the railroad town that became the county seat and Estus as that town's most successful Black business owner. But at that moment, those futures were ahead of them. At that moment, Estus was a young Black man who owned nothing in a Jim Crow world, and Prent was a middle-aged white man who owned everything, acres of rich farmland and old pines and all the rights of citizenship. He could have found a better tenant, a man with a large family who could put many more hands in the field to work the rich land. Yet Prent Berry said yes. The white man who was likely Estus Johnson's father also became his patron.

Sometime in the fall of 1899 or the early winter of 1900, Estus, Rosie, and baby Doretha moved to a small house on Prent Berry's farm to begin sharecropping. Estus's youngest brother, George Herrin, around thirteen, joined them, possibly because Delphia had died. But according to family history, Estus was not satisfied. He wanted to own the land he worked, to be the master of his own small world. Somehow after a year or two, and despite his lack of resources, he persuaded Prent Berry to allow him to rent rather than sharecrop. Over the years, Estus and Rosie were able to increase the acreage they farmed. Their sons worked alongside Estus and the local men he hired. Their daughters helped their mother tend the garden and cook and clean for the family and some of the farm hands who were also boarders.

In good years, they put away money toward their dream. But the kids kept coming. In all, Rosie and Estus Johnson had nine children, including the stillborn twin of Estus Jr. By 1903, when Prent Berry had turned much of his farm into the town of Prentiss, Estus and Rosie may have had to move off the land they rented to make way for the railroad or the new grid of streets. By 1918, when Estus signed his World War I draft registration card with an *X*, he and Rosie were renting from Prent's brother John Berry. They still had not managed to buy. After the war, plummeting cotton prices probably made it even more difficult to save.

Like almost everyone in the Piney Woods, Rosie and Estus Johnson were devout and committed Christians. If the doors of Green Grove Missionary Baptist Church opened, Estus Johnson entered. And it was there one day that he heard the speech that would change his life.

In the early 1920s, the pastor, a Reverend Cook, brought a man who was probably his relative, R. C. Cook, to the church just north of Prentiss to talk to the congregation about establishing a home union. These conversations ultimately turned into the mutual aid society that local Black leaders chartered around this time.

Yet R. C. Cook did not just urge Jeff Davis residents to band together to help themselves. As the owner of a burial association and a funeral home or two, he also tried to sell them burial insurance. In Cook's popular family plans, Black families paid pennies a month, less than a quarter, and then if a covered person died, the policy paid for that person to have a simple funeral.

But in addition to the policies he likely sold that day, Cook came away from the church with something else, too. He persuaded Estus Johnson to come to work for him.

It would not have been an easy job. In rural Mississippi, many Black and white farm families hung on to their relative self-sufficiency by growing what they ate, making what they wore, and otherwise avoiding most purchases that required cash. Yet burial insurance that covered the costs of embalming the body, a nice casket, and an engraved headstone— a set of practices that seemed to permanently plant the remains of a loved one in the ground at their church or family plot—also had great appeal. Cemeteries with proper headstones functioned as community archives, repositories of the information about the members of that separate Black world. While lynching dehumanized and mutilated the bodies of Black people, burial insurance literally helped preserve them, marking a family's existence on the landscape in a lasting way.

Estus probably started by selling policies to his relatives and neighbors and the other members of Green Grove before branching out. Then he used what he had earned selling policies for R. C. Cook to form his own business. In 1928, the Johnson Funeral Home and Burial Association opened in a borrowed building on St. Stephens Road near the Prentiss icehouse. Because he knew J. E. and Bertha Johnson well from church and some of his kids attended the Prentiss Institute, he got permission to store his coffins on campus. It was a perfect Jim Crow business model. Segregation created a niche because white funeral homes did not serve Black customers. And by combining burial insurance and the funeral home business, Black owners potentially profited twice: once when they sold the policies and again when their customers used the payouts for these policies to buy funeral services.

In 1929, the year the US stock market crashed, Johnson was still not a landowner. Then, suddenly, his situation grew worse. A building he was constructing to house his business burned to the ground, and then his wife, Rosie, died. At the end of the year, he married Frankie Weathers, adding two stepdaughters to his family. In the years to come, he and Frankie would have four more children of their own.

Estus Johnson's new family expanded while the economy continued to shrink, because in farm country the Great Depression was already well under way before the market crashed. Falling cotton prices after World War I, floods and droughts, and the boll weevil, which arrived in Jeff Davis in 1907, hammered farm profits. Many Black families got by because their teenage boys and men worked off and on at sawmills or on timber-cutting crews. But Frankie and Estus Johnson prospered. If money could be scraped together for anything, the burial policy got paid. No one wanted to send their loved one to heaven without a proper ceremony. No one wanted to bury a family member in a cardboard coffin in a grave without a headstone.

By the 1930s, Frankie and Estus had saved enough to buy a lot on Fred Street in the Quarters, the Black section of Prentiss. There, across from the gin and the cotton warehouses, they constructed a wood-frame building with space for the funeral home on one side and on the other, living quarters for Estus's son Central—then in his early twenties—and his family. This arrangement enabled a Johnson, Central or one of his brothers, to be available twenty-four hours a day if anyone called and needed the hearse, which doubled as a Black ambulance, to take someone to the hospital or to pick up a body.

Success in the death business had finally enabled Estus Johnson to get what he had always wanted, his own land. And he did not stop with the lot on Fred Street. He also began buying pieces of property west and northwest of Prentiss near where he had lived as a child. By 1940, he and Frankie and their kids lived on their own farm, which shared a long boundary line with the farm where my grandfather Oury Berry had grown up and his parents, my great-grandparents, still lived.

Maybe it was Oury who phoned that day in August 1947 from the Lipsey farm. Whoever called, it was Estus's son Central Johnson who answered. In such a small place, given their jobs and the fact that their families owned adjacent land, Oury and Central must have known each other. What did Central think as he held the receiver to his ear? As he drove the waxed and polished hearse the short mile or so to the Lipsey's place, parked, and walked up to where law enforcement officials still stood over Versie Johnson's body? Somehow, Central picked up the corpse of a Black man a little younger than he was, a person he probably knew at least by sight, a human who had been alive so recently he might have still been warm. Sure, as a trained embalmer, Central was accustomed to death. But given the accusations against Versie Johnson and how he died, this one must have been hell.

4.

BLACK BOY

Sometimes official documents record the lives of Black people, but just as often these archives also erase them. Of the forty-one pieces of evidence I have located that refer to Versie Johnson's life, fewer than ten directly address what he did before his last days. In almost every case, officials struggle to get his name right, rendering it variously Versey, Bursie, and Vernon across three census reports, a birth certificate, a World War II draft registration, and two mentions in a small-town paper. It's not much to work with, fragments rather than a whole, a man described not so much by how he lived but by how he died. And yet it is enough to see the outlines of a time when Versie Johnson had a future.

When I started this research, I did not know whether I would be able to find the right Versie Johnson at all. In a year and a half of research trips to Mississippi, I did not speak to a single current or former resident of Jeff Davis County who remembered him. And the written record was sketchy. The *Prentiss Headlight* article simply called him a "local" Black man, and articles about his death in other newspapers provided contradictory information, sometimes describing him as a sawmill worker and other times as a farm laborer. Few newspapers stated his age, and those that included that detail did not agree. I did not know whether Versie Johnson was married or widowed or single or where he was born or his parents' names. Compounding the difficulties, Jefferson Davis and nearby counties were full of Black Johnsons in the first half of the twentieth century.

I decided to start by looking for a man in his twenties or thirties. A census search turned up both a Vernon and a V. H. Johnson in that age range in Jefferson Davis County in 1940, but I did not even know if he lived there seven years before he died. To find out more, I broadened my search, combing through long lists of Black Johnsons in nearby counties that shared boundaries with Jeff Davis: Covington, Lawrence, Simpson, and Marion. Then I added other nearby counties. When I hit a dead end, I read the original handwritten census tract sheets, which have also been photographed and digitized, to check the spelled-out names against the indexes and account for the not-at-all-rare errors in transcription. Staring at all those names, I grew more and more worried that this search would fail.

Then one day I got lucky. I found a Versie Johnson, age four, living with his parents, Bill and Lizzie Johnson, in the 1920 census for Lincoln County, Mississippi. It was easy enough to find Bill and Lizzie on the same or a nearby rented farm in Lincoln County in 1910, four years before their son was born. Using these names for Versie Johnson's parents, I systematically searched again in broadening circles out from Lincoln County. Remembering that a few papers had said he was a veteran, I searched military records. Those reports were wrong. But I did find a World War II draft registration for "Versey Johnson," living in the town of D'Lo in Simpson County, with a mother named Lizzie Johnson living in Jeff Davis County.

To me, that draft registration coupled with the 1940 census listing for Vernon and his mother living near Prentiss proved this was the right Versie Johnson. But I hired a specialist in Black genealogy, Sharon Morgan, to check my work. When I laid it all out for her, she was skeptical. That 1940 census said Versie Johnson and his mom lived with Reggie and Velma Knight, his brother-in-law and sister, and I had not documented a sibling with that name. Sharon then did more research.

When she found Versie Johnson's sister Eula Mae and her husband, Reggie Knight, through the World War II draft registration of their son Reggie Knight Jr., she emailed me the discovery with the subject line "Eureka!" That find led back to the 1940 census entry that I had found where the census taker had probably gotten Eula Mae's name wrong or listed her under a nickname. Velma had to be Eula Mae. Then Sharon advised me to request the birth and death certificates from the Mississippi State Department of Health to confirm that the elusive Johnson we were tracking was the man who had died in Prentiss on August 1, 1947. When those certificates arrived, it was clear. We had found him.

Putting together these government records for Versie Johnson with the documents that describe his ancestors and siblings, I can tell a story about his birth, his childhood, and some of his adulthood. What I cannot tell you is whether he preferred to spell his name Versie or Versey. I have chosen Versie, because it appears early, in the 1910 census when he was four, and then shows up again at the end, when one of his sisters provided the information for his death certificate. In the absence of more substantial records about Versie Johnson's life, such hints about how he lived—his preferences, pleasures, and pains—are doubly precious.

It was cold for southern Mississippi and probably still dark when Bill Johnson slipped out of his family's cabin near the crossroads settlement of Nola. Lizzie Cooper Johnson's pains had started. Lord willing, this child would be their seventh, and Lizzie's labor was likely to proceed quickly. It was time to get help.

Bill probably hitched the mule to the wagon, drove to the midwife Henrietta Jett's house, and carried her back. If she lived close, he might have walked or sent their oldest son, Willie, then around ten. Their girls Ella and Cora were fourteen and thirteen, but they would have been helping their mother, and Black parents in Jim Crow Mississippi were reluctant to send a daughter out alone before light. Eula Mae, around nine, would probably take care of little Gertrude, two, if she woke up. At six, son Jesse was old enough to mind himself.

Whoever went, the message got through. Henrietta Jett probably arrived sometime that morning. In rural Mississippi in 1915, Black women usually gave birth at home, attended by midwives. Jett, who had lived in that part of what was then western Lawrence County and eastern Lincoln for decades, might have delivered some of Lizzie and Bill's other children, too. So far, all of Lizzie's babies had lived. For a while, at least, this one would be no different.

Around thirty-five and an experienced mother, Lizzie Johnson carried the memory of what to do in her muscles and joints as well as her head. She knew. She also had women there to help her, probably her mother, Clara Cooper, and her sisters, Anna and Ella. When the midwife arrived, she would have put her hands on Lizzie's body to check the baby's position and if necessary, worked to try to turn the child in the womb. If the baby was lined up right, Jett and the other women would have wiped Lizzie's brow, held her hand, and helped her through the contractions. Sometime in the late morning, the circle of Black women would have watched as the little head crowned. A few more hard pushes, and this part of Lizzie's labor at least was done. The Johnsons had a new son.

Versie Johnson's mom probably held him as Jett cut the umbilical cord and then used a soft rag to wipe the blood and vernix from his skin. Taking in her tiny boy, Lizzie would have noticed if he had his father's nose or her brother's mouth or her grandma Rachel's chin. When at last the baby was clean and swaddled and suckling at Lizzie's breast, Jett marked the time. A week later when she filled out the paperwork with the county registrar, she listed the time of birth as 10 a.m. on November 23, 1915, and the place as the Nola voting precinct in Lawrence County, just to the east of the Lincoln County line and near the Fair River settlement where Lizzie grew up.

Lizzie and Bill Johnson favored family names. They called their first child, Ella, for one of Lizzie's sisters, their first son, Willie, after his father, and their second son, Jesse, for Lizzie's brother. It was possible the name they chose for this new baby, their seventh child, was also a family name, too. Alternately, Lizzie, who unlike her husband could read and write, might have come across the name at school or in a book or newspaper. Virginous, the name on the birth certificate, was an unusual choice, and by the time their youngest child was four, his parents would shorten it to Versie.

Growing up in Fair View, Lizzie Cooper completed the eighth grade, at that time the first year of high school—a notable achievement for a Black woman raised in the rural South at the end of the nineteenth century. While Lizzie was still in school, Bill, about five years older, lived with his first wife. People married young in the country. Surviving records do not reveal whether Bill had any children from this union, or what broke up their marriage. Bill's first wife might have died giving birth or left her husband for someone else. Or maybe Bill left her for Lizzie. However that relationship ended, in December 1898 Versie Johnson's parents, Bill and Lizzie, married in Lincoln County, not far from the Nola district of Lawrence County where their son would be born nearly two decades later. In January of 1900 they had Ella.

A few months later, the census taker found the new mother and the baby with Lizzie's grandmother Rachel Baggett. Lizzie's parents lived next door in the house where Lizzie grew up. James and Clara Cooper were probably renters rather than sharecroppers, because they stayed on the same land in the Fair River voting precinct in Lincoln County for decades. This distinction meant the Coopers had resources—their own tools and a mule and other animals—and thus paid a set amount for the land they farmed rather than a percentage of the crop they grew. Rachel Baggett, Clara's mother, had her own separate dwelling on this land, where she lived alone after her husband, Jack Baggett, died sometime between 1870 and 1880.

Lizzie began her life as a new mother there, surrounded by family and at home, in the place where she had always lived. Her grandma Rachel Baggett had been enslaved when she had her own children. But Lizzie's mother, Clara Baggett Cooper, had been able to draw on Rachel's help and wisdom as she gave birth during Reconstruction to her first baby, Anna, and in the years after, to at least seven more children. As Lizzie became a parent, she in turn relied on her ma and grandma as well as her pa, her siblings, and other members of an extended family whose bonds had survived slavery.

But Bill, her husband of about two years, was living elsewhere when the 1900 census worker knocked on Lizzie's grandmother's door. There were many possible destinations that could take a Black man in Mississippi away from his wife and new baby at this time, not all of them good. About twenty miles southwest of Fair River, the Butterfield Lumber Company paid Black men good money, and Bill Johnson might have been away working at their Norfield sawmill or on a crew cutting logs or laying railroad track in southern Lincoln County, trying to earn some money in order to set up a new household with Lizzie and Ella. Alternately, Bill might have been a prisoner. As far as southern law enforcement officials were concerned, Black men were guilty, if not of the particular crime at hand, then of another for which they had not been caught. Penitentiaries and jails needed bodies, people to work the prison farm or laundry or to serve on chain gangs building county roads or to lease out to white landowners or businessmen who used them as household servants, farm laborers, or members of turpentine crews. If Bill was not imprisoned or working in the timber industry, he might have still been living with his first wife despite his marriage to Lizzie. In the 1900 census, I found Bill and Willie and William Johnsons the right age in all these scenarios.

Whatever caused Bill and Lizzie's separation, they started their life as a family apart. Yet the land and the promise of independence from whites that it enabled, even for sharecroppers, would help bring them together again.

At some point between 1900 and 1910, the Johnson family reunited and got a farm, what locals called the process of entering a contract with a landowner to live on and work particular acres for around half of the crop. They were poor, for sure. No one with other options made this choice. The work was endless, the risk high, and the pay as often as not virtually nothing. The children came fast, seven in fifteen years, a period in which Lizzie was almost always pregnant or nursing. Like many sharecroppers, the Johnsons sometimes moved after the year-end settle, looking for richer soil or a more generous landlord. But they did not go far. They had married in Lincoln back in 1898, and census takers found them there, in the eastern part of that county, in 1910 and 1920. When Versie Johnson was born, either they had settled just across the line in western Lawrence County or the midwife had been confused about their location. All these places were close to Lizzie's parents in Fair River.

Like most farmers in Mississippi, the Johnsons organized the rhythms of their collective life around the cotton crop. At times, every member of the family strong enough to hold a hoe or pull the fibers out of the bolls probably labored in the fields. Other tasks—work in the house, the garden, the yard, and the barn—were usually divided according to gender. Lizzie would have taught the girls to piece quilts, sew clothes, and cook and preserve the food they grew, passing along the lessons she learned from her granny Rachel and her ma. The boys would have followed Bill everywhere and learned by watching how to dress fish and game, call out "gee" and "haw" to turn the mule, and pull the teats just right so the cow gave the most milk.

Winter was short in the southern part of the state. By the time the new baby was two months old, his father and oldest brother and maybe a sister or two had started breaking up the soil and setting the rows in the fields, preparing for the planting that would start in early March. After the cotton sprouted, whoever was needed helped with the thinning. In April, they "chopped" the cotton, cutting the weeds away from the crop. As the plants grew bigger, Bill used the mule to plow the rows while some of the kids came behind with hoes, cutting the weeds where the plow could not reach. If the whole family worked the fields, Lizzie or Ella probably tied little Versie on her back and told Jesse, too young to get much done with the heavy hoe, to keep an eye on the toddler Gertrude. When it got hot and sweat soaked through the men's and boys' overalls and wet the back of the women's and girls' dresses, someone—possibly Eula Mae—filled a bucket at the spring and toted it and a tin cup up and down the rows, giving everyone a cool drink.

In late June or early July, the cotton fields were "laid by," the fieldwork there done until harvest, and farm folks had more time for fun. Maybe some Saturday afternoons, the whole Johnson family braved the damp and melting heat to pack into the wagon for the ride to Monticello, the Lawrence county seat, or to Brookhaven, the county seat of Lincoln. Black people from miles around would be in town then to visit and to trade. Lizzie, Ella, or Cora would have carried eight-month-old Versie as family members meandered along the sidewalks, stopping to look in the shop windows or to watch the trains at the depot. Lizzie might have used some egg money to buy the youngest kids a piece of penny candy. Bill probably joined a knot of men talking about the weather and the cotton crop.

Through July and August, the children still had chores. Someone had to gather the eggs and shell the peas and shuck the corn. The garden patch still needed attention. Versie Johnson was too little to help as the middle children squished borer worms and slugs and gathered whatever had ripened, a pan of butter beans or a bucket of bright red tomatoes. He was also too young to go along when the girls set out to pick the blackberries that grew in a tangle of long, thorny limbs at the edges of the fields or the boys went fishing at the deep bend in the creek or on the nearby Fair River. But he was old enough to watch and take in the smells as his mother fried the fish and made the cobbler and then to sit on Lizzie's lap and beg for a bite.

In September, the cotton bolls began to swell and burst, spilling their white fibers out into the Mississippi sun. The youngest member of the Johnson family would have been big enough to crawl after the sacks his parents and siblings pulled down the rows as they picked and to call out "pa, pa, pa" as Bill left in the wagon to haul the cotton to the gin. By the time of the year-end settle, he was one, too young to understand and yet old enough to feel the mood if Bill came home from his meeting with the landlord with his pockets empty.

When Versie Johnson was around six, he followed his youngest brothers and sisters to a rural one- or two-room primary school where an overworked teacher did what she could to open up the wider world—the kind of institution that sent graduates who could afford it on to a place like the Prentiss Institute for high school. His older siblings—Ella, Cora, and Willie—were unable to attend much in their early years, which must have been hard for Lizzie. Perhaps the place she had studied had closed or was too far away from the Johnson home for the kids to walk. Or Bill, who could not read or write, might not have valued education. More likely, the family simply could not make it without the children's labor, and Lizzie taught them what she could by the light of the gas lamp on winter evenings after the chores were done. Cora and Willie caught up, attending school as older teens and learning along with their younger siblings, Eula Mae, Jesse, Versie, and Gertrude. But Bill and Lizzie's first child, Ella, did not. Unlike the rest of her siblings, she reached adulthood without learning to read or write.

Still, before Versie Johnson's birth and for at least a few years afterward, life on the land in their own cabin must have contained some happiness and joy. Inside their cabin, they had each other. Beyond their walls, they had Lizzie's family nearby and possibly some of Bill's relatives, too. They also had Black neighbors and friends and the members of their church. They had a community.

Versie Johnson and his relatives left a few clues in the official records, especially the once-a-decade census. From the information in these forms, I can fill out the bare contours of their existence. Other kinds of sources, firsthand observations of rural life in this period by scholars and writers like W.E.B. Du Bois, explain what rural Black southerners meant when they said they just wanted "to live like folks." Especially useful are the writings of Richard Wright, the rare Black author then who had actually grown up in Mississippi.

Wright was born in 1908 in Roxie, Mississippi, a tiny town in Franklin County, about fifty miles west of Nola, the precinct of Lawrence County where seven years later Lizzie and Bill Johnson were living when they had their son. Wright, too, had an educated mother and a father who could not read or write. Though he moved much more than Versie Johnson did as a child, he spent some of his early years in Mississippi: in Roxie; in the river town of Natchez, where his maternal grandmother oversaw a large household; in Greenwood, a town on the eastern edge of the Delta where he stayed for a while with an aunt and uncle; and in Jackson, Mississippi's capital and largest city. In books like *Uncle Tom's Children* and *Black Boy* that blurred the boundary between fiction and autobiography, Wright explored what he knew firsthand, from the simple delights of childhood to the hard truths about a place where white people called him boy even as he became a man.

In the story "Big Boy Leaves Home" published in 1938 in the collection *Uncle Tom's Children,* Wright describes in all its joy and horror a day in the lives of four Black boys growing up in the rural Deep South. As the story opens, they are walking through the woods calling out the lines of a song. "Yo mama don wear no drawers," one of them sings. Another answers, "Ah seena when she pulled them off." Then another chimes in, "N she washed 'em in alcohol." Then all four voices blend together, "N she hung 'em out in the hall." The barefooted boys laugh as they use long sticks to beat back vines and bushes as the woods give way to pasture. No one remembers the next line of the song. Someone says, "Shucks, what goes wid hall?" The others yell out answers, "Call." "Fall." "Wall." Then the one called Big Boy says, "Quall." Laughing again, they throw themselves down on a patch of warm grass. One of the boys tells Big Boy what they all are thinking, "Yuh crazy as a bed-bug."

A little while later, they hear the whistle of a train. Pounding their heels in the grass, they chant the words of a spiritual. "Dis train boun fo glory / Ef yuh ride no need fer fret er worry / Dis train, Oh Hallelujah / Dis train... / Dis train don't carry no gambler / No fo day creeper er midnight rambler / Dis train." When they stop singing, they laugh again. It's quiet for a moment. Then one of the boys draws out a hum. Another says, "Whut?" The first replies, "Somebody don let win! Das whut!" Big Boy remains silent. The others—Buck, Bobo, and Lester—jump up. Eventually, one of them tells Big Boy he's "rotten inside," as another says, "NIGGER YUH BROKE WIN!" After much ribbing, Big Boy falls back in the grass, closes his eyes, and replies, "The hen whut cackles is the hen whut laid the egg."

My grandfather Oury Berry, around the same age as Richard Wright, grew up with this kind of play as well. On the Brady land his maternal grandpa gave his ma, he would have met Black boys who lived on neighboring farms. Overhearing them "shooting the dozens," competing with one another in rounds of thrown insults, he might even have joined in. Wherever he learned the phrase "crazy as a bed-bug," he used it all his life. If the right situation arose, he also repeated the line about the noisy hen and her egg. He, too, learned to swim in deep spots in creeks and went barefoot when it was warm to save his shoes. And if his atrocious spelling was any indication, he also skipped school. Like other white and Black boys in the rural South, Richard Wright's Big Boy and Versie Johnson and Oury Berry shared the same language, the same pastimes, and some measure of the same poverty though it was certainly better to be a part of a poor landowning family than to be a sharecropper. Jim Crow did not make them different. It just gave many white people too much power, including, in the right circumstances, the authority to decide who lived and who died.

In Wright's story, Big Boy at first resists the decision that sets them all on the path to disaster. When Buck, Bobo, and Lester say they are going to the creek to swim, Big Boy slaps the air with his palm and hollers, "Naw, buddy, naw. N git lynched? Hell naw!" But his friends ignore him and keep walking, and eventually he joins them. At the swimming hole, the friends switch roles. Bobo reminds them that "Ol man Harvey" who owns the place does not let his Black neighbors use it. Lester recalls that Harvey took a shot at a Black man who tried to swim there last year. He also points out the NO TRESPASSING sign. This time it's Big Boy who wants to swim. "Waal, wes here now," he argues. "Ef he ketched us even like this thered be trouble, so we just as waal go on in." He starts to take off his overalls, and the other three follow. Soon they are all laughing and splashing and churning up the water. Then they sit on the bank in the sun to rest and warm up. A train whistles, the number seven heading North, and they talk about going there. One boy says, "They say colored folks up Noth is got ekual rights." They grow silent and pensive, watching a black winged butterfly and listening to the bees and sparrows and thinking. They've skipped school and had a perfect day. Then a white woman appears on the opposite bank of the creek. As the Black boys scramble to get their clothes, she screams, and the world ends. Buck and Lester are shot by her white male companion there at the swimming hole.

The rest of the story unfolds in slow motion the lynching that Big Boy foretold. Only it's Bobo, not Big Boy, who is burned to death that night. Big Boy's punishment is to watch his friend die from where he is hiding, a hole the four boys dug in a hillside a few weeks before. Miraculously, Big Boy gets away. The plan his father and other Black men hatched to save the two boys works for him. On his way north, the place of his and his friends' dreams, all Big Boy can think about is home.

Unlike Wright's character Big Boy, Versie Johnson did not have to leave the land where his family sharecropped. Most days, he followed his father, Bill Johnson, to the fields. He wore clothes his sisters washed. And he ate his mother's cooking. Even on days when he and his father had to keep picking or planting right through dinner, Lizzie brought something to them in the fields, a square of corn bread topped with a slice of fatback, perhaps, or a small crock of peas and greens. Until they left home, he probably shared a bed with his older brothers, Willie and Jesse. When he could be spared from the work, he went to school, eventually in his teenage years making it through the fourth grade. There and at church, he found friends whose lives were a lot like his own.

It was possible that Versie Johnson loved farmwork, the feel of the dirt and the smell of the coming rain, a life bent to the cycles of the seasons and the crops. It was also possible he longed instead for the wider world, for anything that did not require following a mule's ass around a cotton field, for high school or for rambling. After all that farming, he might have wanted to work for wages at a sawmill or a store or a gin. Then on paydays, he could buy a cold Coke or a plug of tobacco or save for a guitar or a new hat for his girl or even a used car. On the edge of manhood, Versie Johnson must have looked at the future and dreamed. But given the meager sources that survive, I simply do not know for sure.

Unless they focus on elites, historians rarely have access to the inner lives of the people they write about. A majority of working people do not keep diaries or family Bibles, and if they save letters and other family papers, these items are often lost over the years. While oral historians have worked to close some of these gaps by interviewing regular folks, not everyone gets a chance to tell their own story and have that record preserved in an archive. Anyone trying to recover the history of rural Black people during the Jim Crow era faces an additional challenge: the way white supremacy shaped the institutions that reported the news, collected the data, and preserved the documents. Even the census, that once-a-decade record of all Americans' lives, sometimes fails to account for Black southerners.

As I worked to finish up what had been several years of research, it began to look like the 1930 census officials had skipped over Versie Johnson's family. Because of this single missing document, I had no idea what happened between two different phases of his life: his childhood in the area on both sides of the border between Lincoln and Lawrence Counties and his young adulthood, when the census taker found him at twenty-four living with his mother and sister outside Prentiss. There, in the years between 1920 and 1940, the trail went cold.

As with most historical research, I finally figured out some of what happened in this gap through a lot of work and a little bit of luck. Mostly, I stared at the 1930 census on my computer screen for hours, scrolling through entries for Black people named Johnson in Mississippi and then nearby states in widening circles until I covered the country. I tried every variation I could think of on his name and found nothing. Then I tried Bill and Lizzie and the related names William, Will, and Elizabeth, and found thousands of entries. More than once, I gave up, and then a few days later, decided to try again. And then one day, before I had gotten to the end of all the possible entries for his parents, it dawned on me that his youngest sister, Gertrude, might still be living with the family, even if his older siblings had likely moved away by then. And the name Gertrude was also not that common. By searching for his sister, I found the family, father William, mother Elizabeth, and daughter Gertrude all the right age living with a fourteen-year-old boy whose name the census taker had mistakenly recorded as Bursie Johnson.

What this document made clear was that between 1920 and 1930, the family made a radical move. It might have been caused by the breakup of Lizzie's family as Clara Cooper, Lizzie's mother and Versie Johnson's grandmother, died. In the aftermath, Lizzie watched her parents' household dissolve as her father, James Cooper, married Carrie, a woman younger than many of his own children, and as her sister Minnie Cooper moved away. Maybe, after all this sorrow, Lizzie and Bill left in order to make a fresh start close to the Johnson side of the family. Alternately, it might have been trouble that chased the Johnsons away: a landlord mad because Bill challenged him over the year-end numbers or a white farmer on a neighboring property with too much interest in Gertrude. Whatever the reason, sometime in the ten years preceding the 1930 census, when Versie Johnson was between five and fourteen, his family left the area in western Lawrence County and eastern Lincoln where they had married and had their children and moved about seventy miles north to Rankin County, where Bill had been born.

There, the family lived on a rental farm, and Versie Johnson went to school and helped his father with the work. Bill and Lizzie's grandson and probably Ella's child, a ten-year-old boy named Mack who had taken the Johnson name, lived with them too and also attended school and worked on the farm. The other Johnson siblings lived elsewhere. In the 1930 census, Mississippi-born Willie Johnsons the right age sharecropped, worked for wages at a lumber mill, a freight depot, and a brickyard, and served time in prison. Multiple Jesse Johnsons worked as farm laborers or sharecroppers. At least some of Versie Johnson's older sisters had gone into domestic service.

One of these siblings was Eula Mae. Sometime after her family moved from the place where she had grown up, she settled in Jeff Davis, the next county east of Lawrence. It would prove to be a fateful choice.

By 1930, Eula Mae Johnson worked as a live-in cook for Fred and Nona Dale and their children in one of the nicest houses in Prentiss, right on the main street, Columbia Avenue. Fred Dale, a navy veteran and former cashier at the Bank of Blountville, owned and ran a large general store in downtown

Prentiss, where his decisions about how much credit to extend to his customers shaped the lives of local Black and white folks. Nona was a Berry, not my grandfather's branch of the family but the wealthy ones. Her father was Prentiss founder P. W. Berry, my grandfather Oury Berry's distant cousin.

In this way, Oury's family tree, which is also my own, has branches that intersect with Versie Johnson's family tree. In a small town like Prentiss, Mississippi, such intimacy was unavoidable.

The Johnson family endured another loss in the next ten-year window between censuses. Sometime before 1940, Versie Johnson's father died: his mother is listed in the census of that year as a widow. The Rankin County household broke up, and mother and son moved in with other family members, Eula Mae Knight and her husband, Reggie Knight, on a farm just outside Prentiss. Around the same time, Gertrude Johnson, Lizzie's youngest daughter, also moved to the area. She headed a household that included herself and two lodgers in the Black section of Prentiss, the Quarters.

Versie Johnson's sister Eula Mae and his brother-in-law Reggie Knight probably met while she worked for the Dales: Reggie Knight likely farmed land he had rented from Nona Dale's relatives. On April 14, 1930, the census taker found Reggie Knight still living with his first wife, but at some point that marriage ended, and Eula Mae and Reggie married. On September 23, 1930, Eula Mae gave birth to their child, a son she named after his father.

The elder Reggie Knight connected his recently arrived Johnson in-laws to long-standing networks of Black and white families in and just outside Prentiss. Born in 1897, before both the town and the county were formed, Knight had lived his entire life near Prentiss with the exception of two years in the army's 326th Labor Battalion, military service that had taken him overseas during the Great War. Back home after the armistice, he tried his hand at farming, renting or sharecropping land near Prentiss, an income he seems to have supplemented through less-than-legal means.

By the time he married Versie Johnson's sister, Knight already had a criminal record. In 1929, Prentiss marshal John C. Sanford arrested Knight for gambling. Judge John Tyrone, then the mayor of Prentiss as well as the county's judge, charged Knight and four other Black men the Jackson paper called "colored boys" with running a "regular five-cornered game" at a nearby mill. About six months later, Marshal Sanford arrested Knight again, this time for making a "keg of home brew" in a thicket of bushes near Prentiss. In 1933, after Reggie and Eula Mae Knight had their first child, Marshal Sanford and sheriff W. H. Mathison arrested him again in a liquor raid. In that case, the court convicted Knight and sentenced him to pay $100 for alcohol possession.

Given Reggie and Eula Mae Knight's history, when Versie Johnson arrived in Jeff Davis County, he moved in with a Black family that local law enforcement officers viewed with suspicion. Yet it was also a Black family with some kind of alliance with the wealthy Berrys, the powerful branch of my own family. Even after Reggie Knight's arrests for gambling and bootlegging, he continued to farm for Dr. W. S. Berry—a first cousin of Eula Mae's former employer Nona Berry Dale and another of Oury's distant relatives. By 1940, Versie Johnson's youngest sister, Gertrude, was working as a cook in a private home, a job with a white family that Eula Mae and Reggie Knight probably drew on their connections to secure. Eula Mae Knight used her own talent in the kitchen, a set of skills she shared with her sisters, to leave the Dales and take a job that paid more, cooking at the Prentiss Hotel.

When this relationship between the Knights and Berrys began is unclear. Possibly, it had roots in the era before Emancipation when some of Reggie Knight's ancestors might have been enslaved by some of my Berry ancestors. Alternately, Knight might have created this connection himself. Born within two years of each other, Knight and W. S. Berry could have gotten to know each other as boys, fishing in White Sand Creek together or hunting squirrels in the pines, the kind of friendship that put a Black man in a position, as long as he stayed "in his place," to ask a white man for a job or for other forms of aid.

These kinds of unequal alliances were not uncommon in Jim Crow Mississippi. Black people got employment and some measure of protection from white patrons whose standing in the community might stave off trouble with other white people. In return, these white benefactors got dependable workers and something less tangible but perhaps even more important: Black subservience and deference, a little taste of the old antebellum mastery. If Knight had this kind of relationship with Dr. Berry, he had something that might be valuable to a Black man who made hooch and gambled: a white man obliged to try to help. But whether or not Versie Johnson had the temperament and inclination to make this kind of alliance with a white man, leaving Lincoln County, where his mom's family had such deep roots, and then also leaving Rankin, where his father had connections, made it impossible. Patronage relationships took a long time to build and often started when white and Black people were young. Versie Johnson likely came to Jeff Davis County to reunite with some of his own family members. But this move all but guaranteed that, if trouble arose, no white person would feel obliged to help him.

In the spring of 1940, Versie Johnson was surviving but he did not seem to be thriving. At age twenty-four, he lived in another man's house. The year before, he made only $180 in wages as a farm laborer, his income as reported to the census taker, at a time when the Labor Department calculated the median income for nonwhite men in the United States at $460. By the fall of 1940, he had moved to Simpson County, a white-majority county with a reputation as one of the most racist places in Mississippi. It was not clear whether he left because of some kind of trouble with an employer or the law or even his brother-in-law or because something better appeared, like an interesting woman or the opportunity to set up a branch of Reggie Knight's bootlegging business in the next county north.

By the time Versie Johnson registered for the World War II draft about six months after the 1940 census, he lived in D'Lo, a former sawmill town in Simpson County surrounded by eroded, stump-filled land, where rents on what had been mill-worker housing would have been low. He must have had a car, because he listed his employer as a white man named Alton White, a farmer and store owner in Pinola, a small town about ten miles away. Whether or not Johnson was bootlegging or even running a card game on the side, his work for White probably included farm labor as well as loading and unloading goods at the store and making deliveries. Johnson was not yet married or he would not have given his mother's name as his contact, the person who would always know his address.

Both the front and the back of Versie Johnson's draft registration provide a great deal of information about him, given the dearth of other sources. But it's the back of the form on government-yellow cardstock that I'm drawn to, the part where the registrar filled in a physical description. It's the closest thing I have to a portrait of Versie Johnson, but like everything else in the Jim Crow era, it is an image that fuses some of what was actually present with all that white people refused to see.

The registrar described Johnson as five feet nine inches, not tall for a man but not short either. She recorded his weight as 175 pounds, again an in-between measure, neither large nor small and an indication that he was not too poor to eat well. She checked the box for black for his hair color and dark brown for his complexion. But it was the eyes that revealed that this description was as much about the white registrar's racism as about the man in front of her. She marked them as black, too. The form gave this impossible option—no one actually has black irises. It set her up. But it seemed unlikely that she really tried. To determine Johnson's actual eye color, this white woman would have had to stare into his eyes. She would have had to consider his particular humanity. She would have had to look.

About a year and a half later, another white official also refused to look when she filled in the form for Johnson's brother-in-law Reggie Knight in Prentiss. When World War II draft registration finally extended to men his age in February 1942, Knight would not have been worried: the local draft board would not call him because at some point since his earlier discharge from the military, he had lost an eye. He signed the required form that listed his address, birth date, and employer—Dr. Berry—with an *X*. It was left to the Jeff Davis County registrar to add his signature in her clear and flowing cursive and then to sign her own name in the same script on the back, Mrs. Grace Berry. That registrar was my grandmother, the person I am named for, Oury's wife.

In 1940, whatever took Johnson to Simpson County, he had lived there long enough to turn up twice in the *Magee Courier,* the local paper. He appeared first in a list of D'Lo men sent draft questionnaires in February 1941. Whether or not the local board tried to draft him, he never served in the military. The problem might have been what happened that summer—the event that got Versie Johnson into the *Magee Courier* a second time. Johnson was arrested and convicted of some criminal charge, probably selling alcohol or gambling because something more serious would certainly have made the newspaper. In September 1941, his name appeared in a list of cases being heard on appeal in that month's term of the Simpson County Circuit Court. No records survive of either the original trial or the appellate proceedings.

After that, Versie Johnson disappeared from the records until after he died. It's unlikely he won his appeal, and he might have served time in the Simpson County Jail or the Mississippi State Penitentiary, better known as Parchman Farm, a prison in the Delta two hundred miles north of Prentiss, where most prisoners served their sentences farming with nineteenth-century tools on land that had formerly been a plantation.

Ironically, it is Versie Johnson's death certificate that tells me the most about how he lived in his last few years. Gertrude Johnson, born just before him in the Johnson sibling birth order, gave the authorities the information they needed to fill out that form. It describes Versie Johnson as a widow [*sic*]. Sometime between 1940—the census then lists him as single—and 1947, he got married, but I could find no record of the date or place. Then, wherever the couple was living, his wife died, possibly in childbirth. If Versie Johnson had kids that survived, they must have been taken in by his wife's family. At some point during these years, either with his wife or alone, he moved back to Prentiss, where his mother and two sisters were still living. Some of his relatives probably helped him get a job, and articles about his death describe him as a sawmill worker or a farm laborer.

For thirty-one years, Versie Johnson lived without leaving much of a trace in the historical record. Then suddenly, when he died, it was different. It made the news. Nothing in Jeff Davis County would ever be the same.

PART II

"Quiet and Orderly"

5.

THE LAW

The first time my grandfather Oury Berry ran for sheriff, his wife and my grandmother, Grace Berry, tried to talk him out of it. In 1943, the Berry name meant something in Prentiss. Forty years had passed since P. W. "Prent" Berry made a deal with a railroad to cut down a pine forest and build a town. He and some of his children, Oury's distant cousins, still lived there. Oury and Grace were not part of their circle, a network of the town's most powerful residents that also included members of white families with names like Dale, Tyrone, and Magee. But they had both climbed far from their impoverished childhoods. Grace did not think it would be enough to win my grandfather the office of sheriff. She feared few people would vote for her husband because his own father drank.

Oury decided to run anyway. He wanted the job with its pay, status, and power. Like those better-off Berry men, he wanted to be a leading citizen. By the time I knew enough to ask him whether he regretted the decisions that led him to the sheriff's office, he was dead.

Oury's father, my great-grandfather Henry Jackson Berry, had always been a problem. In our family history, his alcoholism provided a cautionary tale about the evils of drink. But no one gave many details. Not mentioning anything unpleasant, a kind of lying by omission, was a family tradition. I found out from a newspaper article that sometime before World War I, he lost a limb in a logging accident after the tree his crew was cutting fell on him and smashed his left leg so badly it had to be amputated.

Maybe whiskey made him careless, or he took up liquor after the accident to dull the pain. However his alcoholism began, once he started drinking, H.J. could not stop. Come payday, he drank up what he earned working as a sawmill foreman. More than a decade after his first accident, a load of lumber slid off the back of a railroad flatcar at Haney's sawmill and broke his remaining leg. His drinking got worse.

H.J.'s wife, my great-grandmother Lula Brady Berry, had her pride. Thanks to her own father, who was a successful farmer southwest of Prentiss, she also had the land he had given the couple after they married. In better years, when H.J. laid off the liquor and the weather cooperated, the family might make a decent cotton crop. Otherwise, they ate what they could grow, raise, and catch. Sometimes it was not enough. Sometimes H.J. and Lula's eight kids missed school to work on the farm. Oury grew up hungry.

At the Baptist and Methodist churches that most people in the county attended, the ministers denounced the "demon drink." Locals might not have talked openly about people from respectable white families, but with friends, shelling peas on the porch or sipping a cold bottle of Coke at a country store, they gossiped. In the eyes of most people, H.J. was a failure. He did not fulfill every husband's and father's most important duty, providing for his family. He also sinned. Jesus did not live in intoxicated hearts. But in 1943 in Mississippi, H.J. was also a lawbreaker.

The end of national prohibition laws in 1933 gave states the right to control the manufacture and sale of liquor within their borders. Mississippi remained dry, and law enforcement officials there and in other dry states faced an even more difficult battle stopping liquor production and sales than they had when alcohol had been banned everywhere. In Jeff Davis County, the border with Louisiana, a wet state, was less than fifty miles away.

Never mind that Oury did not drink, other than an occasional secret sip or two of bootleg whiskey at his favorite brother-in-law's farm in Marion County. When he announced his run for sheriff, the most powerful law officer in the county, his alcoholic father became a liability.

Jeff Davis County was formed the year before Oury Berry was born. Beginning with the new Mississippi Constitution ratified in 1890, the state had passed multiple laws designed to prevent most Black men and a significant number of lower-income white men from voting. Disfranchisement was actually central to Jeff Davis County's very existence. Folded into the former territories of Lawrence and Covington Counties, Black residents had little political power. But because of where Black people lived and how the lines were drawn, they formed a majority when Mississippi lawmakers created Jeff Davis in 1906. In that sense, the legislature's decision to name the new county after the Confederacy's only president, a former Mississippi planter, congressman, and senator, was a kind of sick joke.

In 1943, when my grandfather decided to run for sheriff, Mississippi still had a few Black voters. But as in many other southern states, only white residents there could vote in the Democratic primaries. And after the early twentieth century, the Republican Party was so weak in the region that it rarely ran county-level candidates. For voters in Jeff Davis and many other southern counties, the Democratic primaries were the election. Local voters would select their officials in an early August primary and if necessary, a late August runoff. Only a small number of Black county residents managed to get past Mississippi's registration process and pay their annual two-dollar poll tax to the sheriff, who was also the tax collector. But even they would have no say because the race was already decided. Whoever came in first in the Democratic primary had already won.

Whatever the demographics of each particular county, Mississippi as a whole had a Black majority until 1950. Maintaining white supremacy in this context required an aggressive and militant approach. As a result, white politics in the state often revolved around issues of law enforcement. In Jeff Davis County in the mid-twentieth century, virtually every candidate for local office ran on the issue. Even men vying for the job of superintendent of education argued that schools should teach children "respect for law and order."

In Mississippi, sheriffs could not succeed themselves, but during their four years in office they had virtually unlimited local authority. In particular, they could use state laws forbidding the possession and sale of alcohol as a ready justification for arresting, jailing, and even killing other citizens.

While many white and Black Christians sincerely believed drinking was a sin, in practice, laws forbidding the sale of alcohol gave sheriffs, deputies, and police officers a way to control Black people within their jurisdictions. In Mississippi, the issue of prohibition could not be separated from the use of law enforcement to enforce the "law" of inequality and the "order" of segregation. How would voters trust the son of the town drunk with that kind of power?

Yet there was Oury Berry in January, the first man to throw his hat into the ring. If he won, he would not only hold a powerful, important job. He might also be able to repair the damage his father had done to the family's reputation. In his statement published in the *Headlight,* Oury made a point of not making "extravagant promises." He admitted he had never run for office before, but that only made him more qualified since he was not a "professional politician" aligned with any particular political faction. Instead of experience, in "these grave times," with the war on and no peace in sight, he offered hope, his belief "that conditions in this county" could be "better." He understood what was at stake because he had two brothers, Herman and Albert, in the military and two kids—one of them my mother—who would "soon be in the teen age group." Without quite saying it, he reminded voters that his fight against liquor was personal. He kept his platform simple: "the ENFORCEMENT of the laws, and a strict and business-like administration." The *Headlight* gave him the highest possible compliment: "He is known all over the county as being a young man whose life and character are above reproach."

As farmers got their crops in the field that spring, eight other white men joined the sheriff's race alongside my grandfather. Trying to stand out in the crowd, H. L. "Fate" Magee turned his announcement into a poem. In a time and place where most people left the race of people whose ballots they sought implicit, Z. P. Polk made an explicit appeal to "white voters." Most of them promised they would work hard to stop the bootleggers.

Often candidates for sheriff had experience as deputies, town marshals in Prentiss or Bassfield, or district constables. But white voters cared more about what they called character: church membership, a "fine family," and a reputation for honesty and integrity. For in a very real sense, the job of sheriff was different from their own roles in the community by a matter of degree rather than kind: most of the white men there grew up with guns—shotguns and rifles they used to hunt squirrels, quail, turkeys, and deer, firearms they kept in their homes or cars and sometimes carried, symbols of their authority as citizens who mattered, and tools for enforcing their will. Learning to shoot transformed a boy into a man. In their way of thinking, "respectable" white men who grabbed their guns and turned out to help local law enforcement officials were not vigilantes. They were not breaking the law but enforcing it, because the whole point of the legal system was to support white supremacy. When white voters elected a sheriff, they chose a fellow citizen to put his farm or other business aside for four years and make their shared duty to police their community his full-time job.

In a nation at war, it helped that Oury had military experience. In his late teens, he had taken the train to Fort McClellan in Alabama, his first real trip away from home, to spend a month at the Civilian Military Training Camp there. If my grandfather had learned anything growing up, it was that he did not want to be a farmer, and CMTC suggested an alternative: at bases around the country, CMTC offered a kind of summer-camp version of basic training designed to give more young men than could serve in the small, peacetime military some service experience. Oury loved it—he kept the badge he earned there all his life.

Somehow, after this modest military training, my grandfather managed to gain a spot in the navy—an assignment that was all the more improbable since he had never been on a ship. In early 1927, the year after his father's second accident, Oury left home for a career in the military.

The navy trained my grandfather to be a barber. It was not exactly a job at the center of the military branch's mission, but someone had to cut sailors' hair on long voyages and on bases. But after only a few months, Oury caught pneumonia, nearly died, and spent weeks at Norfolk Naval Hospital struggling to recover. Nine months after he left Prentiss, he was back home with a medical discharge, a three-and-a-half-inch scar on his chest, and a missing section of rib where navy doctors had drained his left lung. He would receive a monthly payment of varying amounts "on account of disease of the lungs—peace time service" for the rest of his life, money that helped raise him into the middle class. In the 1930s and 1940s, these $22 to $30 checks were about what Black schoolteachers earned in rural Mississippi.

Memories, a scar, and a stipend were not all that Oury had brought back to Prentiss, however. He also returned with the social capital of having served in the military, something that would work to his advantage in the race for sheriff. And he would soon find another asset as well.

Growing up, Oury had not really had what local whites considered a "fine family"—but back home in Prentiss after the navy, he met a young woman who would help him to change that fact. Grace Keene, who had moved from Sumrall, Mississippi, a sawmill town about twenty-five miles away on the train, to keep the books at the Prentiss Wholesale Company. She and Oury married in September 1932, joined Prentiss Methodist Church, and had a son, Jimmy, my uncle. In 1936, they brought their baby daughter, Joan, my mother, from the hospital to the first home they ever owned, a small wood-frame house they built at the corner of Leaf Avenue and Fifth Street.

Oury raised himself up in the community in other ways as well. Whereas his father had been an on-again, off-again laborer on account of his injuries and his drinking, Oury forged a reputation for himself as not merely a hard worker but also a business owner. When he met Grace, he cut hair and gave men shaves as an employee at an established Prentiss barbershop. After he married, he opened his own place, Berry's Barber Shop, in a small storefront downtown.

Barbering turned out to be good preparation for campaigning. A good barber handled his scissors and razor well enough, but he also knew how to talk. Customers came for the company and the entertainment as much as a haircut or a shave. Oury had a knack for storytelling, and he could play a little harmonica and sing a variety of folk songs and old minstrel tunes. His shop functioned as a kind of clubhouse, a place white men gathered to swap stories, tell jokes, make music, and argue politics. At work, Oury got to know the white men who lived in Prentiss as well as many who lived in the country and came to town to trade.

The year 1942 proved to be a period of transition. The attack on Pearl Harbor and the official declaration of war had occurred in December 1941, but most Americans did not understand until the next year that fighting World War II would require a complete transformation of the peacetime economy and a massive influx of men and even women into the military. Back in Prentiss, young men were joining the service and everyone who could manage was buying war bonds. But Oury was having health problems related to his illness in the navy that made it impossible for him to keep working as a barber. He closed his shop, and he and Grace bought the Sanford Dairy—cows, equipment, and a set of customers along an established delivery route—from Flora Etta Sanford, the widow of J. C. Sanford, a former Prentiss marshal who also worked as a builder and a farmer.

Oury must have known the family that sold him the dairy business. Johnny and his wife, Flora Etta Sanford, and their kids lived on First Street in 1930, though by 1935 they lived just outside Prentiss, on the farm that probably housed their dairy. Though the Sanfords were Baptist and my grandparents were Methodist, Oury might have cut Sanford's hair and shaved his beard. Grace might have bought the Sanfords' milk.

To have a place to run the dairy, Oury and Grace sold their house in Prentiss in June 1942. In August of that year—as German U-boats sank US ships and claimed the lives of many American sailors, including perhaps some of Oury's old mates—my grandparents bought about thirty acres and an old house outside town. Their new farm sat on the western edge of

Prentiss, southwest of the creek locals called the Big Ditch and the main Mississippi Central tracks and out past the dead ends of both Sweet Beulah and First Street. The place had belonged to Oury's great-uncle Pickens Brady, who, when he died in 1938, was the county's last living Confederate veteran. Because they were related and they promised not to cut down Pickens's precious water oaks, Oury and Grace were not required to make a down payment. Instead, they paid the veteran's son Thomas Brady with a series of interest-bearing notes. They planned to keep the cows, bottle the milk, and run the delivery routes from the old Brady place.

This new thirty-acre parcel connected my grandparents and my mom and uncle to Berry family history. But it also pointed ahead to their own and to their descendants' future. Prent Berry's widow, Effie, owned land just north of them along the main railroad track. The Prentiss railroad depot lay a short distance to the southwest. Beside the depot, W. T. Lipsey had expanded the cotton gin he inherited from his stepfather, Henry Bourn, and opened a tractor dealership. His landholdings extended northwest from there, opening out into agricultural fields and rural houses just west of the old Brady place, Grace and Oury's new home. Locals called this area the Lipsey farm.

I never visited the family farm near the place where Versie Johnson would die almost five years to the day after my grandparents signed the deed. In 1951, when my mom was a teenager, they sold it and moved into the house in town, where they lived until my grandfather died and my grandmother grew too old to live alone. By the time I knew enough to look for them, the house and the water oaks and anything else that might indicate the land had once been a farm were gone.

When he announced his run for sheriff in January 1943, Oury put his reputation as a husband and father, a businessman, a farm owner, and a Methodist up against H.J. and his drinking. Politics were just that personal in a place as small as Prentiss. In 1949, the scholar of southern politics V. O. Key famously called this practice "friends and neighbors" voting.

Local campaigns were intimate in other ways as well. Candidates tried to meet every voter, but wartime gas rationing made that difficult. Instead of driving to every farm, the men running visited general stores, daylong shape-note singing schools, and funerals. On Sundays, they turned up at country churches holding "dinner on the grounds" and fixed a plate of fried chicken, butter beans, okra, and pie at sawhorse tables under the trees. And they made a special effort to call on folks who were sick or parents whose "boys" were away in the service. With eight people appearing at the same places and events, the process became comical. Jeff Davis candidates shook voters' hands so much that year that the Jackson paper joked, "Now and then you see an unfortunate brother with his arm in a sling."

In the spring and summer of 1943, after a year and a half of fighting, people wanted to talk about the war. Almost every extended family in the county had someone in the military. Many parents had multiple children serving, including the five sons of local Black couple Mr. and Mrs. D. D. Armstrong and the four sons of local white widow Mrs. J. C. Holland. Men were subject to the draft, but many volunteered. Women also went to work as army nurses or in the Women's Army Corps, which sent recruiters to Prentiss.

For local young people, wartime service looked like an opportunity worth the risk. Being in the military gave them a chance to see the world while also serving their country. Many locals had never really been anywhere farther than Hattiesburg or Jackson. Riding a train north through Memphis and St. Louis and the massive stockyards and skyscrapers of Chicago was an adventure. Maybe they would get to see New York City or San Francisco or the Pacific Ocean or even Paris or Tokyo or Rome. If they were Black, and many of them were, maybe the war would afford them a chance to escape the confines of the Jim Crow South, even if it meant leaving all they knew and loved behind.

During those years, Mississippi farm boys helped liberate the French countryside and German concentration camps. They served in Australia. They bombed cities like Dresden and Berlin. They fought on Pacific islands they could not find on a map. Mississippi farm girls also traveled. They nursed wounded soldiers in hospitals in England and France. They managed supplies and did the office work that kept military bases running from California to Georgia.

For those young people fresh off the farms who were Black, wartime service came with an additional challenge: navigating extreme and often violent discrimination. The Marine Corps banned Black men entirely. The navy limited most Black recruits to menial work in the mess. Only the army offered Black men—and, in the Women's Army Corps, or WAC, Black women—a wide array of jobs. But the largest branch of the military also built and maintained separate barracks, bathrooms, dining rooms, post exchanges, and bomb shelters. Working together, the Red Cross and military officials even segregated the blood supply.

As part of their service, Jeff Davis men and in some cases women studied communications, accounting, and aviation. They learned to type reports, repair radios, treat wounds, load bombs, fire artillery, and fix engines. They wore smart uniforms, received free health care, and earned good wages. Of course, some of them felt homesick. Many were scared. Most felt a sense of pride in doing something that mattered. To travel that far into the unknown, they had to be brave. Many of them died.

Jeff Davis people also left the county for jobs in war industries. Like Arlene Berry, Oury's sister and my great-aunt, many went to Pascagoula to work at the massive Ingalls Shipyard. Others moved to Mobile to work at the Alabama Dry Dock and Shipbuilding Company. Some left the region entirely, taking the train to Detroit or Chicago or Los Angeles, where they built airplanes, jeeps, tanks, bombs, and guns.

"Going among strangers," as many rural southerners described their experience, young people discovered unimagined worlds beyond their small towns and farms. Americans from outside the region also experienced life in the South. Within a hundred miles of Prentiss, old military facilities like Camp Shelby and new bases like Camp Van Dorn and Jackson Army Air Base housed thousands of soldiers. In the course of doing their jobs, soldiers and defense workers came into contact with people they never would have met before who lived in ways they did not always understand. The fact that the taken-for-granted aspects of life could be so different in other places suggested that things could be different at home, too. Many Black southerners embraced this idea eagerly and understood the war as a global battle against white supremacy. Many white southerners feared it.

As they moved around the country, Black defense workers and soldiers occasionally violated local segregation laws and conventions. Sometimes, they did so because they did not understand the mostly unwritten rules. Other times, they acted intentionally. Either way, white law enforcement officials, including sheriffs and military MPs, as well as white civilians, responded by attacking them.

At least six civilian race riots, twenty military riots, and between forty-five and seventy-five lynchings occurred in the South during World War II. Outside the region, southern white soldiers and migrants also attacked Black people. At Fort Dix in New Jersey, Private James Greggs, a white MP from the South, shot and killed Private David Woods, a Black soldier from Chicago, because he refused to go to the back of the line at a theater. In Detroit, an influx of hundreds of thousands of Black and white southern migrants fueled tensions that exploded into a three-day riot after Black men and women moved into federally built housing. Nine white people and twenty-five Black people died. Most of the Black victims were shot by white police. At Camp Shenando in Pennsylvania, white soldiers kicked a Black soldier in the face and destroyed one of his eyes for having the audacity to visit a segregated PX. As Black soldiers organized to fight back, six truckloads of armed white soldiers in battle fatigues arrived, shot out the streetlights, and began firing into the crowd. Black soldier Dempsey Travis was shot three times. As two white soldiers drove him to the hospital in an ambulance, Travis overheard one of them ask, "Why we doin' this to our own soldiers?" The other soldier replied in a strong southern accent: "Who ever told you n*****s were our soldiers. Where I come from, we shoot n*****s like rabbits."

This unnamed white soldier was not wrong. At Fort Benning, Georgia, white men lynched Black private Felix Hall by binding his arms and legs and hanging him from a tree. At Camp Claiborne near Alexandria,

Louisiana, white MPs and civilian police killed ten Black soldiers and wounded at least twenty-one after a white MP slapped a Black soldier's girlfriend and Black soldiers fought back. Alfred Duckett, a Black soldier there, remembered being told by a white officer, "We want you to know we're not taking any foolishness down here, because we don't shoot 'em here. We hang 'em." White war workers in Mobile rioted after Black workers were promoted to shipyard jobs formerly reserved for white men. In Centreville, Mississippi, a white sheriff shot and killed William Walker, a Black private from Chicago, near the entrance to Camp Van Dorn. Black soldiers serving at Jackson Army Air Base in Mississippi's capital complained, "We are treated like wild animals here, like we are inhuman....Even the officers here are calling us n****r." As the writer James Baldwin explained, Black parents felt "a peculiar kind of relief when they knew that their boys were being shipped out of the south, to do battle overseas. It was, perhaps, like feeling that the most dangerous part of a dangerous journey had been passed and that now, even if death should come, it would come with honor and without the complicity of their countrymen."

As the nation mobilized to defeat the Axis powers, sheriffs and other law enforcement officials across the South fought a war within the war, a home-front battle to enforce local conceptions of white supremacy. Other white men joined them. The fall before Oury entered the sheriff's race, white folks in Piney Woods counties near Jeff Davis lynched three Black men in less than a week. A mob of local men hung teenagers Ernest Green and Charlie Lang from a bridge near Shubuta in Clarke County first. Then, five days later, another mob hung Howard Wash from a bridge near Laurel in Jones County.

As Clarke County sheriff Lloyd McNeal explained to a northern white reporter, "We're all for law and order here. But of course, we got some good folks who get kind of wild. Them n*****s is gettin' uppity." Asked whether the FBI, sent in to investigate, would find anything, the sheriff replied, "You know how it is. People don't like to tell on their friends." A "responsible" Laurel businessman reported that he was against lynching but that there were "extenuating circumstances....The 'n*****s' have been giving Laurel a good deal of trouble lately. Shootings. Stabbings. They get drunk, the 'n*****s' do, on Saturday nights. The whites are getting worried, with their young menfolk going off to war and leaving the white women unprotected... We've got to keep the n*****s in their place."

As Mississippi governor Paul Johnson explained, white residents were upset because more white men than Black men were leaving the state to serve in the military. No matter that white southerners were mostly at fault for this disparity: Mississippi spent so little on Black education that many Black recruits could not pass the army's limited literacy tests, and others were rejected for health problems related to poverty. The governor argued that given the state population was "50 per cent Negro," white residents were not wrong to be worried. "I'm not defending lynching," he told the reporter. But outsiders, including "the President's wife," Eleanor Roosevelt, have to stay out of the state's business. "We're a very proud people in the South, in Mississippi, and you just make us mad that way."

White southerners' concerns about Black men on the home front only intensified as the draft expanded in 1943, sending even more white men away from home. The *Prentiss Headlight* urged white county residents to "declare war on the home front this year." While bootleggers went about their business openly, F. A. and Ruth Parker's editorial lamented, white men fought to save the nation. One Black bootlegger plying his trade for years despite multiple arrests and trials "has had the gall to purchase a Taxi License in order to be eligible for all the tires and gasoline he needs to run his business of bootlegging!" After calling this "nauseating," the paper urged people to act: "If the LAW CAN'T stop such, then people, in righteous indignation should!" Without a doubt, the editors of Jeff Davis County's only paper believed vigilante violence was justified.

That June, in a letter he wrote to a New Yorker who had criticized his racism, Mississippi senator Theodore Bilbo told the story of an incident he said happened near Mississippi's Camp McCain. According to Bilbo, six Black soldiers stopped a white couple, held a knife to the white man's throat, and raped the white woman twelve times. Rapes were soaring, the senator argued, because white people outside the South made "the negro believe that he is as good as the whites" and would receive "full and complete social and political liberty when this war is over." Along with Black leaders like Walter White and "A. Randolph Phillips," Bilbo's mangling of A. Philip Randolph's name, these Americans were "laying the foundation for a racial war when this war is over."

Challenging Bilbo for the title of most racist man in Congress, Mississippi representative John F. Rankin condemned the Selective Service for sending white men away while leaving Black men at home to rape white women. Acutely aware of Jeff Davis County's Black majority, many white locals agreed, though they seemed more worried about a labor shortage than rape. The *Prentiss Headlight* repeatedly blasted idle Black men and women lounging on the streets of Prentiss and urged white law enforcement officials to use force if necessary to put them to work. The Jackson *Clarion-Ledger* joked that the local judge down in Jeff Davis would soon force everyone "that can be swung by the neck" into the fields to get "the soil in shape for planting."

This kind of casual reference to lynching confirmed what Black journalists had been arguing since before the United States entered the war. The NAACP's magazine *The Crisis* put it bluntly in 1940: "The only essential difference between a Nazi mob hunting down Jews in Central Europe and an American mob burning black men at the stake in Mississippi is that one is actually encouraged by its national government and the other is merely tolerated." Two years later, a white northern journalist investigating lynchings in Mississippi offered another damning observation: "The lynching spirit means more than mob law. It means the inability of so many white southerners to keep their fists, their clubs, or their guns in their pockets when a colored person stands up for his legal rights." A reporter for the *Chicago Defender* made his argument clear in his 1943 headline "War Bound to Improve Mississippi Since State Cannot Be Any Worse."

In July, after the Detroit race riot but before the Democratic primary, the *Headlight* published a rare editorial directly addressing "the race problem" in Jeff Davis County. Struggling to walk a thin line, editors F. A.

and Ruth Parker admitted being a little worried about local race relations. "Outstanding Negro leaders round about the county" had assured them that Black residents "are satisfied with their status and want no change." Yet the Parkers still offered a "warning" to their Black readers to shun like "a rattlesnake" outsiders like Eleanor Roosevelt who "endeavor to stir up racial hatred and poison your minds with stories of race equality." Their advice to their "colored friends" was to stop "loafing" and "work, work, work." "White supremacy has always prevailed and always will," the editors argued. "God who designed and brought into being the faculties of both the white man and the negro willed it so."

Across the region, white southern leaders repeated this point. Liberal Tennessee journalist and FDR ally Mark Ethridge put it politely: "The Southern colored man must recognize that there is no power in the world— not even in all the mechanized armies of the earth, Allied and Axis—which could now force the Southern white people to the abandonment of the principle of social segregation." The secretary of the Birmingham Chamber of Commerce spoke more crudely. "There's one thing you can put in your pipe and smoke," he told a white northern journalist. "There's no white man down here goin' to let his daughter sleep with a n****r, or sit at the same table with a n****r, or go walkin' with a n****r. The war can go to hell, the world can go to hell, we can all be dead—but he ain't goin' to do it." Either way, the message was the same. For many white people, nothing, not even winning the war, was more important than white supremacy.

Late in 1942, shortly before Oury Berry entered the sheriff's race and the same month that white residents of the Piney Woods lynched three Black men, a Swedish economist and sociologist named Gunnar Myrdal completed *An American Dilemma: The Negro Problem and Modern Democracy*. Drawing on his own travels and fieldwork as well as the research of a brilliant team of Black and white collaborators, Myrdal bluntly revealed the lie at the center of American political and social life: in their treatment of Black Americans, white Americans were not living up to their own stated ideals of liberty, equality, and the rule of law.

For Black citizens and their allies in the white left, Myrdal's conclusion was not news. But not looking and therefore not seeing—forms of lying camouflaged as denial—were old American traditions. Myrdal's work made it harder for the majority of white Americans not to see—and therefore not to know—this truth: that their efforts to uphold white supremacy belied their professions of patriotism.

When Myrdal arrived in America in 1938, the director of the Carnegie Corporation, the organization that had commissioned his study, urged the scholar to start his research by traveling across the country and especially the South. Myrdal never forgot that trip. As he later wrote about his two-month journey, "I was shocked and scared to the bones by all the evils I saw, and by the serious political implications of the problem." In *An American Dilemma,* Myrdal described "a pattern of illegality . . . firmly entrenched in Southern politics and public morals."

In Myrdal's analysis, the problem had roots in the years during and after Reconstruction when conservative white men took back control of southern statehouses in a process they called "redemption." Because the Thirteenth, Fourteenth, and Fifteenth Amendments to the Constitution guaranteed Black Americans equal rights as citizens, white southerners working to restore white supremacy had to pretend. They had to govern under the fiction that Black people possessed full and equal protection under the law. They had to lie. In this context, they developed a unique form of politics, in Myrdal's phrase, a conservatism "harnessed to the practice of illegality."

This illegality was even more pernicious because it was upheld by purported agents of the law—white men (and they were all men) like the sheriff that my grandfather was, at this time, aspiring to become. Sometimes law enforcement officials simply ignored the law, like when they refused to charge lynchers with murder. Other times, politicians wrote state laws that hid their true aims, like the so-called grandfather and understanding clauses that disfranchised Black voters because their ancestors had not voted or they had not interpreted the state constitution to the satisfaction of local registrars. What Myrdal called "illegality" flourished because almost all white people, including many federal judges serving in the region, supported this fiction of equality to "comply" with the Reconstruction Amendments that guaranteed Black citizenship rights.

As Myrdal explained, sheriffs and their deputies, constables, marshals, police officers, and state highway patrolmen upheld a civic order only partially defined by formal laws. Mississippi had the most racially restrictive system in the nation and yet the fewest formal segregation laws of any southern state. More important were the shadow laws, unwritten codes and conventions that upheld the real civic order of white supremacy. Not infrequently, enforcing white southern ideas about "law and order," especially in Deep South states, meant doing things that were technically illegal under federal and sometimes also state laws. Sheriffs routinely beat Black suspects and deprived them of adequate representation and due process. They also turned their Black prisoners over to lynch mobs, or, as that practice decreased in the 1930s, shot them outright themselves on questionable charges of resisting arrest or attempting to escape. Because it was the sheriff's duty to support white supremacy, this kind of violence was simply part of the job.

For this reason, a series of Supreme Court decisions in the 1920s and 1930s aimed at improving criminal procedures in southern states had little impact in cases of Black on white crime. The 1923 decision *Moore v. Dempsey* outlawed criminal convictions obtained in courthouses surrounded by howling mobs. The 1936 decision *Brown v. Mississippi* outlawed the use of testimony acquired when law enforcement officials tortured suspects. Other decisions strengthened the right to timely counsel and made it easier to prove Black men and women were being excluded from juries. But in many jurisdictions, sheriffs and other law enforcement and court officials ignored these rulings and instead lied about what they did. Constitutional rights were just not worth that much in a world in which the collective desires of local white people mattered more than the law as interpreted by distant federal courts. By the time my grandfather Oury ran for sheriff in 1943, calls for law and order had long functioned as assurances that candidates would uphold not the Constitution but rather white supremacy. For far too many white southerners, this was where true loyalty lay.

When white residents of Jeff Davis County went to the polls in August 1943, they worried about not just the war overseas against the Axis powers but also the race war at home. A community of farmers, they feared that efforts to compel local Black folks to work (like Prenitiss' wartime mayor and the *Headlight*'s editor F. A. Parker's recently announced "Work or Fight" order calling for strict enforcement of vagrancy laws) would still not deliver enough hands for the harvest. But beyond this immediate concern lay a broader anxiety about whether Black residents, including returning veterans, would openly challenge Jim Crow segregation. White voters wanted a sheriff who would do whatever was necessary to uphold their understanding of the law.

Grace Berry turned out to be wrong about her husband's chances of victory. Oury won the first primary by doing very well in Prentiss and Bassfield, the only other town of any size in the county, while holding his own in the countryside. But with nine candidates in the race, no one received a majority. Leading up to the second primary, Oury and his opponent, J.R. McInnis, fought each other through political ads in the *Headlight*. J. R. tried to use the fact that he had sons in the military to his advantage. Oury countered that he had served in the navy and had an "Honorable Medical discharge." Since the military could not make use of him, he was "offering" himself "for service on the home front." Anyone reading the paper would have known what he meant.

Trying to dispel potential voters' concerns about the health problems that had forced him to close the barbershop, my grandfather promised "not to sit behind the office desk" but to be "outside doing my job as a sheriff." Like other white voters, he was "nauseated at the sight of the negro bootleggers riding all over the county in their fine cars, plying their trade, causing no end of trouble to the farmers' work hands by drunkenness and its accompanying evils" while "our boys" were "fighting and dying on the field of battle."

Without saying it directly, my grandfather promised to rid Jeff Davis of all that his white neighbors were afraid of: Black men and women who were idle, independent, drunk, or rich and who refused to defer to white people's authority. Black people who did not fit white stereotypes because they owned large farms or ran successful businesses were especially threatening to white people because they exposed the lie of white supremacy. In a different way, Oury's alcoholic father did the same. As a result, my grandfather's candidacy rested on this implicit premise: Who better to fight all the threats these bootleggers represented than a candidate for sheriff who had grown up in a home wrecked by drink?

The day after his daughter, Joan, my mother, turned seven, Oury Berry won the August 24, 1943, Democratic primary runoff, 1,770 to 864. He won in the towns and in the farming areas, beating his opponent in every precinct except Clem and Williamson Mill, rural areas north of Prentiss where J. R. McInnis and his friends and relatives lived. The race wasn't even close. Oury won by a wider margin than every other Democrat on the ballot. With the November general election a formality, in September, not much more than a year after buying the Sanford Dairy, he sold the business with its daily milking demands but kept the land and house he had bought from the Bradys. The son of the town drunk, as Oury's wife, Grace, had put it, could actually become a sheriff in dry Mississippi. Oury would not have to be a farmer after all.

When Oury took office in early January 1944, Mississippi sheriffs held a kind of absolute power. Inside their jurisdictions, no one could really tell them what to do. In places where many men still avoided "public" work—a job with a boss and a salary like Oury's father had held—in order to remain the lords of their own households, farms, and businesses, the sheriff sat at the pinnacle of white masculine independence. Sheriffs were the lords of the county.

The job of sheriff came with too much power—but in Mississippi counties where sheriffs were also tax collectors, the position also came with too much work. As the number one law enforcement official in a county, the sheriff was responsible for public safety and for preventing crime across a wide territory. He managed the jail and delivered prisoners to court in the county and elsewhere and attended local criminal proceedings. He also conducted sanity hearings and transported locals to state institutions for the mentally disabled. And he collected all local taxes, licenses, and fees, including property and poll taxes and car registration fees. He even enforced the requirement that dogs be vaccinated for rabies.

A Mississippi sheriff did the work of a police officer, a social worker, an accountant, an animal control officer, and an executioner. He also managed an office and a staff, men who worked as deputies and women who helped with the office work and tax collection. Successful sheriffs hired competent people for these jobs. Oury was lucky on this front. He put his wife to work running his office. My grandmother Grace had "book learning"—a two-year degree in business from Mississippi Woman's College in Hattiesburg—as well as related work experience. She did her job so well that a later sheriff hired her to manage his office, too.

Like the farmers who voted them into office, Mississippi sheriffs did not get a salary, and thus it is extremely difficult to estimate how much any of them, including my grandfather, earned. Instead, sheriffs paid themselves, the expenses of running the office, and the wages of their employees out of a share of fees they collected and payments the county made for services like attending court. In counties where they were also the tax collector, they earned money for that work, too, including ten cents out of every poll tax paid. To encourage enforcement of prohibition, Mississippi gave sheriffs one third of a fine that the state charged people convicted of selling or possessing alcohol—what people often called the whiskey tax. Some conservative Christians like F. A. and Ruth Parker, the editors of the *Headlight,* denounced this tax as immoral. In a state that prohibited all use of alcohol, they argued, it did not make sense for the government to profit from the "demon drink." In practice, the whiskey tax also encouraged fraud. A sheriff earned more money charging people with selling alcohol than he did prosecuting other crimes.

The year 1944 was a particularly difficult time to take over as sheriff. Property tax receipts were down in Jeff Davis, not just because they had decreased everywhere as a result of the Depression but also because the cutover land had little value. Whiskey taxes brought in the most revenue, but they were unpredictable. With so many young men away for war work or military service, the crime rate fell across the country, and it likely declined in Jeff Davis County, too.

Partly because these sorts of contingencies made the pay so variable, and partly because sheriffs could not serve back-to-back terms, most men who held the office kept their farms or other businesses. But Oury had sold the dairy, and without it, he could not expect to make much off his small acreage. During the first year of Oury's four-year term, fees and taxes covered the expenses of running the sheriff's office without much left over for him. The county's Board of Supervisors started paying him $40 a month to cover the gap.

The money helped, but it did not begin to solve all the challenges Oury faced. In 1942, Gunnar Myrdal had predicted major changes in American race relations. Two years on, in Jeff Davis as in many parts of the South, Black residents were increasingly defying the laws and conventions of Jim Crow segregation. For people like my grandfather, whose livelihoods depended on enforcing white supremacy, this growing Black resistance posed a near-existential threat.

Prentiss was too small to develop a separate Black business district beyond the Johnson Funeral Home, a Black barbershop, and a few short-lived ventures including several Black-owned cafés. This meant that many Black people also frequented white-owned businesses, which was good for white business owners. To turn a profit in Prentiss and many southern towns, they needed Black customers.

But the result was integrated commercial areas. To manage racial interactions there, white people created and enforced a variety of mostly unwritten conventions that governed how Black people should act in situations like encountering white pedestrians on the sidewalk or seeking service from a white store clerk. In Jeff Davis, a majority of Black residents lived in the countryside. When they came to town, they mostly followed the rules. During the war, some of them, like their counterparts in larger southern cities like Birmingham, decided to stop.

In Prentiss, white residents were accustomed to seeing Black people shopping and swapping local news and gossip with relatives and friends on Saturday afternoons. The crowds could grow thick, filling the space between the crepe myrtles on the sidewalks on both sides of brick-paved Columbia Avenue. Children caught up with friends near the railroad depot. Old folks sat on benches made of wood planks at a corner on Columbia called the buzzard's roost, a place reserved on other days for white people. Sweating folks with spare change bought icy Cokes and Pepsis in returnable bottles at the back door of the Palace Drugs soda fountain. Banned from sitting down inside, they sipped their drinks out on the streets, laughing, talking, and enjoying their own company.

During the war, as young people had more money to spend, some of them began violating local segregation rules, staying in town late into Saturday night, openly drinking and gambling, and refusing to yield the sidewalk to white people trying to push through the crowds. The *Headlight* complained about idle Black men and women hanging out in town on weekdays. Just as Oury took office as sheriff in January 1944, a letter "To the Colored People of Jeff Davis County" from a Black farm owner named Paul Exposé appeared on the paper's front page. More directly than the Parkers had done, he condemned local Black folks for crowding into town on Saturday nights to drink whiskey and gamble. He informed his "colored friends" that "Mr. Garraway," owner of a large general mercantile, had to close his soup kitchen because "we wouldn't obey." The Parkers saw Exposé as an ally, a Black man willing to tell other Black people to do what white people wanted.

Not surprisingly, people like the Parkers seized statements like Exposé's to claim most Black southerners were satisfied with segregation. But his statement just as likely expressed his own Christian concern for his Black neighbors' souls as well as their bellies. During the war, Black people found ways to resist second-class citizenship, to occupy spaces denied them, to wage a guerrilla war against Jim Crow even in a tiny town like Prentiss. "How do Negroes feel about the way they have to live? How do they discuss it when alone among themselves?" Black writer and Mississippi native Richard Wright asked in his 1940 essay "The Ethics of Living Jim Crow." "I think this question can be answered in a single sentence. A friend of mine who ran an elevator once told me, 'Lawd, man! Ef it wuzn't fer them polices 'n' them of lynch mobs, there wouldn't be nothin' but uproar down here!'"

Many Black southerners registered their opinions about Jim Crow by migrating out of the region. In other parts of the country, they still might face racist law enforcement and vigilante violence, but they also became voters. Black newspapers widely read in Mississippi like the *Chicago Defender* argued that a more powerful federal government and a global war gave Black Americans a unique opportunity to mobilize this growing electoral strength to demand equality. Activists like NAACP head Walter White agreed.

As the war raged, a Supreme Court decision in 1944 opened up the possibility of meaningful Black voting in the South, too. Before this decision, in many parts of the South, the Democratic Party ran primaries open only to white voters. *Smith v. Allwright* declared that state and local branches of a political party and the primaries they ran could not be segregated. It gave Black southerners who somehow got past racist registrars and paid their poll taxes every year a chance to participate in a meaningful way in the electoral process. Over the next decade, about thirteen hundred Black citizens of Jeff Davis County would become registered voters.

In making this decision, the eight Supreme Court justices in the majority had refused to indulge the usual white southern lies about segregation. Instead, they had stated what was obvious, that southern states had violated Black people's right to vote as guaranteed by the Fourteenth and Fifteenth Amendments. The NAACP had won its first landmark victory against the Jim Crow South. In what he always called his most important case, NAACP lawyer Thurgood Marshall made the Supreme Court that he would later join stop not looking and actually see.

For white southerners living in areas with a Black majority like Jeff Davis County, the 1944 *Smith v. Allwright* decision was particularly troubling. Three days after this Supreme Court decision, the Parkers wrote another editorial condemning Eleanor Roosevelt. If the president's wife cared about the country, she would "button up her lip" and stop preaching "racial equality and such rot." With "her flair for publicity, unadulterated asininity and pure, downright ignorance," the first lady had "done more to spread racial unrest" than any other American. Nowhere did the editorial mention *Smith v. Allwright* directly. But the closing paragraph made clear the real subject of this rant. "This is the SOLID SOUTH...and it is going to remain so, regardless of Eleanor Roosevelt or any decisions handed down by the United States Supreme Court!"

Oury Berry likely agreed with the Parkers, who had supported him for sheriff early and in a crowded field—an alliance that would last through all three of my grandfather's terms. F. A. Parker died in 1958, but my grandparents remained friends with Ruth Parker, who continued to publish and edit the *Prentiss Headlight* by herself until she retired in 1970. What I do not know is whether my grandparents and the Parkers knew they were lying or whether they had pretended for so long that they thought their lies were the truth. Either way, they had to work hard to not see. There had never been any "racial peace" in Jeff Davis County or any other part of the South for Eleanor Roosevelt to disturb.

Sometimes Oury loved being sheriff. Before Christmas recess, he dressed up like Santa and visited the kids at Prentiss Elementary, the school that his daughter, my mother, Joan, attended. But at other times, the job could be extremely difficult.

Executions were particularly tough. Sheriffs spent four years praying no one received a death sentence on their watch. Oury did not make it half a year before his prayers failed.

On the afternoon of May 4, 1944, Oury Berry transported L. R. Phillips from the mob-proof Jackson jail to the new local jail Jeff Davis County had used WPA money to build in 1940. The local court had convicted Phillips, a white man, of murdering "Uncle" Dock Broom, an eighty-two-year-old widowed white farmer who lived alone south of Bassfield. For his crime, Phillips had been condemned to die.

Phillips asked for a last meal of "beefsteak, French fried potatoes, and Black coffee," according to an article the following week in the *Prentiss Headlight,* and he ate it "with a relish." He spoke to a minister but made no formal, public statement except to claim that he was innocent. Offered a stimulant—a practice understood as an act of mercy to help a condemned man hold on to his self-control and retain his dignity—he refused.

Just after midnight, Phillips walked unassisted up the stairs and sat down in Mississippi's mobile electric chair, housed with its batteries in the back of a truck parked at the courthouse. My grandfather did his duty, what his job required. After strapping Phillips in, he put a hood over his head and threw the switch. Whether or not Oury looked, it would have been impossible for him to avoid the sounds and smells in the minutes it took for Phillips to die.

My grandfather's initiation into the gruesome realities of the job, Phillips's execution was Jeff Davis County's third. The first two had occurred four years earlier. All three of these executions would lay the groundwork, in subtle yet important ways, for what was to come.

GONE UNDERGROUND

S even years before my grandfather executed L. R. Phillips and a decade before Versie Johnson died on his watch, a double homicide occurred in Mississippi that made headlines across the nation. In this case, the executioners were not law officers. Instead, a mob of white men lynched two Black men in Duck Hill, a tiny town in the red clay hills of Montgomery County, about 160 miles north of Prentiss, just as Congress debated the fate of a federal anti-lynching bill.

This incident would transform both the practice and the politics of lynching and change how white southern men exercised their power. Before Duck Hill, lynchers in the Deep South often bragged about what they had done. After Duck Hill, they lied. In this context, the job of law enforcement officials like my grandfather Oury Berry—and the pressures upon them—changed. Public acts of torture and murder ruined a town's reputation. If a sheriff could not or would not stop them, killings needed to be done quickly and quietly.

Three years later, the effects of the Duck Hill lynchings played out in another highly publicized case in Jeff Davis County. In a series of incidents there in 1940, my grandfather's predecessor as sheriff succeeded

The author (left) and her grandfather Oury Berry beside his patrol car sometime during his 1970–1973 term as sheriff

The young town of Prentiss, Mississippi, as seen on a postcard produced not long after the town's 1903 founding as a stop on the Pearl and Leaf Rivers Railroad

Timber workers and a manager near a steam skidder (a huge engine that used long cables to drag cut pine trees to a railroad car) in south-central Mississippi sometime between 1918 and 1920. By 1930, timber companies had cut down almost all of the old-growth longleaf pine trees in Jefferson Davis County.

One year after the creation of Jefferson Davis County in 1906, Black residents recruited J. E. and Bertha LeBranche Johnson to move to Prentiss and help establish the school that became the Prentiss Institute. This photograph shows the graduating class of 1938.

Built in 1926, the Prentiss Institute's Rosenwald Building contained classrooms, offices, and an auditorium and served as the center of the Prentiss Institute's expanding campus.

Four generations of a Black Jeff Davis County family, the Magees, at the Prentiss Institute, where they all took classes

On his birth certificate, Versie Johnson is called Virginous. The form records his father, Bill Johnson, as working in farming and his mother, Lizzie Cooper Johnson, as working as a housewife.

On October 16, 1940, Versie Johnson met with a registrar, who filled out his World War II draft registration card. The back of the form offers the only known physical description of Johnson.

STANDARD CERTIFICATE OF DEATH

State File No. 12325

STATE OF MISSISSIPPI

Registrar's No. #69

1. PLACE OF DEATH—
County Jeff Davis | City or Town / or Street and Number Prentiss, | Inside or Outside Corporate Limits? Outside / or Rural Precinct

Hospital _____ (b) In this Community

Length of Stay Before Death, (a) In Hospital _____

2. RESIDENCE BEFORE DEATH—
State Mississippi. | County Jeff Davis | City or Town Prentiss | or Rural Precinct

3. (a) FULL NAME Versie Johnson

If Foreign Born How Long in U. S.? _____ Yrs.

3. (b) If veteran, 3 (c) Social Security

name war _____ No. _____

MEDICAL CERTIFICATION

20. Date of death: Month 8 day 1th year 1947 hour _____ A. M. or _____ P. M.

4. Sex Male | **5. Color or Race** Negro | **6 (a)** Single, widowed, married, divorced Widow

21. I hereby certify that I attended the deceased from _____, 19_____, to _____, 19_____;

that I last saw h_____ alive on _____, 19_____;

6 (b) Name of husband or wife _____ | **6 (c)** Age of husband or wife if alive _____ years

and that death occurred on the date and hour stated above.

7. Birth date of deceased Nov (Month) 23th (Day) 1916 (Year)

Immediate cause of death *Killed by Officers of Jefferson Davis Co.*

DURATION

8. AGE: Years 30 | Months 9 | Days 8 | If less than one day _____ hr. _____ min.

Due to *Shot* 3 - 166

9. Birthplace Lawrence County, (City, town, or county) Miss (State or foreign country)

Other conditions (Include pregnancy within 3 months of death) *G. O. Berry — Sheriff*

10. Usual occupation Puble work

PHYSICIAN

11. Industry or business _____

MAJOR FINDINGS: Of operations _____

FATHER {

12. Name Willie Johnson

13. Birthplace Rankin County, (City, town or county) Miss (State or foreign country)

Of autopsy _____

Underline the cause to which death should be charged statistically.

MOTHER {

14. Maiden name Lizzie Cooper

22. If death was due to external causes, fill in the following:

15. Birthplace Lincoln County, Miss. (City, town, or county) (State or foreign country)

(a) Accident, suicide, or homicide (specify) _____

16 (a) Informant's signature Gertrude Johnson

(b) Date of occurrence _____

(b) Address Prentiss, Mississippi.

(c) Where did injury occur? _____ (City or town) (County) (State)

17 (a) Burial (Burial, cremation, or removal) | (b) Date 8-2-47 (Month) (Day) (Year)

(d) Did injury occur in or about home, on farm, in industrial

(c) Place First Baptist Cemetery

place, in public place? _____ (Specify type of place)

18 (a) Signature, funeral director Central Johnson

While at work _____ (e) Means of injury *Gunshot*

(b) Address Prentiss, Miss.

23. Signature *G. O. Berry (Sheriff)* M. D.

19 (a) 8-18-47 (b) Lela McHease (Date received local registrar) (Registrar's signature)

Address _____ Date Signed _____

Versie Johnson's sister Gertrude Johnson provided the personal information about him included on his death certificate. His immediate cause of death is listed as "killed by officers of Jeff Davis County due to shot, G. O. Berry, Sheriff."

The Jefferson Davis Courthouse, flanked by the county jail, as it existed at the time of Versie Johnson's arrest

The author's grandfather Oury Berry and grandmother Grace Keen Berry in front of a load of pine logs on a railroad car or wagon, sometime before or soon after they married in September 1932

The author's grandfather Sheriff Oury Berry, sometime during his second term as sheriff (1953–1956), and other officers pour liquor into "the ditch" beside the courthouse, with the county jail in the background.

The author's grandfather Oury Berry wore this Jefferson Davis County sheriff's badge.

The place where Versie Johnson was killed is now the Prentiss Christian School's football field.

Federal examiner C. A. Phillips administers the oath to Joe Ella Moore at the Magnolia Hotel in Prentiss on August 25, 1965, three weeks after the passage of the Voting Rights Act.

Downtown Prentiss today, showing one of the few remaining businesses, Palace Drugs

in stopping multiple lynching attempts. Very possibly, he was inspired by the example of Duck Hill and the negative publicity that the town and its officials earned in the aftermath of that horrific killing.

This 1940 case of a thwarted lynching, too, influenced what happened later—but in a different way. White people in Jeff Davis were angry that the sheriff opposed their lynch mob. Their traditional representative of law and order, the law enforcement officer whom they had chosen to uphold white supremacy on their behalf, no longer seemed willing to do his job or to let the white men of Jeff Davis take the law into their own hands. This meant that they would have to push even harder for that time-honored "right" the next time they wanted to exercise it.

In this way, the double lynchings at Duck Hill in 1937 and the thwarted lynchings in Prentiss in 1940 profoundly shaped the events that led to Versie Johnson's 1947 death. These events, taken together, established much of the context for the killing that would follow.

The first crime in the series of offenses that led to the blowtorches happened around dark. George S. Windham, a white shopkeeper, stood in the back of his store about six miles east of Duck Hill, Mississippi, and ate a can of sardines and some crackers. His wife and two kids were still away visiting relatives for the Christmas holidays. Rather than rushing home for family supper, he stayed at the store and caught up on his work, checking his books to see which families still owed.

Like most rural store owners, white and Black, Windham probably sold food and a wide collection of other merchandise, from overalls and suits to tractor and car parts. But he also made money as a lender, by supplying credit. Few people in farm country had cash, so families charged what they needed at a local store and paid higher prices and interest in return. Farm owners and renters usually settled their accounts at the end of the year, after they got their cotton ginned. Sharecroppers paid after getting their settlement from their landlord unless the land they worked was owned by the storekeeper or the landlord paid the account directly.

On December 30, 1937, Windham would have had a lot of cash on hand. Anyone who had worked at a country store or even settled their own account might have known this. Someone clearly did.

In Mississippi, where most people still worked the land, the Great Depression simply added to the ongoing economic misery and to poor people's desperation. During the Great War, cotton had hit a high of 35.2 cents a pound. As peace returned, prices began a long decline, reaching a June 1932 low of 4.6 cents a pound, less than the cost of growing the fluffy white fibers. Boll weevil infestations did not help, as farm owners and sharecroppers faced lower yields and had to pay for insecticides to treat the pest. The worsening crisis threw the rural South's credit and labor arrangements into turmoil. Almost every family owed at least one store owner. Farm owners lucky enough to have access to credit took out loans to buy seed, fertilizer, other farm supplies, more land, and increasingly tractors. Sharecroppers owed the owner of the land they farmed and sometimes multiple merchants, too. Despite a deeply rooted sense of themselves as independent and self-sufficient farming folk, many rural people during the Great Depression were drowning in debt. Black and white farmers' shared belief that landownership meant economic security turned out not to be true.

In the mid-1930s, new federal farm programs began paying farmers to reduce cotton production to try to raise prices. The white officials who calculated crop reduction payments sometimes cheated Black landowners. But all people who received these payments were required to share the funds with their sharecroppers and renters. Many owners evicted their tenants instead. White and Black families thrown off the land faced starvation because they could not grow their own food, and without a cotton crop as collateral, store owners cut off their credit. In the depths of the Depression, settling up—paying off the store account at year end—would have been particularly fraught.

On that December night, a car pulled up outside the place Black locals called "Mr. Sam's store." About ten minutes after that, neighbors heard a sound they thought was a firecracker. Fifteen minutes later, the car pulled away.

At first, no one thought much about it. By then, cars had become common in the rural South, and that time of year, firecrackers were also plentiful. It was a store. Every day except Sunday, people walked or rode or drove up, shopped, and then went away.

It took another hour and a half before anyone noticed anything unusual. People living near the store heard groaning and went to investigate. They found Windham lying on the floor bleeding, with the back of his head and his right shoulder full of buckshot from a shotgun blast through a window. He died in the back of a car on the way to the hospital. The killers had stolen the money from the drawer and taken the cash from the wounded man's pockets before ransacking the store. Their bloody footprints covered the floor.

The hunt to find out who pulled that trigger ended in a double lynching so horrible that it made the town's name synonymous with barbarity. In a forest near that country store, white men with an old vision of their personal right to enact the law confronted a new fact. Federal relief—the only thing enabling some white families to keep their land and others to eat—was dissolving the agrarian independence—never more than a partial truth—that they so valued and that had been central to their sense of themselves for generations. They took their fury out on local Black people, who in truth shared their economic misery. In the course of those actions, they found a new instrument of torture, the blowtorch. The use of this "modern" tool changed everything.

Someone had to pay for the murder of a white man, but Montgomery County sheriff Edgar Wright had no good leads. So he tried something new. The Jackson police force had opened what they called a bureau of identification, an early version of a crime lab, and Wright sent shards of glass and the looted cash register there for analysis. He also employed a more traditional tool of southern law enforcement. He brought in the dogs.

A practice rooted in centuries of slave patrols, the use of what many white southerners called "Negro dogs" did not disappear after Emancipation. Instead, landowners put dogs to work tracking sharecroppers fleeing debt, and sheriffs and vigilantes used them to hunt alleged criminals, especially Black people accused of crimes like rape and murder. Musicians evoked the horror of being chased, cornered, and attacked by snarling dogs—the hellhounds of the blues. Being tracked by dogs became a metaphor for all the ways Black men suffered in the Jim Crow South and for the possibility of violent death always at hand.

Over the next few days, Wright and his deputies used the dogs as well as other leads to arrest multiple men. One of them told a reporter for the Jackson *Clarion-Ledger*, "Heaven knows I'm innocent." Sobbing visibly, he insisted that every Black person in the county loved the white store owner. "If my own father or mother had anything to do with killing Mr. Sam," he pleaded, "I'd sho' tell the sheriff." But the case remained unsolved, and Wright and other law enforcement officials threatened and assaulted Black people within a large radius of the crime scene and used any pretext to make arrests.

This kind of behavior was not just a regional problem. Across the country, American law enforcement officials routinely violated the rights of the people they policed. Often, they employed what they called "the third degree," a euphemism for their systemic infliction of pain and suffering on suspects. Black people in the Jim Crow South were particularly vulnerable to this abuse because they were disfranchised. Elected sheriffs and constables had little incentive beyond their own consciences to treat Black southerners fairly, and in practice, these officials' inner sense of morality proved mighty weak. Sheriffs, deputies, constables, town marshals, and police officers routinely punched suspects and hit them with batons and whips in police cars, courthouses, and jail cells and at lonely spots along county roads. Some officers practiced what they called "the water cure," using a hose to force water into suspects' mouths or noses until they agreed to talk. Others shocked suspects with live electrical wires. Just across the Mississippi border in Helena, Arkansas, a sheriff and his deputies rigged up an improvised electric chair to extract confessions.

As bad as being in custody could be, sometimes being released was worse. It was not uncommon for southern sheriffs to threaten to turn their

Black prisoners over to lynch mobs. Sometimes they actually followed through on those threats. But some southern sheriffs—my grandfather included, according to my mom—resisted those mobs.

By late January, Sheriff Wright began focusing on a new suspect. Officials piled up a lot of what they called "circumstantial evidence" linking Roosevelt "Red" Townes to the crime. Townes, a "known" thief and bootlegger, lived with his wife in Elliott, just five miles north of Duck Hill, they claimed, and he had escaped from jail just before the murder. Officers also said he had stolen a gun on the afternoon Windham was killed and that he had gotten another person to purchase shotgun shells for him, the same kind that killed "Mr. Sam." Wright seemed to think Townes's motive was too obvious to talk about: a poor Black man needed money, so he killed a white man who had cash.

A person familiar with what passed for criminal justice in the Jim Crow South might have called this a frame-up. When a white person died and there was a possibility a Black person had played a role, law enforcement officials were under tremendous pressure to solve the crime quickly. The NAACP would later discover ample evidence to support this argument by sending in Howard "Buck" Kester, a white union organizer and minister they had previously employed to investigate the 1934 lynching of Claude Neal in Marianna, Florida. In Mississippi, Kester used what he described to NAACP head Walter White as a "passport" for cover. This fake letter from a Memphis attorney explained that he had employed Kester to locate the heirs of a dead man who had lived near Winona, the seat of Montgomery County, earlier in the century. Using this explanation as a pretense, the undercover investigator interviewed "all manner of people" who might have knowledge of the current case: men, women, and children, teachers, ministers, and reporters, as well as farmers, road workers, and clerks. The work put twelve hundred miles on his car, and he "ate enough hamburgers and drank enough Coca Cola to kill an elephant." But he worked fast. Twenty-five days after the double lynching, he mailed Walter White his report.

Locals told Kester that Townes had mostly lived in Memphis. Unable to find steady employment there, he traveled to Mississippi looking for work and met Robert "Bootjack" McDaniels, who lived in the Duck Hill community. Together, they began selling "white mule"—illegally distilled corn liquor—to local Black folks.

But in the red hills of northern Mississippi, white men claimed bootlegging as their "prerogative." White vigilantes caught the Black men selling liquor and whipped them before warning them to leave town. Because taking anything valuable like livestock was also a criminal act reserved for white men, Townes and McDaniels turned to stealing corn. Again, white vigilantes caught the two men and whipped them, this time more brutally than the first. The men who administered the beating also told them to leave Montgomery County immediately or "they might die of 'sudden pneumonia,'" a euphemism for lynching.

According to the NAACP report, Sheriff Wright decided Townes was guilty because he had returned to Duck Hill briefly from Memphis around the time of Windham's murder. But as the weeks became months and Townes evaded arrest, a frustrated Sheriff Wright offered a $500 reward for Townes's capture. Finally, in early April, authorities in Memphis took him into custody. Townes allegedly confessed, according to Kester under brutal torture. Sheriff Wright then quietly transferred him from Memphis to Jackson, Mississippi, and its famously mob-proof jail, a facility located on the top floor of the million-dollar, five-story Hinds County Courthouse built in 1930. That Mississippi needed this facility made clear the pervasiveness of vigilante behavior across the state. Townes would stay at the jail in Jackson until he had to appear in court in Winona.

Back in Montgomery County, local leaders faced a dilemma. Southern courts believed they had done their job well if a defendant was not lynched but instead experienced what a Mississippi paper called "the forms of the law," a quick trial followed immediately by a legal execution. But beginning in the 1920s, the US Supreme Court had decided to try to enforce the deeper meaning of the Constitution. Avoiding a lynching was not enough. Rather, criminal courts must weigh the evidence and actually adjudicate guilt or innocence. In 1936, as part of an effort to bring southern criminal procedures in line with the law, the Supreme Court had ruled in *Brown v. Mississippi* that convictions based on confessions extracted through torture were unconstitutional. It was not yet clear what effect this ruling would have on local trials. Beyond Townes's confession, Wright had no solid evidence linking Townes to the crime.

On April 13, 1937, the last day they would live, Roosevelt Townes and his alleged accomplice, Robert "Bootjack" McDaniels, spent less than an hour and a half in the courtroom in Winona. Townes must have retracted his confession, because both men insisted on their innocence and pleaded not guilty to the charge of murdering Windham. The judge appointed attorneys to represent the accused men. Then he adjourned the court for the midday meal.

The fact that Wright did not handcuff the prisoners as he and two of his deputies led them from the courtroom on their way back to the jail provided a clue that the sheriff knew what was coming.

Twelve white men, a self-appointed jury, met the officers and their prisoners at the courthouse's north exit. A report at the time said one of the vigilantes might have called out "Let's get them" before one or two of them pointed guns at the sheriff or a deputy, though eyewitnesses disagreed about the details. Whatever happened, Deputy Hugh Curtis later told a reporter, "It was all done very quickly, quietly, and orderly." Yet despite the calm, none of the officers could identify any of the unmasked vigilantes. Maybe the sheriff and his deputies closed their eyes or turned their backs. Somehow, while not looking at their assailants, the armed officers gave up their prisoners without a fight. Here, as elsewhere, when whites claimed not to see, they were not simply not looking. They were lying.

Wright's behavior was not unusual. A 1933 study of one hundred lynchings found that law enforcement officials participated in half these killings, and in 90 percent of the others, they either "condoned" or "winked at" mob action.

Someone working for Montgomery County had been worried enough to issue an order prohibiting people from parking automobiles around the courthouse. After a driver left a school bus in the no-parking zone, several people tried to move it. No one could find the key. It turned up mysteriously just as the twelve vigilantes hustled Townes and McDaniels on board, no doubt to a seat at the back.

As the school bus traveled north on Highway 51 to Duck Hill and then east to Windham's store—a trip of about twenty miles, some of them unpaved—automobiles idling at intersections or parked along the rocky shoulders of the road joined the growing caravan. On a back road, "Uncle" Jim Christian, an elderly Black man who had lived in the area since the Civil War, saw hundreds of cars traveling "in a cloud of dust." As he told a reporter for the *Baltimore Afro-American,* "They were honking horns and singing and shouting and looked like they was off to a picnic or a barbecue." His white neighbor noted the school bus in the lead and told him it must be a festival. The two old men only learned the truth later when another car drove by, and someone inside asked Christian's neighbor if he wanted to come see the lynching.

At the end of that drive in a lonely forest of oak and pine, a crowd variously estimated at two or four or five hundred men, women, and children waited. These spectators watched as the lynchers pulled Townes and McDaniels off the bus and chained them to trees about ten feet apart. Then one of the lynchers lit a blowtorch, a tool commonly used by plumbers then to weld metal pipes.

The "jury" applied the blue-white flame to McDaniels first. It did not take long for him to say whatever the white men wanted. At some point, he implicated another Black man named Shorty Dorroh, and a few members of the mob left to find him. Satisfied at last with McDaniels's confession, the lynchers shot the still-conscious man in the head.

Townes watched McDaniels die. Then the lynchers turned to him. They tortured him for about an hour, dragging out his agony. At some point while Townes was still alive, one of the lynchers got a camera and took pictures. Later, a Grenada photography studio would sell these grue-some images to the press. Since the nineteenth century, participants and spectators had routinely collected lynching photographs as well as links of chain or shards of flesh, a finger perhaps or a bone, as souvenirs. While Black newspapers had made a practice of publishing lynching photographs in order to expose the barbarity of white supremacy, this time two of the country's most popular magazines, *Life* and *Time,* as well as a white newspaper, the *Memphis Press-Scimitar,* printed the images along with articles denouncing the killings. The *Baltimore Afro-American* offered a fitting caption, "Mississippi civilization, 1937 style."

In the woods, the lynchers tired. They gathered sticks and limbs and piled them at Townes's feet and poured a five-gallon can of gasoline over his head. Someone lit a match. A sheet of flame enveloped the still-conscious man. And then, at last, it was done. A little over two and a half hours earlier, McDaniels and Townes had been in court. By 3:30, they were both dead.

Word reached the lynchers that Governor Hugh White had called out the National Guard, an action anti-lynching activists often called on southern state leaders to take but that in this case came too late. At some point during the torture of Townes, the group had returned with Dorroh, but instead of lynching him, too, they horsewhipped the terrified Black man, told him to leave the state, and let him go. As the crowd dispersed, the woods grew dark. Clouds piled up on the horizon. A light rain started to fall. Underneath Townes's body, the still smoldering coals smoked for a while and then went out.

Most white southerners knew that murder was wrong. Still, politicians and white newspaper editors there had a way of talking about degrees. A lynching that mimicked the forms of a legal execution was, to some people, excusable, not a murder but a death sentence carried out by the people. There were things white southern men could not be expected to tolerate. A burning, on the other hand, was always bad.

In a competition that never should have existed, Duck Hill became known as one of the worst lynchings ever committed because of the way the murderers used a modern, industrial tool to burn their victims and because white magazines and newspapers published the pictures the participants took, giving them a wide circulation. Despite all the press coverage, neither the state nor the county ever investigated these crimes. According to Kester, Sheriff Wright had "personal friends" among the mob members. A former Winona mayor told the NAACP investigator that "a thousand people in Montgomery County...can name the lynchers." Yet not one member of the mob was ever held accountable.

On the day of the Duck Hill lynching, word of what had happened in that Mississippi forest reached the floor of Congress as representatives were debating the Gavagan-Wagner anti-lynching bill. Michigan's Earl Cory Michener read a press report. Black spectators who had packed the gallery grew silent. Two days later, the legislation passed, even as 106 out of 123 House members representing southern states voted against it as a violation of states' rights. Sixth District Mississippi congressman William Colmer, who represented Jeff Davis County, was one of them, and he denounced the bill in a regular column he wrote for local papers like the *Prentiss Headlight*. In June, as the Senate prepared to consider the bill, the NAACP sent every single senator as well as all the major newspapers a copy of a report based on Kester's undercover reporting.

By 1937, the NAACP had succeeded in making federal anti-lynching legislation what *Time* called "a permanent sectional issue." Sponsors offered at least one bill every legislative session. In 1937, they proposed fifty-nine. The House of Representatives first passed a bill of this kind, the Dyer Anti-Lynching Bill, in 1922. It died in the other chamber after southern senators used the filibuster to hold the floor for twenty-one days. In 1935, another anti-lynching bill passed the House, and southern senators filibustered for six days, killing it, too.

After repeated delays, the Senate's version of the Gavagan-Wagner bill finally came up for a vote on January 6, 1938. A senator from Utah and another from Idaho joined fifteen southerners in a six-week filibuster that shut down all congressional business, including urgently needed economic relief. Anti-lynching legislation opponents turned the debate into what an NAACP official called a racist "harangue." One by one, southern senators stood and asked what could possibly be next. Black patrons staying at white hotels? Equal funding of Black and white schools? Federal supervision of elections in the region, an admission of just what it would take for Black citizens to be able to exercise their right to vote? If all that was not bad enough, Mississippi senator Theodore Bilbo attacked Walter White directly as he reminded listeners of the rape myth, the traditional excuse for white vigilante violence. "What senator...will not understand the underlying motive of the Ethiopian who has inspired this proposed legislation?" According to Bilbo, White desired a federal law "with a zeal and frenzy equal if not paramount to the lust and lasciviousness of the rape fiend in his diabolical effort to despoil the womanhood of the Caucasian race." White's goal, Bilbo argued, was "to become socially and politically equal to the white man." In a rare moment of clarity, the Senate's most racist member got at least that last part right.

The NAACP put a majority of its resources into the fight to pass a federal anti-lynching law. As White wrote to another NAACP official, "The situation in Mississippi is so bad that beyond publicity...there is nothing we can do in the Mississippi courts." The only thing that might stop white men from killing Black men there was a federally enforced law. Yet once again, in February 1938, southern senators who answered only to white voters used the filibuster to prevent a vote on anti-lynching legislation that a majority of their colleagues supported. What happened in Duck Hill had not been enough to change the minds of southern senators. Congress would not pass a federal anti-lynching law until 2022.

But decades of anti-lynching activism did change what white southerners thought and how they acted, even in Mississippi. Increasing numbers of white people in the region began to publicly oppose lynching, and southern white women founded the Association of Southern Women for the Prevention of Lynching to put pressure on sheriffs and other law officers to stop the practice. White papers in the state had always covered lynchings. By the 1930s, as a result of this pressure, they had to actually condemn them as well. Even the *Prentiss Headlight* complied.

Black activists and their white allies knew that lynching was an exceptional kind of violence and yet also a part of a pattern of white behavior that incorporated a variety of extralegal acts. Yet the NAACP's lobbying effort had a hard time conveying this complex reality. In contrast, sensational acts of violence like Duck Hill, in which lynchers tortured and killed their victims while an audience watched, proved particularly useful in rallying support for federal legislation. A white person did not have to support racial equality to see this brutality as a violation of Black people's most basic human rights. As the Raleigh *News & Observer* put it, "What must a decent Southern white man feel when he thinks of men of his race not merely killing in anger but making a slow and sadistic festival of human torture."

Because no community wanted to be the next Duck Hill, white southern men changed how they killed Black people. As the *Baltimore Afro-American* argued, "The South hushes up its lynchings now because it knows that there will be a drive on to pass an anti-lynching bill in the next Congress." The NAACP reported three more hidden killings in Mississippi in 1938.

Most Americans welcomed what official statistics suggested was a decline in lynching as progress. But some activists—including NAACP officials— worried that their focus on this particular form of violence had created unintended consequences. Rather than eradicating what many Americans who opposed the practice called the lynching spirit—white men's right to act without legal authority—anti-lynching activism had instead steadily pushed this vigilante tradition underground. White men intent on taking the law into their own hands increasingly did so in secret. It was difficult to fight what no one in an official capacity would admit happened. Lying became as essential to law enforcement as nightsticks and guns.

Worried about a possible increase in unacknowledged lynchings, the civil rights organization again sent Howard Kester undercover to Mississippi to investigate. He quickly learned about four killings near Cleveland and two near Canton that local authorities had also managed to keep secret. Undoubtedly, there were others. In his report, published by the NAACP in January 1940, three years before my grandfather was elected sheriff of Jeff Davis County, Kester argued that lynching was "entering a new and altogether dangerous phase." Rather than aiding and exonerating participants in public lynch mobs, local officials arranged and took part in or worked to cover up quieter murders. In Duck Hill, Kester reported, officials had gone a step further and actually appointed a small committee of white men to handle privately and without publicity any future lynchings. While the overall number of lynchings across the region was decreasing, in some parts of the South, like rural and small-town Mississippi, the lynching spirit had simply gone underground.

This change did not mean that vigilante violence was invisible. Everybody who lived near a lynching knew. Instead of being in the papers, the news traveled by word of mouth. But the message of white supremacy carried. White men could still act with impunity. They did not have to stop killing. They just had to stop talking in public.

Underground lynchings preserved what was for many southern white men a central characteristic of their conception of themselves as citizens, their right to be the hands of the law. The alternative—actually following the law and allowing the court system to operate—ironically undermined this authority. Another murder that occurred in Prentiss in 1940 showed just how seriously southern whites took any challenge to their power, and also helped set the stage for Versie Johnson's murder seven years later.

In 1940, three years after the Duck Hill lynching, extended families across Jeff Davis County sat down together on New Year's Day for dinner, the big midday meal. Black and white people ate corn bread or biscuits and, if they had it, meat—quail the men and boys brought home from a holiday morning hunt, smoked ham from a hog butchered as the weather had turned, or chicken, golden fried pieces of a young rooster or an old hen. Many tables also held a big bowl of black-eyed peas for luck.

In 1940, almost everyone needed some good fortune. In the aftermath of the Duck Hill lynchings, racial terror had not stopped in many parts of rural Mississippi. Instead, it had taken on a new, more hidden character. At the same time, the Great Depression battered residents of the poorest state in the nation's poorest region.

Despite years of New Deal programs—payments to farmers to decrease cotton production and combat soil erosion, commodity price controls, rural electrification and road paving projects, and a new farm credit agency—Jeff Davis County residents were still struggling. The big timber companies had cut the last of the longleaf pine forests, shut down their sawmills, sold off their railroads, and gone, taking their jobs with them. Locals who had realized their dreams of farm ownership by buying the cutover acres could not fall back on the old practice of selling a little timber to pay their taxes.

Instead, farmers dug into the muck of creeks or rivers looking for what they called deadheads, logs of old-growth pine or cypress that had escaped from rafts floated downstream to mills before the coming of the railroads. Then they sold these old logs for cash. Other farmers dynamited up the pine stumps that dotted their fields and hauled the pieces to a plant in Hattiesburg that extracted turpentine from the dead wood. A few local people got "public" jobs on WPA projects, like the men hired to tear down the old Jeff Davis jail and build a new one, and my great-grandpa, Oury Berry's father, Henry Jackson Berry, who worked as a timekeeper on a road-building crew. But the number of acres sold on the steps of the Jeff Davis courthouse for back taxes soared. Many families, white and Black, lost the most important thing they had after each other: their land.

No tax sales took place during the holidays, but every four years at the courthouse on the first weekday after New Year's, officials swore in Jeff Davis's new elected officers: the sheriff, town marshals, and district constables as well as members of the Board of Supervisors and the super-intendent of education. That year, S. Gwinn Magee, a farmer and former circuit clerk who had served a term as Jeff Davis County's sheriff a quarter of a century earlier, took up the job again. The next sheriff elected in Jeff Davis would be my grandfather, Oury Berry.

If Magee ate black-eyed peas at his holiday dinner, the magic beans had not worked. By the time he started his second term, his luck had already soured. An attempt on New Year's Day to arrest four Black men allegedly running liquor through the county turned into a shoot-out that left a former Prentiss marshal named John C. Sanford dead. Between then and the October execution of one of the two Black men convicted of this killing, Magee stopped multiple lynching attempts and made a lot of local white people mad. The next time, they would not be thwarted.

The series of crimes that left two men dead started with a phone call. On New Year's Day, a young Black man named Willie Barnes went to Columbia, the seat of Marion County just south of Jeff Davis, for what he later described vaguely as "a number of purposes," one of which was to see "a girl." In Columbia, he stopped at the Y, a café run by its Black owner, Jerome Franklin. A Black man Barnes knew named Fred "Doc" Polk worked there, and the two men started talking. According to testimony later provided by Barnes, Polk told the younger man that he and Jerome Franklin were taking a load of whiskey to Prentiss that night. Polk asked Barnes to join them.

In some parts of the South, white people claimed the right to sell illegal spirits to both Black and white customers. As had happened in Duck Hill in 1937 according to the NAACP's report and would happen again at Moore's Ford in Georgia in 1946 when two Black married couples— George and Mae Murray Dorsey and Roger Malcom and his wife, Dorothy Dorsey Malcom—were lynched, white men killed Black people who did not respect their monopoly on the bootlegging trade. But in the Piney Woods, bootlegging remained a fairly segregated business. Black bootleggers mostly sold cheap corn whiskey to other Black people who ran small, illegal bars or to individual customers. Franklin made a living during the Depression by selling alcohol under the table to his café customers and to other juke joints and restaurants nearby.

Sometime after Barnes left Franklin's café, he walked to the Columbia telephone exchange to call Prentiss marshal Hance Polk, who the next day would be sworn in for another term. Barnes had been working as a laborer in Prentiss's electric light department for about two years. He also served as an informant, helping Polk catch Black people who sold liquor in Prentiss. That day, Barnes told Polk the suspects would leave Columbia in a car loaded with four ten-gallon kegs of liquor around sundown on their way to Prentiss. He also warned him to "be careful."

How exactly Franklin, Doc Polk, and Barnes connected with Hilton Fortenberry was never made clear. But Willie Barnes later testified that the four men drove to Franklin's house, where the café owner picked up his 32-caliber Winchester rifle. Sometime around dark the four Black men set out for Prentiss in Franklin's car with Franklin's liquor and Franklin's gun. They took a roundabout route, stopping in Silver Creek and other places to make sales. When they finally reached the Jeff Davis county seat at about ten o'clock that night, a roadblock awaited.

Accounts differ, but a group of white men—current and former law enforcement officials and probably others, too, civilians who wanted to help—waited in the dark for hours behind two cars positioned to block the highway coming into the town of Prentiss. Sheriff A. H. Polk, then serving the last few hours of his term, was there along with reelected officers Marshal Hance Polk and Constable Fred Burroughs and Johnny Sanford, a former marshal. Incoming sheriff Gwinn Magee was not present. No one seemed to worry about whether people who were not law enforcement officials should be participating.

White men in Jeff Davis County had always been the hands of the law. Before they held their first election or built the courthouse, they had lynched a Black man, Wood Ambrose or Ambrose Wood. Twenty years later, after two white men robbed the Bank of Blountville in 1935, Sheriff W. H. Mattison and Sanford, then Prentiss marshal, quickly organized a manhunt. As the *Prentiss Headlight* reported, "All other officers and citizens who could get a gun and desired a chase joined in." Even white teenagers participated in the search. After Joe Dale, Prentiss founder "Prent" Berry's grandson, and three friends heard the news in the Prentiss High band room, they left the school and took off in a car looking for the bad guys. The bank robbers eventually escaped the county by stealing a Ford coupe and taking two "prominent citizens" hostage. After the kidnapped men were freed, the *Prentiss Headlight* praised them for risking their lives "obeying an invitation to enforce the law." What some people called vigilante behavior, many white residents of Jeff Davis understood as the highest duty of white male citizenship.

Five years after the bank robbery, on New Year's Day in 1940, the car carrying the suspected bootleggers reached the roadblock on the outskirts of Prentiss and slowed. Together, Hance Polk and Sanford, current and former Prentiss marshals, identified themselves as "the law" and walked toward the vehicle. Jerome Franklin immediately began to turn his car around. As Sanford crossed in front of the headlights, someone in the car started firing. Barnes said that it was Fortenberry and that he knocked the gun out of the older man's hands after he shot Sanford and then took aim at Hance Polk. The marshal testified that as the first shots rang out, he dropped to the ground and fired back at the liquor car's tires. However the gun battle unfolded, Sanford was shot multiple times. A father of four daughters, a contractor, a Mason, and an active member of Prentiss Baptist Church, where he had attended services the day before, he died at the scene.

Officers arrested Jerome Franklin, the café owner, before daylight. He claimed he had been "too busy driving to do any shooting" and that though the gun was his, it was Hilton Fortenberry who had fired. He had only fled because, as he said later, "I knew a nigger wouldn't have a chance at a time like that." When the four Black men got back to Columbia, Franklin told officers, a drunk Fortenberry took the money and left in the car. Fortenberry was later arrested. Because Barnes was an informant, officers protected him. It was not clear what happened to Doc Polk.

Over the next several days, white mobs tried to storm the Marion County jail in Columbia, where Franklin was held on at least two occasions. Early on January 5, 1940, Marion sheriff O. J. Foxworth told a crowd gathered in the dark, "I am going to make every effort to protect this negro and any attempt at mob violence will be met with the full force of my office." Later that morning, Foxworth moved Jerome Franklin to the most secure facility in the state, the Hinds County Jail in Jackson.

While in jail in Columbia, Franklin would have been able to see and hear armed white men on the street from the window of his cell. As a Black man living in Mississippi, he would have understood what mobs could do. The atrocities in Duck Hill three years earlier had made it brutally clear.

Even behind the walls of that Jackson jail, Jerome Franklin did not feel safe. The forty-two-year-old man confessed to a *Clarion-Ledger* reporter who interviewed him there that he was a longtime corn whiskey seller but "never in no other trouble." "For 18 years, I worked there in Columbia. All the white folks know me," Franklin said. "But this Hilton Fortenberry...he was bad. He'd been in cutting scrapes and fights." If the other man had not been along, Franklin would have been arrested again for bootlegging. He would have been jailed and fined and eventually released. And Sanford would be alive. Franklin used the reporter to try to plead for mercy.

While mobs were trying to lynch Franklin in Columbia, authorities caught up with Hilton Fortenberry in Houston. Mississippi highway patrolman Vance Strickland went to Texas to pick up the accused man and bring him back. According to Strickland, Fortenberry confessed on the drive. Back in Prentiss briefly before being taken to the Brookhaven jail in nearby Lincoln County for "safekeeping," the Black suspect also allegedly confessed to Sheriff Magee. Probably, Strickland and Magee tortured Fortenberry, threatening and assaulting him until he said what they wanted. Yet even then, what Fortenberry offered never really explained what had happened. He admitted firing one shot through the rear door of Franklin's car. None of the other Black men had a gun. Yet somehow the undertaker found three holes in Sanford's body.

Over the weekend, a large number of white men held a mass meeting in Jeff Davis County, probably at the courthouse, to debate Fortenberry's and Franklin's fates. Eventually, they reached a consensus "not to attempt to interfere with the regular procedure of a trial."

If Sheriff Magee did not attend this meeting, he certainly heard about it. Either way, he relied on the decision made there as he brought both Fortenberry and Franklin back to Prentiss that Monday. But clearly not all local white men agreed to let the trial proceed. As a newspaper reported, "crowds of farmers and town citizens from miles around, many of them armed, began milling around this county seat" as soon as the prisoners arrived. As the streets around the courthouse filled, Magee told reporters he would do everything possible to ensure his prisoners' safety. He quickly sent the accused men away again to "undisclosed" jails and called Governor Hugh White.

Maybe politics explained why Sheriff Magee moved his prisoners to more secure facilities elsewhere and asked the governor for help. As events unfolded in Jeff Davis County, Congress was considering another anti-lynching bill in Washington. Neither Governor White nor Sheriff Magee wanted Prentiss to be the next Duck Hill. Maybe that was enough.

But there were always some white southerners who understood the law as a set of abstract rules. It was possible that Magee was one of them and as a result, he took his duty to protect his Black prisoners more seriously than many southern sheriffs.

Whatever motivated Magee, his call for aid worked. Before sunrise the next morning, three companies of national guardsmen armed with tear gas and riot guns arrived at the Jefferson Davis County Courthouse. After they were set up, Magee brought Fortenberry and Franklin back to town for their arraignment. Given the realities of Jim Crow justice, a sure-to-be-all-white jury would most likely convict the Black men. A guilty plea was less risky, even if a Black man was innocent, because it sent a message to white men that a lynch mob was not necessary. But Jerome Franklin pleaded not guilty. Even more surprising, so did Hilton Fortenberry. As word spread around town that locals were organizing another mass meeting to plan a lynching, Sheriff Magee again acted decisively, this time sending his prisoners to the fifth-floor, mob-proof jail in Jackson. To prevent lynchings, sheriffs had to quickly move the men in their custody to other facilities. My grandfather's predecessor clearly was willing to go to the trouble—and to risk the consequences.

Because of Magee's efforts, Franklin and Fortenberry lived to stand trial at the Jeff Davis courthouse ten days after Sanford's death. National guardsmen set up posts outside at all four corners of the building and searched everyone who entered for weapons. As the proceedings unfolded, the sounds of hammers and saws from a construction project just outside on the lawn filled the courtroom.

New structures for law enforcement were taking shape in the county. At the end of 1939, the circuit court had convicted Cleveland Holloway, a local Black man, of slaying another local Black man named Fred Magee after an argument in a café. But around the same time, Jeff Davis officials had received funds from the WPA to build a modern, secure jail. Before the court sentenced Holloway to death, local men employed to work on the project had demolished the old jail with its execution chamber, a room with a built-in trapdoor for hanging prisoners that had never been used. Scheduled for early February 1940, Holloway's hanging would be the first legal execution in county history. In the wake of Sanford's death, carpenters building the gallows enlarged the platform to include multiple trapdoors. As Fortenberry and Franklin's trial took place, officials were already planning how they would carry out the not-yet-convicted men's death sentences.

Despite their lack of time to prepare, Fortenberry's court-appointed attorneys managed to raise substantial questions. One lawyer attacked Willie Barnes for turning state's evidence. It was Barnes who persuaded the bootleggers to go to Prentiss that night so that Hance Polk, the Prentiss marshal, could arrest Fortenberry and Franklin. The whole sordid business, the lawyer argued, was a setup. In court, the young Black man denied it, insisting that he had not even expected to be paid for his information but instead tipped off the officers out of "love for his town and county." Even less information came out about Fred "Doc" Polk, who was indicted but not arrested. Given his long ties to the area and string of bootlegging arrests in Jeff Davis County, he may also have been an informant. The fact that neither Barnes nor Polk paid for their participation in the killing of Sanford suggested that they were both working for law enforcement.

Fortenberry's other attorney tried to undermine confidence in the identification of Fortenberry as the shooter. Undertaker B. G. Walton had found two small bullet holes and one large one in Sanford's body, all in the right chest. The prosecutors proposed an extremely unlikely scenario, that four shots hit Sanford but one of them entered a hole formed by another bullet and enlarged it. The much more likely explanation was that bullets from two different guns made the holes. Because none of the other Black men had a firearm, one of the other white men must have shot Sanford, too.

Instead of following this line of questioning, Fortenberry's second lawyer tried another approach: "You've got a bunch of n****rs in that car, not one. Can you put your finger on the proof that it was Fortenberry who fired the fatal shots?...The lowdown cur that killed Mr. Sanford ought to be hung, but who are you going to say did it?" The killer might have been any of the suspected bootleggers, Fortenberry or Barnes or Doc Polk. What the lawyer neglected to say was that it might also have been the white marshal, Hance Polk.

The most concrete evidence against Fortenberry was his confession that he had fired one shot. The 1936 Supreme Court decision *Brown v. Mississippi* outlawing confessions obtained through torture probably invalidated its use in court. But neither of his lawyers raised the issue.

Meanwhile, Franklin either had money or white patrons willing to help because he hired his own attorneys. Sure that no justice could be had in the town where Sanford had lived, his lawyers focused on setting up grounds for an appeal to a higher court. As the trial wrapped up, they argued for hours with the judge and the prosecutor about how the jury should be instructed. But none of this work would matter if a mob lynched their client before they could file.

As multiple mobs formed over multiple days, Ruth and F. A. Parker at the *Prentiss Headlight* seemed to understand their job as suppressing anything that made white residents look bad rather than reporting the news. "No move has been made to harm the negroes," they insisted repeatedly, and the few armed men who did appear in the streets of Prentiss were from elsewhere. "THE PEOPLE OF JEFF DAVIS WANT JUSTICE METED OUT BUT THEY WANT IT LAWFULLY! They are willing to let the court try the negroes with the assurance that they will be tried fairly, and without harm." Somehow, despite the fact that a person could stand in the office of the *Headlight* and see the courthouse across the street, no one who worked there ever saw the throngs of armed local white men who repeatedly gathered around the building.

Sheriff Magee might have been unlucky, but he succeeded in protecting Franklin and Fortenberry. The fact that he denied his efforts to thwart mob action in the *Prentiss Headlight* after having described them to reporters from other towns suggested he knew his actions were not popular in his home county. The next time voters got to choose a sheriff, they would pick someone who would let them be the law. That person would be my grandfather.

On Saturday, the second day of Franklin and Fortenberry's trial, the jury went out around 8 p.m. About half an hour later, they were back. Twelve white men found the two Black men guilty and sentenced them to death. As the guardsmen stood watch, Magee escorted the convicted men out of the courthouse and into a patrol car for the sixty-mile ride back to the Jackson jail. For the moment, they were alive. They were scheduled to hang on February 23.

Many white residents were probably satisfied with this verdict. Some opposed lynching on principle. Others worried a mob murder would hurt Jeff Davis's reputation as a majority-Black county with, in Mississippi terms, decent race relations—only one recorded lynching thirty-four years earlier, the killing of Ambrose Wood in 1906. Jeff Davis, white residents liked to tell themselves, was not like the Delta or some nearby, majority-white Piney Woods counties. Jeff Davis was civilized.

As expected, Fortenberry's lawyers appealed, claiming twenty-one assignments of error in the trial. In June, the Mississippi Supreme Court denied every claim. A Black man had fired at a group of white men. A white man had died. Franklin and Fortenberry had to pay.

But the Mississippi legislature had passed a bill that spring that added further delays. Many states had decided to electrocute rather than hang or shoot people sentenced to death. In Mississippi, earlier attempts to adopt this modern method of carrying out capital punishment had gotten hung up on the objections of legislators from the Delta who did not want these executions to take place at the state penitentiary at Parchman. Mississippi law enforcement officials had always carried out death sentences in the counties where prisoners had committed their crimes. So the sponsors of the bill came up with an ingenious solution: a mobile electric chair.

Then state officials ran into a problem. No one actually built and sold a portable version of this execution technology, and yet without this piece of equipment as well as a portable generator to run it, the state could not conduct executions. The state finally found a company that agreed to try to build the device, and it was mid-September before they succeeded. Then Mississippi state officials put their one-of-a-kind electric chair on display at the capitol building.

As Mississippi struggled to restart executions, Jeff Davis officials gave up on electrocution. People sentenced to death before the new law passed had the right to choose how they wanted to die, but neither Fortenberry nor Franklin had ever expressed a preferred method. On Monday, October 7, 1940, ten months after the death of John Sanford, Sheriff Gwinn Magee and District Attorney Sebe Dale announced that the state attorney general had approved their plan to hang the convicted men. The execution would take place that Friday.

For months, the gallows had stood waiting on the courthouse lawn as workers completed the new concrete and steel jail and the county used another grant of WPA funds to enlarge and renovate the courthouse and install modern plumbing and electricity. Now, at last, the condemned men would die.

Then suddenly, without any warning, only two days before the scheduled execution, Mississippi governor Paul Johnson commuted Franklin's sentence to life in prison. Fortenberry would face the gallows alone.

The clemency extended to Franklin was not about justice. It was about politics. Johnson claimed he was only following the recommendations of several state supreme court justices and unnamed citizens of Jeff Davis and Marion Counties. Franklin, it turned out, had powerful white supporters, including possibly Governor Johnson's own son. This kind of patronage sometimes protected Black men who had the opportunity to participate in these paternalistic of relationships and the temperament to perform the required deference. Many Black men did not. But the governor's decision left many white Jeff Davis residents even more shocked and angry than some of them had been after law officers had thwarted local mobs.

That night, they called yet another mass meeting, this time to challenge the governor's action, a fact only admitted by the *Headlight* a decade later. As the resolutions drawn up there stated, Sanford had been "willfully, wantonly and maliciously killed and murdered by two Negro bootleggers, Jerome Franklin and Hilton Fortenberry, at a time when he...represented the majesty of the law and was attempting to make Jefferson Davis County a better and safer place in which to live."

But the governor ignored these men who considered themselves good citizens. In upholding a vision of the law as a set of abstract rules, he deprived them of what they understood as their right to *be* the law. Local leaders including Sheriff Magee had been wrong. The "regular procedure" of the courts did not result in what these white men understood as justice. That Friday, they would execute Fortenberry, but Franklin, a Black man they believed they had the right to kill, remained beyond their reach in the Jackson jail. He would live.

Jeff Davis would hold on to its distinction as a one-lynching county for a while longer, but Fortenberry's execution, the last legal hanging in the state of Mississippi, did not go well. At midnight, thirty national guardsmen, four state highway patrolmen, Sheriff Magee, District Attorney Sebe Dale, two other Jeff Davis officials, and the Black man white locals called "Sac" Fortenberry left Jackson. In Prentiss, in the unfenced backyard of the courthouse, the huge gallows waited.

As the officers escorted Fortenberry toward the platform, the trouble started. At least fifty men and several women "elbowed their way up the stairs and circled the trap, directly under the knotted noose." In 1936, twenty thousand people had watched the State of Kentucky hang Rainey Bethea, a young Black man convicted of raping and killing an elderly white woman. Disgusted by this spectacle, the few states that still conducted public executions outlawed such audiences. Mississippi allowed only officials and crime victims to watch hangings, and Sanford's widow had decided to stay home. No one else should have been present.

Sheriff Magee grew frustrated. Twice, he gave the order for these white spectators to "clear out." Each time, the crowd refused. A man yelled, "We are entitled to see it." Sheriff Magee had prevented them from lynching Sanford's alleged killers. He would not stop them from watching one of the Black men die.

Finally, the people who wanted to watch agreed to move back against the walls that ran around the platform in order to give the officers room to work, and the sheriff relented. Hundreds more who did not make it onto the platform crowded around the base of the gallows and filled the courthouse lawn. My grandfather might have been among those spectators on or near the gallows. Still a barber then and living in the first house he and Grace owned in Prentiss, it would have been easy enough for him to walk the three blocks to the courthouse. Even if he was not present, he would have heard about what happened. He would have had a sense of what the job of sheriff entailed.

The officers brought Sac Fortenberry up onto the gallows. Then District Attorney Sebe Dale, a resident of Marion County who served the multiple-county Fifteenth Judicial Circuit and knew the man he was executing, gave a short speech: "It's now the painful duty of Jeff Davis county officers to perform one of the most tragic duties, the duty of putting a man to death. But the situation is made more tragic by the fact that the man who got him into it has gone free. The fact that you, Sac, have been lied on and must die while he escapes is one of the most damnable things that has ever occurred." Some of the spectators offered a chorus of "amens." Then Dale concluded, "Eighteen men indicted you, twelve men convicted you and six men affirmed your sentence, but nobody here wants to take your life."

In heavy silence, the deputies put the hood over Fortenberry's head and used a clothesline to tie his legs. Then the district attorney secured the noose around the Black man's neck and asked Sac to let him know "if it gets too tight." After a muffled response, Dale told Fortenberry to stand up. Sheriff Magee put his hand on the lever. Dale gripped the chair, paused, and said, "Ready!" Magee pushed the lever forward. At 2:24 a.m., Fortenberry plummeted through the trap. The drop did not break his neck. Under the hood, Fortenberry moaned. For eleven long minutes, white people watched as the Black man's body twitched and swayed. And then, at last, it was done.

A LIE

When a mob of white men tortured and killed Roosevelt Townes and Robert McDaniels at Duck Hill in April 1937, Versie Johnson would have heard the news. Black papers published in Jackson, Chicago, and elsewhere reached Black people in Jeff Davis County, and most white papers in Mississippi, including the *Prentiss Headlight*, covered these lynchings. Townes, a Mississippi native, had been twenty-five, only a few years older than Versie Johnson, who was then twenty-one. What I do not know is how Versie Johnson, a young man in his prime with his whole life ahead of him, felt about this gruesome reminder of the ever-present danger of white violence.

By the fall of 1940, when my grandfather's predecessor as sheriff, Gwinn Magee, presided over the execution of Hilton "Sac" Fortenberry, Versie Johnson had left Jeff Davis County and moved north to D'Lo, a former sawmill town located in Simpson County. There, he worked for a white man who owned a farm and a store in another town. Unlike many single men in their twenties, he did not serve in the military during World War II, perhaps because he was arrested and convicted of a not particularly serious crime. And at some point, he married and then his wife died.

I can only repeat the outlines of his adult life here because these bare facts, so much less than the full measure of Versie Johnson's young adulthood, are all that survive. What I want to know is how he met his wife and whether or not they had children and where they lived and why she passed away. What I want to know is how, exactly, he lived. Instead, what the documents tell me the most about is how in 1947 he died.

Because the *Prentiss Headlight* came out on Thursdays and my grandfather and other law officials shot Versie Johnson in the afternoon on August 1, a Friday, it was almost a week before any notice of the killing appeared. But on the front page on August 7, between a report about the latest federal farm programs and the local results in Tuesday's Democratic primary, the local paper published that single-column, seven-paragraph article that I had first read on a visit with my grandmother all those years ago. Most people who lived in and around Prentiss and who had not actually witnessed the shooting would by then have already heard some variation of the news via word of mouth or other newspapers. Instead, the *Prentiss Headlight* provided the official version of what local white leaders wanted outsiders and future readers of the county's paper of record to know, the story of how and why law officers killed a Black man in their custody. It was the paper's job to organize the lie.

The why was easy. Under the headline "Negro Killed by Officers in Scuffle for Gun," the paper acknowledged that local residents were "shocked to their very foundations when it became known that a local Negro, Versie Johnson, had raped a young white woman, an expectant mother, on he [*sic*] W. T. Lipsey farm." The unnamed woman had identified him as the man who threatened her with an iron bar, raped her in the woods near her home, and then made her promise not to tell. As far as the *Headlight* was concerned, a Black man had committed the crime white people most feared. His guilt was not in doubt.

Yet the paper took care to explain how he died. That, too, happened at the Lipsey farm, the *Headlight* reported, where my grandfather, the sheriff, and two officers in the Mississippi state highway patrol, Spencer Puckett and Andy Hopkins, had taken Versie Johnson. As Oury Berry told the *Headlight* and other newspapers, the accused man had asked to travel to the scene of his alleged crime so he could describe what happened, and once there, he tried to grab patrolman Spencer Puckett's gun. The officers had no choice but to shoot.

That was the story. The first time I read it, I knew it was not true. But knowing that what the newspaper presented as reporting was a lie did not tell me what had actually happened. The only reason I ever figured it out was because some people refused to stick to the official account.

At least two white women talked. One of them was Virginia Hartzog, a clerk who seemed to go off script when a reporter from outside Prentiss called the sheriff's office. My grandfather Oury Berry quickly corrected her, and not a single white newspaper questioned the sheriff's account. But some of those papers printed her description of what happened at the jail as well as Berry's denial.

The other white woman who talked, in her own way, was my mother. She was ten years old when Versie Johnson died, too young to be told what actually occurred on the Lipsey farm so close to her own home. But she hung on to a version of the event that made sense to a girl who loved her father. And she shared it with me.

Of course, local Black people also talked at the time, and in far greater numbers—and the stories they told reporters working for Black newspapers came closer to describing what actually happened. The *Baltimore Afro-American,* the *Pittsburgh Courier,* the *Jackson Advocate,* and others drew on unnamed local sources as they worked to reconstruct the story. Two civil rights organizations, the NAACP and the Civil Rights Congress, picked up on this reporting and demanded that the US Department of Justice look into Versie Johnson's death. Precedents existed for a federal investigation. After white residents of two Piney Woods counties north of Jeff Davis County lynched two Black teenagers, Charlie Lang and Ernest Green, and a Black man, Howard Wash, in less than a week in October 1942, the US attorney general sent in the FBI. Five years later, the FBI investigated the lynching of a Black man named Willie Earle near Greenville, South Carolina. But when Versie Johnson died six months after Earle, the federal government did nothing.

But people continued to talk, even well into the new century. Because

I could not go to Jeff Davis County during the pandemic summer of 2020, I began conducting phone interviews with journalists, current and former politicians, writers, and scholars with ties to Mississippi. Among the most helpful of these Mississippi experts was Ralph Eubanks, a writer and professor who had grown up on a farm his family owned in Covington County, just east of Jeff Davis. He told me his family had gone to Prentiss often. One of his mom's best friends from her childhood in rural Alabama had ended up teaching English at the Prentiss Institute, where her husband also held various jobs, and the two families were tight. Eubanks became very close to the son. His friend Alvin Williams still lived in Mississippi, where he spent years working as a marketing professor at the University of Southern Mississippi in Hattiesburg.

When I interviewed Alvin Williams, I learned that his family lived right on the edge of the Prentiss Institute campus, on a street of houses owned by faculty and staff from the school. Like Ralph Eubanks, he was born after Versie Johnson died. But he offered to put me in touch with a ninety-four-year-old Black man who had been his high school history teacher and his mentor as well as his neighbor. This man had ended up living on the same street as the Williams family because his wife taught music at the Prentiss Institute. If anyone would know about this killing, Williams assured me, it would be this man: Mitchell Gamblin.

The problem was the pandemic. When I reached Mitchell Gamblin on the phone, he was eager to talk, but understandably, given the gravity of the topic, he wanted to sit down in person. And, he said, given his age, he did not want to wait. Yet with the pandemic raging and no vaccine yet available, I was worried about how an interview might endanger his health. I also faced another problem. My university had halted all research travel. After I explained the situation to my department chair, she agreed that my interview, given its timely nature, qualified for an exception. With her approval, I waited a few months until the fall, when we might be more comfortable talking outside and COVID-19 numbers were low in both Virginia and Mississippi. Then I enlisted one of my daughters to help with the driving and recording.

We made the nine-hundred-mile trip in two days and arrived on October 8 in time to meet Mr. Gamblin in the early afternoon. He insisted on taking us to the Jeff Davis County Public Library, still in the same building I visited so often as a child. There, sitting socially distanced around a table in the empty reading room, he told me what he knew. Then we spent several hours walking around the old downtown as he filled in more details. The next morning, we all got in his car, and he showed us the place where law officers, including my grandfather, shot Versie Johnson. Then we talked some more as we drove around the countryside and ate a take-out lunch together in Longleaf Trace Park.

A lifelong resident of Jeff Davis County, a dedicated activist and member of the NAACP and other organizations, and a devoted Christian, Gamblin remembered Prentiss after the war quite clearly. Drafted by the army in 1945 when he was eighteen, he worked in Munich transporting German prisoners to a medical facility set up in the former Dachau concentration camp. He returned home early in the summer of 1947. While he did not witness Versie Johnson's death, his good friend Central Johnson picked up the body at the Lipsey farm. Gamblin shared with me what Central told him he had heard white people there talking about after he arrived. The former history teacher also recounted what Black people in Prentiss believed about the killing at the time. Versie Johnson, he said, did not die in an escape attempt. He was lynched.

When white people described what happened on that August day, they focused on the rape. The Jackson *Clarion-Ledger* and the *Chicago Daily Tribune* both reported Johnson's killing in front-page articles the day after he died, and they cited my grandfather as their main source. Five days later, the *Prentiss Headlight* published its own version. In the detailed accounts provided by these three newspapers, a simple, sordid story emerged.

In this description of the events that led to his death, Versie Johnson went to the door of a house on the Lipsey farm on the morning of August 1 and asked the pregnant white woman who lived there for a match. After she gave him one, he grabbed her throat and attacked her with an iron bar. She screamed and offered him ten dollars, all the money she had in the house. Instead of releasing her, he dragged her to a wooded spot and raped her. After the assault, Johnson led the white woman to a small farm building nearby. He drew a cross on the wall and placed her hand on the symbol of Jesus. Then he told her she must not tell anyone and left.

In this version of the story, unlike my mom's, the unnamed white woman did not get a ride but instead walked one to two miles to town to find her husband, who worked as a laborer there. Together, they went to see the sheriff. Because the Lipsey farm was close to Grace and Oury Berry's place, my grandfather probably knew the couple. They were, in rural terms, neighbors.

When the couple arrived at the sheriff's office, my grandfather sent the woman to the doctor. Then he and his deputies rounded up and arrested Johnson and eight other Black men they found near the white woman's house, most of them probably employees in the industrial area around the nearby railroad depot, the site of three cotton gins, including one owned by the same Lipsey family that owned the farm, a sawmill, and several warehouses. How exactly the white woman identified her attacker among the nine Black men at the jail was left vague. The *Chicago Daily Tribune* put it this way: "The woman selected Johnson from the group, Berry said."

When Black people described what happened, they told a different story, according to Mitchell Gamblin—a tale not of rape but of a relationship. Versie Johnson and the unnamed white woman had sex, according to this account, but it was consensual. They were, in Gamblin's words, "lovers."

Relationships across the color line were not uncommon. Despite the fact that white lawmakers wrote a ban on interracial marriage into the 1890 Mississippi Constitution, Mitchell Gamblin remembered interracial couples and even interracial marriages in Jeff Davis and nearby counties. According to him, Black people knew about the affair between Versie Johnson and this white woman long before other local white people became aware of it.

The way local Black people understood it, the events that led to Versie Johnson's death started with a white man named Thompson who worked at the Lipsey cotton gin. Thompson saw Johnson and the white woman together at her home on the nearby Lipsey farm. Afterward, he told any white man who would listen that the white woman had a Black "angel," by which he meant that she had a Black lover. Because the cotton was laid by, farmers and gin workers had time on their hands. Over the course of about a week, the story spread. Because many white people refused to believe any white woman would willingly have sex with a Black man, a growing group of white men that probably included the white woman's husband began accusing Versie Johnson of rape. They also demanded action and made it clear that if law officers were not up to the job, they were more than willing to do it themselves. In response, according to the version of the story that spread among Black residents living in and near Prentiss, my grandfather arrested Versie Johnson.

No one willing to talk to me remembered the name of this white woman. Census documents reveal who lived in the houses near the Lipsey farm in 1940 and then again in 1950, but given the mobility of those years, there is no way to know who occupied those places in 1947. It was certainly possible that in 1947, the white woman was indeed a victim, just like Versie himself. If she was a young woman at the time, she might still be alive as of this writing. She might have her own story to tell.

But in the quest to understand what happened to Versie Johnson, the white woman is actually a distraction. In focusing on her, both the official story and the Black community's alternative locate the attempt to make sense of Johnson's death in the terms set by the rape myth. They shift the focus from Johnson to the white woman, from what has been done to a Black male body to what has been done to a white female one. Concern about her fate still works as many white southerners intended then—as a diversion, a way to deflect and deny the cruel, cold-blooded violence of white supremacy.

In August 1947, clerk Virginia Hartzog dared to describe what was obvious. From the windows of the Jeff Davis County sheriff's office where she worked, she surely had seen the white men gathering outside her window on the courthouse lawn near the jail. She told at least one reporter that a mob of about seventy-five men had "given the sheriff until 8 o'clock" the night of August 1 "to get a confession" from Versie Johnson. Left unstated were the implications of the threat. If her boss failed, the mob would take over the job themselves.

In his conversations with reporters, my grandfather denied his own clerk's statement. "About 75 people did gather around the jail as they will in any small town—out of curiosity," he told the *Clarion-Ledger*. "But they were quiet and orderly and did not make any threats nor set any deadline by which I must determine which Negro was guilty of the crime." By the end of September, Hartzog had left the sheriff's office.

Oury Berry worked hard to control the release of information, but the story my grandfather told the press did not quite make sense. His clerk's counternarrative was one complication. The bloodhounds and the timeline he offered were others.

The Jackson *Clarion-Ledger* reported that my grandfather sent word to a white man in Crystal Springs to bring his hounds the fifty miles or so to Prentiss. When the pack arrived, Johnson had already been arrested. Instead of using them to try to track suspects, the animals "were allowed to sniff Johnson's shoes and were then taken to the scene of the crime," where my grandfather hoped they would pick up the accused rapist's scent and thus provide additional evidence. "But because of weather conditions and the lapse of time, the sheriff said, nothing definite could be ascertained from their actions." At their next meeting, held about a month after Versie Johnson died, the Jeff Davis County Board of Supervisors authorized a payment of fifty dollars for the bloodhounds, making it clear that they were indeed brought to Prentiss. But the *Headlight* left the animals out of their account entirely, perhaps because, for a careful reader, they raised questions about the story. The weather might have been a factor—hounds have trouble following scents when they are panting heavily, and it was hot that day, with a high of around one hundred degrees. But if Johnson had been so quickly arrested and identified by his alleged victim, why did my grandfather even need to call in the hounds?

The official timeline was also a problem. A longer period of time between the alleged rape and Versie Johnson's arrest might help explain the puzzling story about the cross: the strange scene described by both local and national newspapers in which Versie Johnson allegedly brought the white woman out of the woods following the rape, drew a cross on the wall of a nearby building, and swore her to secrecy upon it. Maybe the white woman or someone close to her made up the tale, with its implication that the alleged victim made a promise not to talk, to explain why, as Gamblin suggested, events unfolded over several days.

Beyond the odd tale of this oath, my grandfather's official account of what happened constructed an impossible chronology. Berry told reporters that Versie Johnson arrived at the white woman's house about 9 a.m. on Friday morning, August 1, and was killed that afternoon. That left only six to eight hours for a long list of things to happen: the alleged rape, the pregnant and injured woman's long walk to town, her visit to the sheriff's office and then the doctor, the hounds brought in from more than an hour away and then used, the nine men arrested, the woman taken to the jail to see the suspects and identify Versie Johnson, the gathering of armed white men on the courthouse lawn, the calling in of the patrolmen, members of the state police force whose help my grandfather would have had to ask for and one of whom lived twenty miles away, the trip back to the Lipsey farm, and the shooting during the alleged escape attempt.

Mitchell Gamblin described the story as Black people at the time understood it, including a more plausible course of events that took place over about a week. In his account, tensions built around Prentiss as Thompson spread his story about seeing Johnson and a white woman together in an intimate embrace that other white men turned into an accusation of rape. At some point, my grandfather acted. If Versie Johnson left something like his shoes behind at the white woman's house, Oury Berry might have tried to use the hounds to track him. But it was also possible that he had already arrested Johnson and called in the pack to provide corroborating evidence by locating the Black man's scent in or near the white woman's home. It is worth noting, though, that neither of these efforts would have been necessary had the white woman confirmed Thompson's story and accused Versie Johnson of rape. In Jeff Davis County as in many parts of the Jim Crow South, the white woman's word would have been enough.

Whether or not Virginia Hartzog was right about the mob's ultimatum, my grandfather would have had to consider his options while watching a crowd of armed voters, many of them people he knew, standing on the lawn outside his office. As he made his decision, he probably thought about the example of his predecessor, Sheriff Magee. But he also would have understood that some local white men were angry at Magee for his diligence in protecting the Sanford murder suspects. If the two convicted men had been executed as planned, Magee would have been forgiven. But the governor's last-minute pardon of one of them meant that a Black man had gotten away with killing a white man, considered by those who knew him a leading citizen. In that light, the former sheriff's success in protecting his prisoners looked to some local white men like a miscarriage of justice. Some of them were probably still mad. My grandfather might even have shared this feeling. And in the eyes of many whites, the current allegation that Johnson had raped a white woman was even worse than the accusation that Fortenberry and Franklin had killed a white man. What all this meant in 1947 was that if some of those armed and angry men on the courthouse lawn wanted to lynch Versie Johnson, they would not have been easily turned aside.

As my grandfather understood the situation, he would have had two main options. One choice was to give up and simply let the armed white men take Versie Johnson from his jail. The other was to follow Magee's lead and do everything he could to protect his prisoner through the process of a trial and a legal execution. But whether he decided to send Versie Johnson away to an undisclosed jail in a nearby county or to the mob-proof Hinds County facility in Jackson or to hold him in his own jail, this path had significant obstacles. Versie Johnson, alternately identified at the time as a farm laborer or a sawmill worker, probably did not have the money to hire his own lawyer, so the judge would have to appoint an attorney. Then county officials would have to call a jury, the attorneys would have to select the jurors, and the judge would have to run a trial. Even in the rigged system of Mississippi justice, these proceedings would take a few days. Oury and his deputies would have to guard Johnson either in the Jeff Davis jail or in transport. They would also have to secure the courthouse and its surrounding grounds for the preliminary proceedings and the trial.

If my grandfather managed all this successfully, he would still face what he would have understood as another problem. In a trial, the pregnant white woman—his neighbor—would probably have to testify. Many white southerners would have argued that no white woman should be put through the trauma of having to face the Black man who had allegedly violated her and describe what happened to a courthouse full of people—the lawyers, the judge, members of the jury, and the spectators. Few white folks would have considered that it might have been hard for entirely different reasons, because she might have to look at Versie Johnson and lie.

In my grandfather's mind, there was likely yet another difficulty. Given the place my grandfather lived, the job he held, and the man he was, he would have known one thing for certain. A trial of a Black man who had been accused of raping a white woman had only one possible outcome— conviction, and it was highly unlikely given the alleged crime of rape that the current governor would overturn the death sentence. After the court had gone through the motions, the state would send the truck with the mobile electric chair to Prentiss. Berry and his deputies would strap Versie Johnson in, and then my grandfather would throw the switch and watch and listen as another man died in agony. If this was the best possible out-come, my grandfather probably wondered, why go to all the trouble?

Oury might also have considered how, five years earlier, white men in the Piney Woods town of Laurel, about fifty miles east of Prentiss, had lynched Howard Wash, a Black man who had already been convicted of murdering his white employer. What happened with Wash made it clear a mob could act at any point, even after the trial. And if a lynching occurred, newspapers all over the country would report the story, and the FBI would probably investigate. If members of the mob engaged in torture, Prentiss would become the next Duck Hill—and both the town's and my grandfather's reputations would suffer accordingly.

But if my grandfather saw his choice as not how to protect Versie Johnson's life but how to manage his death, then he almost certainly would have known that there was a third path: an alternative to handing Versie Johnson over to the lynch mob or keeping him safely imprisoned until he could be executed—another course of action that adhered to a different concept of law and order.

On August 1, 1947, my grandfather, Sheriff Berry, would have weighed the rights of a man Jim Crow had taught him to ignore against the future of the place he had spent most of his life, a county then experiencing a postwar economic boom. He also would have considered how his authority had already been undermined by men vying to replace him as sheriff. At least one candidate had attacked Berry's record. Rumors had spread. Twice, it had gotten bad enough that my grandfather felt compelled to address the public. In February, the *Prentiss Headlight* published his words on the front page under the headline "Sheriff Makes Public Statement to the People": "I want you to know that I appreciate everything you have done for me. I also want you, the people of Jefferson Davis County, to know that I have done the very best I could. I have made mistakes, but I assure you that they were honest ones." He did not say what exactly these errors were, and my research has turned up no explanation. But my grandfather assured local citizens, "I have enforced the law the very best that I knew how and have fought the selling of liquor as hard as I could. And I expect to fight it as long as I am in office." He asked white citizens to "help me and my deputies make this the hardest year the bootleggers and law-breakers have ever had." And he closed with a plea "I will appreciate your co-operation to the end."

In June, two months before he arrested Versie Johnson, my grandfather made another public statement. "It has come to my attention by rumor that there is now being operated in the Town of Prentiss on Main St., an open saloon.... This rumor is being spread by a candidate for the office of Sheriff of Jeff Davis County. I challenge this man, or any other person in Jeff Davis County, to substantiate this claim. I stand ready at any time, day or night, to raid any place, white or colored, rich or poor, on information that liquor is being sold at such place or places." Again, he gestured at the vigilante actions so much a part of life there: "I have never refused to go with anyone or any group of people in the enforcement of the law, for better living and moral conditions." Then he defended his work, in case people had forgotten all the notices in the *Headlight* describing Berry and Prentiss marshal Curtis Chance pouring hundreds of gallons of liquor into the concrete ditch beside the courthouse. "When I took the oath of office four years ago, I found conditions in regard to law enforcement in Jeff Davis County bad. In 1944, I made one thousand and twenty searches, personally delivering search warrants." He ended by expressing his regret "that I am forced to protect my record as sheriff, but my books are open to any citizen of Jeff Davis County who might want to see a list of fines, arrests, and convictions that I have made in the last four years."

Versie Johnson's case offered my grandfather a chance to burnish his reputation just as primary voters chose his replacement. Given my grandparents' financial circumstances—both Oury and Grace would be out of a job in early 1948 and they had sold the dairy—his reputation was not merely a matter of preserving his dignity. It was also the central qualification he would bring to any future livelihood. He could not serve two consecutive terms as sheriff, but after his replacement had run out his time in office, my grandfather would be eligible to run again. Proving himself capable of delivering what the white citizens of Jeff Davis County wanted now would help Oury Berry ensure that he'd get another chance to serve them later, as a future sheriff or in some other elected or appointed government position.

As my grandfather decided Versie Johnson's fate, he most likely consulted other local leaders, members of the Jeff Davis County Board of Supervisors perhaps and possibly the mayor of Prentiss. At some point, he must have spoken with F. A. and Ruth Parker at the *Headlight*. He also called in those state police officers, Patrolman Spencer Puckett who lived in Prentiss, and Patrolman Andy Hopkins, who had to come from Mt. Olive, a town in neighboring Covington County. Whether or not he sought the counsel of any of these people as he planned his course of action, he would need them to help him carry it out. And he would need them to stick to the story.

I'd like to think that my grandfather's choice was hard, that he made it reluctantly, that he did not want to do what he ultimately decided his personal interests and his duty as sheriff required. But no evidence survived to suggest that was true. In the Jim Crow South, only a fool or a saint would put the interests of a doomed Black man before the interests of white friends and neighbors who also happened to be voters. My grandfather was not a fool, and he would run and win two more times, serving as sheriff from 1952 to 1956 and from 1970 to 1973. Despite being a dedicated member of Prentiss Methodist Church, he was also not a saint. He did not seem to think about what Jesus would do. Neither did he discover within himself a heroic measure of character. When tested, he acted as many, perhaps most, white people would have acted. Without really looking at it closely, he upheld the racist order in which he lived and worked. He managed the situation.

My grandfather might not have been a hero as my mom remembered, but she was right about one thing. He did not turn Versie Johnson over to the mob at the courthouse. Instead, in what must have been a premeditated plan, he and the two patrolmen, Puckett and Hopkins, took Versie Johnson out of the jail and carried him to the Lipsey farm themselves.

While it was possible that the armed men from the courthouse lawn followed my grandfather's car there, it was more likely that my grandfather told them what he intended to do. However they figured out what was happening, some of them also drove to the Lipsey farm, where they would serve as an audience as that plan unfolded. Ultimately, my grandfather would not let them kill Versie Johnson, but he was willing to let them watch.

Later, my grandfather explained to reporters that he, the patrolmen, and Versie Johnson ended up back at the scene of the crime because the Black man asked if he could show the officers what had happened. In other words, they had transported their prisoner there at his own request. I know this statement is a lie. No Black man accused of raping a white woman in Mississippi would ask to be taken out of the relative security of a jail cell, through an armed "crowd," and out into a field on the edge of town.

What I do not know is whether my grandfather alone came up with the plan and shared it with others, like the patrolmen Puckett and Hopkins, or whether all three officers and possibly other white leaders collaborated on this course of action. I also do not know exactly what happened when my grandfather, Versie Johnson, and the two patrolmen got out of the car after the short drive from the courthouse to the Lipsey farm. Did they go right to the spot where the alleged rape had occurred, or did they park near the house where the white woman and her husband lived and walk from there? Did my grandfather actually ask Versie Johnson to explain what had happened, so that the assembled white men could hear his "confession"? Did all these preliminaries take a while or did he and the two patrolmen get to the business at hand quickly? Did the armed men watching stand back from the knot of officers around Versie Johnson or did they push in close?

One thing is clear. Versie Johnson knew. From the moment they arrested him, he would have realized it was a possibility. By the time they took him out of his cell, he would have been sure. As he sat handcuffed in the back of a car as one of the officers drove him to the Lipsey farm, Versie Johnson would have understood that my grandfather had made a deal with the mob. He knew he was about to die.

In logistical terms, for the white men, it was easy. The three officers fired three shots directly into Versie Johnson's body. Protected by their allegation that Johnson tried to escape, they openly stated afterward that they shot him. They even admitted that there were witnesses, some or all of the people who had made up that mob, although an investigation conducted by justice of the peace C. V. Sutton after Johnson's death never determined how many. The biggest challenge for my grandfather would have been getting the spectators who witnessed the killing to agree that Johnson had tried to escape. Maybe that had been an explicit part of the deal, that mob members could watch as the officers killed Versie if they promised they would not interfere then or talk about what happened afterward. As long as most white residents and the local paper stuck to the story, Oury Berry could be confident he and the highway patrolmen would get away with killing their prisoner. For a time, he was right.

The *Jackson Advocate,* a Black newspaper published in the state capital about sixty miles away, worked hard to expose the flaws in Sheriff Berry's account. One of their reporters reached an undertaker at the Johnson Funeral Home, most likely Central Johnson, and got a description of Versie Johnson's wounds: a shot in the chest accompanied by "powder burns on the skin to show that it had been fired at close range," a shot in the back of the neck, and a shot in the lower left arm. This information must have been attached to Versie Johnson's death certificate at one point, as a faint stamp marked "see slip attached" appears on the line asking for major findings from any autopsy. That paper slip, like so much other evidence, has disappeared.

The *Advocate* also reported that Black people who lived near Prentiss did not believe that Versie Johnson "had confessed to the crime of rape as reported." Instead, they argued, local white men followed "the traditional pattern": "A negro involved in such a case is killed immediately in order to keep certain facts from coming to light." The Civil Rights Congress, a left-wing civil rights organization founded in 1946, boldly stated what many people thought even if they were afraid to say it in public: "It is impossible to believe that the hoary defense that Johnson tried to seize a weapon from the heavily armed police officers can stand any kind of adequate FBI investigation."

But in the end, it did not really matter if the lie made sense. The FBI, which sometimes investigated these crimes, had close ties with the Mississippi Highway Patrol, the state's police force. Given the involvement of the two state police officers, at least some bureau officials probably knew what had happened. But whether or not the federal agency had this information, the lie provided cover. Because the Parkers at the *Headlight* and Prentiss officials agreed to the story, there was no reason for the FBI to send anyone to Prentiss.

No doubt, some people even today will argue that Versie Johnson's killing is not a lynching. This, too, is a well-practiced white southern kind of deflection.

When my grandfather Sheriff Oury Berry, Patrolman Spencer Puckett, and Patrolman Andy Hopkins shot Versie Johnson in front of a crowd of white men in a field at the Lipsey farm on August 1, 1947, the killing met all the qualifications for what the civil rights organizations and the Black press called "underground" lynchings, a practice in which local officials arranged, participated in, or helped cover up killings carried out by white men in the name of justice. And unlike many of these quieter affairs, it was also a spectacle. It had an audience.

Seventy-three years later, Mitchell Gamblin still remembered what his friend Central Johnson said back in August 1947. When the undertaker arrived to pick up the body, he told Gamblin, many white men who had witnessed the killing were still at the Lipsey farm and they were talking about what happened. Central Johnson also heard my grandfather and the other officers say that they shot Versie Johnson.

Mostly, Gamblin reported what he knew about this tragedy calmly and quietly. But when he made his final point about that day, he became animated. He really wanted to make sure I understood that in Jeff Davis County then, as he put it, "the vast majority of white people...would murder people." Why, he insisted, would Johnson have tried to escape? "All those whites with guns calling him the N-word, where was he going to run?"

8.

THE COST

J eff Davis County officials lied about what they did, but they kept careful records about what they spent. Typed figures appeared in the minutes of the Board of Supervisors' September 1947 meeting: $50 for the bloodhounds, $126.50 for the Johnson Funeral Home's services preparing and burying the body, and $609 for various court expenses related to the manslaughter charges brought by District Attorney E. B. Williams against my grandfather and the two state police officers, and the preliminary hearing, which resulted in the dismissal of these charges because of what the court called "insufficient" evidence. Another payment appeared in the minutes for the October term, $50 to Sheriff Berry for what the clerk described in the account book as "extra service for the entire year." In the aftermath of the lynching of Versie Johnson, county leaders gave my grandfather a bonus. Along with his accomplices Spencer Puckett and Andy Hopkins, he had saved the county the expense of a trial, eliminated the need for an FBI investigation, and protected the county's reputation. If county leaders were not thanking him for this specific work, they certainly were not penalizing him for it. Voters later rewarded him, too, electing him sheriff again in 1951 and in 1970.

Yet the real cost of killing Versie Johnson was impossible to calculate. In the summer of 1947, for white residents, Prentiss's prospects had looked as sparkling and clear as the chlorinated water in the new town pool that opened July 4 behind the white Prentiss elementary school. Two decades later, that public pool would be gone, destroyed by county leaders who would rather fill it in than allow Black residents to enjoy it. And the desire to preserve segregation even when it meant whites, too, would suffer would destroy more than that pool.

Johnson's lynching and the subsequent cover-up were not the cause of everything that happened in those years. History rarely works like that. Instead, they were the hinge. The murder and the lie set the tone, dividing local time into a before and an after. They made it clear just how far white county residents were willing to go to preserve white supremacy.

In October 1947, President Truman's Civil Rights Committee issued a report that laid out an alternative direction. *To Secure These Rights* called for "a broad and immediate program" to eliminate all forms of legally sanctioned segregation and discrimination, including the repeal of the poll tax, passage of laws to require states to end racial inequality in education, bans on discrimination in the armed forces and on police brutality, and the passage of a federal law outlawing lynching. It also proposed a civil rights division in the Justice Department strong enough to enforce these changes by investigating violations and denying federal money to institutions that practiced racial discrimination. The Black and white authors of this report believed that the segregationist doctrine of "separate but equal" that prevailed across the South had been tried and found guilty of perpetuating inequality and cutting against "the equalitarian spirit of the American heritage." There were Americans then who knew what had to be done. There were Americans who understood what it would cost not to act.

It would take more than two decades of activism by Black Americans and their allies, but the federal government would eventually force places like Jeff Davis County to integrate the public schools, the franchise, employment, and businesses and other facilities. Black people would win the enforcement of these citizenship rights. But paradoxically, in winning on one front, they would in time lose on another. Civil rights victories prompted a white backlash against the parts of the federal government that tried to guarantee Black rights. By the end of the twentieth century, Black residents of Jeff Davis County would find themselves holding on to the hollowed-out shell of what had been: crumbling public schools, civic buildings, and infrastructure that had previously been supported by local, state, and federal funding but after integration were slowly starved of resources. Across the nation, too many white people reacted to the civil rights movement by turning against the very concept of the public. Rather than accept integration, they rejected democracy.

My grandfather played a role in these battles. He served two additional terms as sheriff, one from 1952 to 1955 and another from 1970 to 1973. In between, he worked as a state fire marshal investigating arson in Mississippi's southern district at a time when white supremacists were burning and bombing Black churches. In both these jobs, Oury Berry supported white supremacy, even when that meant weakening or eliminating the economic, social, and civic practices and institutions that had previously nurtured local life. On some level, my grandfather and the other white men and women who led Jeff Davis in those years must have known that what they were doing was shortsighted and wrong. But when confronted with a choice between sharing their world with their Black neighbors or tearing it down, they chose destruction. They chose the feelings of personal power that flowed from white supremacy. They chose to live in the ruins.

That public pool in Prentiss did not last long enough for me to swim in it. I came into the story that started at the Lipsey farm late, and I was too young to understand what was happening. But after years of research, I learned something important. However much Prentiss looked like the past to me then, in important ways it was actually the future. It was a stark illustration of changes that would eventually play out in other parts of the nation, sometimes more subtly but always with a disastrous impact on democracy as the very idea of a common life.

In the mid-twentieth century, Black families in Mississippi who lost relatives to lynchings sometimes protested. But if members of Versie Johnson's family talked to reporters for the Black newspapers or otherwise made demands, they did it off the record. They kept their names out of the press. Given my grandfather's involvement and his position as sheriff, speaking out would have been dangerous.

Hoping to put the killing behind them, county officials instructed the Johnson Funeral Home to act quickly. Versie Johnson's death certificate says he was buried the day after he died at the cemetery at First Baptist Church. Local officials probably used the cemetery at this church, adjacent to the Prentiss Institute campus, when they needed a place to bury Black people because the town cemetery beside the school with its pool was also for white people only. Genealogists completing a cemetery survey in the late 1980s found many graves without headstones or other markers at First Baptist. One of them belonged to Versie Johnson.

Someone at the sheriff's office contacted the family, perhaps with the help of Central Johnson, who in his role as funeral director signed the death certificate. The fact that this document listed Gertrude Johnson as the person who provided the information about her brother's life suggested she was still in Prentiss when he died. His mom, Lizzie Johnson, was also nearby, still living with his sister Eula Mae Knight. His mother and these siblings and possibly other relatives and friends might have gone to the funeral home and the cemetery.

Because there was no way to know that the violence would stop with one killing, it was also possible that Lizzie and Gertrude Johnson and Eula Mae Knight did not stand watch as Versie Johnson's body was lowered into that warm earth. These rituals were not a given. When something like this happened, relatives often had to stay away.

For Lizzie Johnson, a woman in her late sixties, the death of her youngest child cut another hole in the fabric of her family. In the aftermath of the wrenching loss of their younger brother, Eula Mae stopped working at the Prentiss Hotel and Gertrude moved away or died. For all three of them and perhaps for his siblings living elsewhere, worry and grief must have fused. Maybe for this reason, they did not commission and install a headstone. They might have worried about drawing attention to their connection. It was also possible that Versie Johnson's family members could not afford a permanent marker to replace the temporary tag left by the funeral home. In 1940, his two sisters earned little working as cooks—$8 a month for Gertrude and $12 a month for Eula Mae Knight—and Lizzie Johnson did not have a job. Even if their earnings had improved in the seven years between the census and their brother's death, they were likely still struggling. But that did not mean that they forgot.

Before Versie Johnson's lynching, activists who worked to improve the lives of Black people in Jeff Davis County had conducted themselves like Versie Johnson's grieving family. They moved quietly. They kept their names out of the news. But all that changed in the late 1940s. After Versie Johnson's death and despite the risk, some Black residents became more willing to act in public.

Most of these activists were farm and business owners, teachers, professors, and preachers. Unlike these county residents, Versie Johnson spent much of his short life working for white people as a laborer. His sisters worked as domestic servants. Part of the precarious Black working class, the Johnson siblings lived on the margins of that separate world built and run by better-off Black people. Despite the fact that Jim Crow segregation officially recognized only racial categories—Black versus white—class divided Black residents from one another. Differences in income played a role, as well as a mix of other factors, including property ownership, the length of time lived in a community, kin networks, and education levels. It was possible that, during his lifetime, Johnson had resented the more financially secure inhabitants of this separate Black world. And some of these people, in turn, might have had little sympathy for a Black man they understood as foolish enough to get involved with a white woman or to put himself in the wrong place when white men were looking for a scapegoat. But in the end, it did not really matter what any of them felt. None of them could stop the sheriff or the mob. Once white men had their hands on Versie Johnson, Black people could not save him.

This violence must have made many Black residents of Jeff Davis County think hard about local law enforcement. And two facts would have been absolutely clear. Sheriffs were elected by voters, and Black people were a majority. Before *Smith v. Allwright,* it had made little sense to go to the risk and expense of registering and paying poll taxes. But in opening up the Democratic primary, the only real election in Jeff Davis County, to the participation of Black registered voters, that 1944 Supreme Court decision had transformed these calculations. Even if only some Black people in the county voted, if they stuck together, they might create a constituency that white candidates had to consider. If other Black people saw that voting made a difference, they too might participate. Given the population of the county, someday there would be enough of them that they could elect their own candidates.

Before Versie Johnson died, Black activists in Jeff Davis County had favored a discreet and pragmatic approach. Prentiss Institute founders J. E. and Bertha LaBranche Johnson followed an uplift model of Black advancement in which middle-class leaders promoted education and self-help and made quiet appeals to sympathetic whites. After founding a local women's organization, Bertha Johnson became a leader in the Mississippi Federation of Colored Women's Clubs, which had some success politely lobbying for a more equitable distribution of social services, including libraries in Black schools and a "colored wing" of the state tuberculosis sanatorium. In the 1920s and 1930s, J. E. Johnson ran a statewide Black leadership organization he and his wife had helped found, the Committee of One Hundred. Under Johnson's direction, the organization worked for "the general improvement of the Negro race" by employing moral persuasion, behind-the-scenes negotiation, and appeals to white self-interest. As more Black residents of Mississippi joined the NAACP in the late 1940s, the Committee of One Hundred disbanded.

In Jeff Davis County, where many Black residents had attended the Prentiss Institute, sent their children to the school, or worked there, the Johnsons exerted a powerful influence. But the service of at least 667 Jeff Davis County Black men and some women in World War II transformed how many locals understood the world. They had seen what the federal government had done to support democracy overseas. They wanted their government to work for democracy at home, too. And they were unwilling to ask white Americans quietly to give them what they believed they had already paid for or earned.

In the postwar period, the NAACP worked hard to expand its presence in the South, but it took courage to join, much less found, an NAACP branch in rural Mississippi. About six months after Versie Johnson's lynching, Black residents of Jeff Davis County created the Prentiss NAACP. Though chapters in rural places usually carried the name of their county, members likely chose "Prentiss" instead to avoid having to refer to their outpost of the great civil rights organization by a Confederate general's name. P. J. Polk, a landowner in Mt. Carmel who had grown up with landowning parents and grandparents, served as longtime chairman. To keep the identity of its members secret, the group met quietly at Black churches, including Mt. Zion Missionary Baptist Church between Prentiss and Mt. Carmel and Oak Grove Baptist Church, about six miles northwest of Prentiss. Membership grew from fifty-nine men to at least seventy-nine men and women over the branch's first six years, a not insignificant number given the county's size and the fact that Black people who joined risked white retaliation.

The Prentiss NAACP was a tight-knit group, made up of people who were often related by birth and by marriage. Like P. J. Polk, many members came from old Black landowning families. Others were the children of men and women like Will and Mary Otis Gray, World War II veteran Wardell Gray's parents, who had more recently acquired farms. Some were ministers like Reverend R. Terrell and Reverend A. D. Gray. Starting in 1950, the branch allowed women to join. Some, like Essie Hartzog who taught school, were married to male members, in her case Isaac Hartzog. Others were widows or single women. Schoolteacher Susie Polk joined after her husband died. She lived in Mt. Carmel with her daughter and her mother, Mary Hartzog, another widow and also a landowner. At least one member worked for the federal government, A. J. Godbolt, the county agricultural agent for Black farmers. Ernest Lockhart was the principal of the Black school in Lucas.

As landowners, members of the Prentiss NAACP knew that they and other Black people paid property taxes. Yet they also knew that many Black people in the county still lived on unpaved roads. Most were ignored by law enforcement when they were victims of crime. And when the federal government paid for programs like rural electrification, they were the last to receive these services. As teachers and the parents of students, these Prentiss NAACP members also knew that Black children attended primary school in facilities without running water, adequate heat, or books and other supplies. They understood that Black parents had to pay tuition for their kids to attend the Prentiss Institute while the county ran at least four white public high schools. From their perspective, Black people had been asking quietly in Jeff Davis since the founding of the county. If they wanted equality, they would have to become voters. Elected leaders paid attention to people who cast ballots.

In the spring of 1951, before the crepe myrtles that grew all over downtown Prentiss had bloomed, two extraordinary petitions addressed to the "Citizens and Taxpayers of Jefferson Davis County" were filed with the Board of Supervisors. As the local paper of record, the *Prentiss Headlight* was required to publish them along with all other Jeff Davis County legal notices. In these documents, Black parents, some of whom were NAACP members, called out white officials for their grossly unequal distribution of school funds. The fact that county officials were promising more money in the future "if everything works out" was not good enough. "Our children are suffering now," D. F. Powell and Ford Hartzog argued. "Not for cafeterias and gymnasiums but for the simple comforts of school life. We have buildings with no window panes, no seats but high benches, not a map or a globe. 2487 white children receive approximately $41,153 for maintenance, per year from taxation which is paid by white and black alike, as compared to about 3100 Negro children [who] receive not one cent." Technically, these Black residents of the county were still "asking" for help. Their petition and accompanying note appealed to "citizens and taxpayers" for relief. But this approach was not careful or circumspect. It announced that white officials were breaking the law and put them on notice. It was direct.

In the aftermath of Versie Johnson's lynching, some Black residents of Jeff Davis County founded a civil rights organization and put its membership to work strengthening Black institutions and increasing the number of Black voters. The two goals were intertwined. Black institutions nurtured Black independence, which enabled more people to cast ballots without fear of white retaliation. If enough Black people voted, they could elect a better sheriff.

The year 1951 turned out to be something of a turning point in county history. It was also the year my grandfather ran again for sheriff. When his first term ended in early January 1948, Oury Berry had gone back to running a dairy on the land he and Grace owned close to the Lipsey farm. But in January 1951, a month before he formally announced his candidacy, they sold that property. Two months later, before Oury had started actively campaigning, he and Grace paid $7,500 for the sprawling, one-story wood-frame home where years later I would visit them. The then run-down house at the corner of Second Street and Pearl Avenue dated back to the early days of the town when its double lot a block off Columbia Avenue would have been a fashionable address. By the time they bought it, members of the town elite were building suburban-style homes on the edges of Prentiss. But the house was a short walk from the sheriff's office in the courthouse.

In his second campaign, Berry made the same pledges he had made when he ran the first time: to stand against corruption, to enforce the laws, including prohibition, and to spend the taxpayers' money frugally. Again, he listed his qualifications as his family, his faith in God, and his character. But this time he also ran on experience, on what he had done. As he told voters in his announcement for the office on the front page of the *Prentiss Headlight,* "My record as your former sheriff is open for inspection at all times." In a sense, my grandfather was not hiding anything. He seemed confident that killing Versie Johnson was not a liability.

As it turned out, he was at least partially right. Oury Berry won the first primary on August 7, 1951, easily. He won the second primary, too, but it was not a landslide. People who had voted for others in the first round seemed to come together around his opponent, Shelby L. Mikell Sr.

It was not clear what attracted so many voters to Mikell, my grandfather's opponent in the second primary. But one thing stood out in the precinct vote counts: the poll numbers from Mt. Carmel, a community about nine miles northeast of Prentiss. Because Mt. Carmel had once been a white-majority town, it had a polling place. After most of the white people moved to Prentiss to be near the railroad, Mt. Carmel lost its charter. Over the years, Black people bought up the houses, other buildings, and surrounding land, and the former town became a thriving Black settlement. For years, county officials allowed Black people in Mt. Carmel to run a voting precinct there in the general election but did not give them a ballot box for the Democratic primaries. But after *Smith v. Allwright,* Mt. Carmel residents could not be stopped from voting in the primaries, too.

While Black voters also cast their ballots in other precincts, virtually everyone who went to the polls in Mt. Carmel in 1951 was Black. Tallies from this precinct provided a measure of which candidates Black voters preferred. In the first primary, Oury Berry got 3 votes out of the 110 ballots cast there, while Shelby Mikell got 83, and three of the other four candidates picked up the rest. In the second, Berry got 7 votes in contrast to the 93 earned by his opponent. In Mt. Carmel at least, Black voters did not support my grandfather, and the lynching of Versie Johnson must have been one of the reasons.

Oury Berry still won the second primary, and subsequently the general election, securing a second term as sheriff. But a majority of Jeff Davis residents had always been Black. If local Black folks kept registering and voting, things in Jeff Davis County were going to change.

Over at the *Headlight,* editors F. A. and Ruth Parker noticed this shift. Endorsing Hugh White for governor ahead of the second primary that would see my grandfather narrowly advance to the general election, they condemned the other leading candidate, Paul Johnson, because of his association with President Truman. White voters, the Parkers warned, should "take all the issues into consideration, including the vote at Mr. Carmel when 103 Negro voters cast their ballots for Paul Johnson with only eleven voting for the other candidates." If elected governor, Johnson would pay back his supporters by helping force "Harry Truman's despicable civil rights program," the very plan laid out in *To Secure These Rights,* "on a free people. IT MUST NOT HAPPEN HERE!" Two days after the second primary, the Parkers were even more direct, calling Black voters "puppets" and condemning what they called "bloc voting by the Negroes of Jeff Davis County."

Of course, Black voters were simply doing what white voters had always done. After church, outside at the store, before choir practice, at the family table, and anywhere else they gathered, they talked to one another and shared information as they decided which candidates to support. In the wake of Versie Johnson's death, increasing numbers of Black residents had been registering to vote and paying the poll tax. And they were determined to have a say in local politics.

During my grandfather's first years as sheriff, his father Henry Jackson Berry's behavior had been an embarrassment. My mom told me that Prentiss marshal Curtis Chance had asked her father's deputies to let him know if H.J. was drinking in public so he could take care of the situation quietly and save my grandfather from having to arrest his own dad. But in early January 1952 just as Oury Berry took the oath of office for the second time, his father died. Even if H.J. had been a liability, he was also Oury's father, and the loss hurt. My grandfather began his second term as sheriff under his own cloud of grief. And as a man who always did what he understood as his duty, my grandfather now had the added task of looking after his mother, Lula Brady Berry, an educated woman for her generation of rural white southerners and a person who never quite fit into the world in which she had to live.

During my grandfather's second term as sheriff, the Supreme Court issued their May 17, 1954, decision in *Brown v. Board of Education* outlawing segregation in public schools, and white people across Mississippi reacted in shock and anger. Mississippi senator James O. Eastland was defiant. "The South will not abide by nor obey this legislative decision by a political court," he stated baldly. "We will take whatever steps are necessary to retain segregation in education." In the short run, the *Brown* decision did not integrate public schools in Jeff Davis County or many other places in the Deep South. What it did instead was inspire a more organized and militant defense of what many white southerners called "our way a life," the segregationist movement.

About thirty-five miles east of Prentiss in Brookhaven, Thomas Pickens Brady, a lawyer-turned-circuit-court-judge, became a leader of this resistance. Judge Brady was Oury's cousin—their grandfathers were brothers—and Grace and Oury must have known him. They had bought the farm near town, "the old Brady place," from his father, also Thomas Brady, and after he died, they paid off their debt to Thomas Pickens Brady.

In a series of "Black Monday" speeches denouncing the *Brown* decision that he later published as a book, Brady fused legal arguments for states' rights with racist anthropology as he called on white Americans to eliminate public schools and outlaw the NAACP. He also helped turn the White Citizens' Council, a group founded in Indianola, Mississippi, about 150 miles northeast of Prentiss, into the leading segregationist organization. Brady's book, *Black Monday,* became the movement's handbook. At their peak, Citizens' Councils and allied organizations had as many as two hundred and fifty thousand enrolled members. Jeff Davis County residents organized a branch. It met at the courthouse.

No membership lists survived for the Jeff Davis Citizens' Council, but the Parkers were probably involved as well as my grandparents. I remember my grandfather later denouncing the Klan for its lawlessness, but he would have liked the Citizens' Council, with its aura of respectability and its claim to be an organization made up of law-abiding citizens. If he joined, he likely did so because he believed in the mission: enforcing segregation laws and customs and preserving white supremacy without resorting to blatant terrorism.

Critics captured its character perfectly when they called it the "country club Klan." Most of the time but not always, members of local branches of the Citizens' Council preferred economic pressure and other kinds of bloodless vigilantism to acts of violence. They threatened Black families who tried to vote or to send their kids to white schools with the loss of a job, the recall or denial of a loan, or the refusal to supply credit or goods.

But as the segregationist movement grew more militant, acts of terrorism increased across Mississippi. What Mitchell Gamblin said about white residents of Jeff Davis County and their willingness to murder Black people applied to much of Mississippi. In May 1955, as campaigning began for the August primaries, two shotgun blasts from a passing car killed Reverend George W. Lee, a voting rights activist in Belzoni, Mississippi. Together, Lee and grocery store owner Guy Courts had worked to get Black residents of Humphreys County to pay their poll taxes and register to vote. Ninety-four out of sixteen thousand Black people of voting age there succeeded in completing the process. But that was too many for some white locals. Humphreys County officials said Lee had died in the car wreck that happened after he was shot. When an autopsy found lead pellets in Lee's neck and jaw, the sheriff suggested they were "fillings from his teeth."

In August 1955, between the first and second Democratic primaries, the violence only accelerated. Someone shot and killed voting rights activist Lamar Smith in front of the Lincoln County Courthouse in Brookhaven. Smith had succeeded in getting about five hundred Black people in Lincoln to register and vote by absentee ballot, and it was possible that some of these people were related to Versie Johnson, since he spent time there growing up and his mother's family had lived in the area since at least 1870. But the white men who witnessed Smith's daytime murder would not talk. Despite being present at the courthouse when Smith died and telling people he had seen a white man whom he named "leave the scene of the killing with blood all over him," the sheriff charged no one. It had nothing to do with voting, but two weeks later two white men, J. W. Milam and Roy Bryant, lynched fourteen-year-old Emmett Till. When Till's body was found in the Tallahatchie River about 180 miles north of Prentiss, the sheriff denied that the corpse belonged to the boy and argued instead that it had been planted as part of an NAACP plot. In November just after the general election, someone shot George Lee's ally Gus Courts, the only Black person still on the voting rolls in Humphreys County after a harassment campaign drove the others away. Courts survived and fled to Chicago. In Mississippi in the 1950s, white men resisting integration continued to see themselves as the hands of the law. Sheriffs continued to lie.

No voting rights activists died in Jeff Davis County in these years. A key factor was the sheer number of Black voters. Would-be vigilantes and law enforcement officials would have had trouble choosing a target. The Jeff Davis voter rolls at the end of 1954 contained almost thirteen hundred Black names, out of a Black population over twenty-one years of age in 1950 that numbered approximately 3,923. Organizing by NAACP members had played a part in encouraging people to become voters, but so had other networks, like kinship and church membership. Somehow, Circuit Clerk Larkin Davis had allowed not just a few Black people whom white residents approved of but also hundreds of others to register successfully. There were simply too many voters to threaten them all and no clear leaders of the registration effort to kill.

It did not save Versie Johnson, but the separate world Black people had built in Jeff Davis County did offer some protection from the economic threats segregationists used so effectively in other parts of Mississippi like the Delta. The many successful Black farmers in the area were hard to intimidate. The federal government set cotton prices, and the fiber, unlike many agricultural products, did not spoil. Neither did timber. Someone would gin what they grew and buy any second-growth trees they cut, and they could sell any surplus corn, vegetables, and livestock above what their families needed to their Black neighbors. Some Black professionals like public school teachers were vulnerable as government employees. Others like ministers were not.

At the Prentiss Institute, professors and staff were safe, too, as long as Bertha Johnson, who ran the school after her husband died in 1953, did not disapprove of their actions. Because she operated a private institution that got some money from the county to educate Black high school students, Johnson might have been a moderating influence. In 1958, white officials were on good enough terms with her to buy the land where they opened Prentiss's first Black high school from the Prentiss Institute and to name it J. E. Johnson after her husband. But her son A. L. Johnson, the dean of the Prentiss Institute in the 1950s, was a member of the NAACP. And 1958 and 1963 reports from the Mississippi Sovereignty Commission, a spy agency created by the state in 1956, portrayed the Prentiss Institute as a "hot bed" and a "beehive" of NAACP activity.

Because intimidation had failed, Jeff Davis officials tried another strategy, one Citizens' Councils were advocating across the state in 1955 and 1956. In February 1956, James Daniel, the newly elected circuit clerk, simply voided the county's voter registration rolls and required everyone to reregister. Black residents like Daniel S. Ross, who had been voting for about five years; Dudley Hawthorn and Genora Holloway, who had been voting for eight to ten years; and even John E. Barnes, who had been voting for forty, suddenly found themselves rejected because they failed to interpret the Mississippi Constitution to Daniel's satisfaction. The circuit clerk made most of them take the new written test, a provision that voters had to be able to read a passage and write a "reasonable" explanation of it as set out in an amendment the state passed in 1955 to tighten voter restrictions. The new law clearly said that people who had been registered before January 1, 1954, could qualify under the old law, which did not require literacy, making Daniel's actions illegal. But few understood these details, and Black people who did had little leverage. Daniel could just as easily administer the oral test and say they failed that one as well. In Jeff Davis County, the number of Black voters dropped from over 1,220 in 1954 to about 100 in 1956.

Across Mississippi, Black registration declined from approximately twenty-two thousand in 1954 to about eight thousand in 1956, a tiny fraction of the 497,354 Black people in the state old enough to cast ballots. Activists claimed that at least thirty-one Mississippi counties did not allow any of their Black residents to vote. Aided by state NAACP officials like Medgar Evers, local NAACP chapters urged rejected applicants to respond to these voting roll purges by trying again. In Jeff Davis, members of farm-owning families and people associated with the Prentiss Institute put on their church clothes and drove or caught a ride or walked to Prentiss and made their way down the neat, brick-paved Columbia Avenue to the columned courthouse. Sometimes Daniel said he was too busy and sent them away. Other times he made them wait for hours and then gave them the test and flunked them again. On rare occasions, he actually passed a Black applicant. Rejected applicants noted the date and the time and the names of any witnesses. They were not just trying to get on the voter rolls. They were also gathering evidence.

In 1958, an NAACP legal team led by Constance Baker Motley used affidavits provided by Black residents of Jeff Davis to file *Darby v. Daniel,* the civil rights organization's first Mississippi voting rights case. At a time when the threat of segregationist violence and the certainty of economic reprisals kept many Black residents of the state from coming forward, Prentiss NAACP members and their relatives and neighbors somehow found the courage to fight. The lead plaintiff in the case, Reverend H. D. Darby, had become a voter around 1950, soon after he moved to Prentiss so his children could attend high school at the Prentiss Institute. The family lived in a farmhouse on the school property, and Darby occasionally did day labor there, like driving a tractor for the school, while continuing to pastor an African Methodist Episcopal (AME) church in another county. He was also a member of the Prentiss NAACP.

When Darby tried to reregister in June 1956, Circuit Clerk Daniel rejected him. Daniel failed him again in November 1956 and in June 1957. Yet despite the evidence from Darby and other former voters rejected in the reregistration, the federal district court found in favor of Daniel in a decision handed down in November 1958. The NAACP legal team, assessing the odds of a victory in relation to their limited resources, decided not to appeal.

It had taken them almost a decade, but as a result of the lawsuit, Jeff Davis County officials finally discovered the existence of the local NAACP branch. By that point, my grandfather had finished his second term as sheriff, and Shelby Mikell had won the next election and taken over the job. In early 1959, Circuit Clerk Daniel reported to the Sovereignty Commission that he and Sheriff Mikell had learned "the NAACP was operating underground at Prentiss." Soon afterward, Mikell and Daniel got hold of a copy of the Prentiss NAACP's minutes for the years 1948 to 1954 from someone inside the organization, and the circuit clerk sent those to the state spy agency, too. The Sovereignty Commission put the names of Prentiss NAACP members in their files and kept them under surveillance. Back in Prentiss, Daniel rejected the voting application of anyone he suspected of being an NAACP member.

Black residents like dairy farmer and Prentiss NAACP president Wardell Gray and Lucas schoolteacher and likely NAACP member Mabel Walker Armstrong did not give up. Neither did elected county officials, who kept spending tax dollars and even breaking the law to stop them. The Justice Department eventually took over the investigation of voting discrimination in Jeff Davis County and filed a case called *United States v. James Daniel*. In hearings held in 1962, Jeff Davis attorneys Joe Dale and Donald Kruger tried to rattle Black residents brave enough to take the stand. They called men and women by their first names like they were children and were especially rude to Black women, interrupting them repeatedly to say they could not understand them. More seriously, Dale and Kruger demanded the names and addresses of all Black residents who had talked to the FBI about voting discrimination in Jeff Davis County. After the Justice Department was forced to file an amended complaint including the names of the people involved, the *Prentiss Headlight* published the list on the front page, a release of information that made it easier for white county residents to retaliate. *United States v. James Daniel* remained open until the Voting Rights Act became law on August 6, 1965, and settled the issues it had raised.

Oury Berry did not play a role in either the NAACP's or the Justice Department's Jeff Davis County lawsuits. If the sheriff worked with local members of the Citizens' Council to harass Darby or the other Black residents trying to vote, and he probably did, that sheriff was not my grandfather. Instead, Oury—whom the rules had prevented from running for another term in the previous election—was busy trying to build a new career through his position as an assistant state fire marshal, a political appointment that Jeff Davis County leaders must have helped him get. Versie Johnson's relatives were probably not involved in these voting rights lawsuits either. Their names do not appear among the affidavits signed by rejected voters or as potential witnesses in any documents associated with these legal actions. It would have been virtually impossible for Black residents who made their living working as agricultural laborers, domestic servants, or perhaps bootleggers to participate in such a public challenge to white supremacy.

But Oury Berry was involved in supporting "the southern way of life" in other ways. In the early 1960s, segregationists increasingly began to use bombs and set fires in their fight against Black rights. Any time a suspicious fire occurred, the state fire marshal's office investigated to determine whether it was the result of arson. Sometimes the FBI got involved, too, especially when bombs were suspected. In the summer of 1964, as activists working with the Student Nonviolent Coordinating Committee (SNCC) and the Congress of Racial Equality (CORE) flooded the state as part of the Mississippi Summer Project, thirty-seven Black churches, the most visible Black institutions in the state, were burned or bombed. In some but by no means all of these cases, congregations had been involved in organizing or had allowed activists to use their facilities. In others, church members played no role in the civil rights movement. I have found no evidence of church burnings in Jeff Davis County, but as assistant fire marshal for the southern district of Mississippi, my grandfather was involved in investigating these crimes elsewhere.

In July, Virgil Downing, an investigator for the state Sovereignty Commission, wrote a report about a meeting he attended with Adams County law enforcement officials and my grandfather to talk about two recent burnings of Black churches in the countryside outside Natchez, Bethel Methodist Episcopal and Jerusalem Baptist. Sheriff Odell Anders said he had contacted the pastors and associated stewards and deacons, and all of them denied they had hosted NAACP meetings or participated in any activities like voter registration drives. Berry had no suspects and "in his opinion...whoever set these churches on fire did it in a hurry and immediately left the vicinity." Sheriff Anders ended the meeting by promising to track down every lead, but around Natchez, he revealed, white people were saying the churches had been burned by a radical member of the NAACP "for publicity purposes." No one present disagreed.

White officials in Jeff Davis County never did give up trying to enforce white supremacy at the ballot box. But the activism of Black southerners and their white allies created a political context in which the federal government forced whites there and elsewhere across the region to recognize the citizenship rights of their Black neighbors.

About two weeks after President Lyndon Johnson signed the 1965 Voting Rights Act, the Justice Department sent four federal officials to Jeff Davis County. Worried that local leaders might try to block their work or that potential voters might be afraid to brave the courthouse, the federal registrars looked for an alternate space. It took a federal court order for them to gain access to four rented rooms at Prentiss's Magnolia Motel. As the window air-conditioning units chugged and gurgled, trying to cool the hot, wet air, the registrars set up their tables and posted their signs. The United States of America, not Jeff Davis County, would assess Black residents' voting applications, and federal law would at last apply.

Soon people started arriving on foot and in cars, knots of kin and neighbors, old folks leaning on younger people for strength. Some drove in from all-Black settlements and Black country churches. Others walked over from the Black part of town still called the Quarters or from the Prentiss Institute. Grandparents who had lived their entire lives on land not far from where their own parents and grandparents had been enslaved filled out forms along with young adults who had just become old enough to qualify. Some had voted before and had been fighting since that 1956 purge to return to the rolls. More than a few had helped make this all possible through their willingness to stand up to the intimidation and the ever-present threat of violence and participate in the voting rights lawsuits. But there were many who had never had the money to pay the poll tax, now also gone, or the time or the courage or the job security to try to register. People understood the ritual as a solemn occasion, and some were probably afraid, but for all of them who had fought so long and so hard for their rights, there must have been smiles and tears of joy, too. If they all voted, they would have law enforcement that worked for them and nice schools, too. They would run this place.

On August 25, 1965, a Hattiesburg photographer drove over to Prentiss to capture this historic undertaking. In one of his images, Joe Ella Moore, a Black woman old enough to be a grandmother, stood in front of a registrar in one of those Magnolia Motel rooms. Wearing a white straw hat with a wide brim and a Sunday dress she might well have made herself, she pursed her lips, looked straight out through her glasses, and raised her right hand to seal her oath. The federal government had finally decided to enforce the Fifteenth Amendment in the South. Progress toward racial equality was possible. The camera caught the exact moment when it happened, when Joe Ella Moore became a Jeff Davis County citizen.

Five years later, I was in kindergarten and my then sixty-three-year-old grandfather had recently retired from his job as fire marshal when the Jeff Davis County sheriff, Kermit Hawthorn, suddenly resigned. In April 1970, the Jeff Davis County Board of Supervisors appointed Oury interim sheriff and tax collector until a special election could be held on June 2, 1970.

My grandfather, a symbol of massive resistance to integration given his participation in the lynching of Versie Johnson and other actions as sheriff and state fire marshal, decided to run for his old job. Candidates for two offices, sheriff and Beat 2 constable, were on the ballot. All of them were men. Two of them were Black. Wardell Gray, a World War II veteran, then president of the Prentiss NAACP and a successful Black farmer who owned a great deal of land and operated a dairy, ran for constable. Ambrose White, also a World War II veteran and a farmer who owned his own land, ran for sheriff. His father, Willie White, had been one of the rejected voters who filled out the affidavits used in the NAACP's and the Justice Department's Jeff Davis County voting rights cases. The *Prentiss Headlight* published photographs of Gray and White but not the other candidates so white voters would know they were Black. Both Black candidates lost, though White did well enough to face my grandfather in a runoff.

Just like with the franchise, white residents of Jeff Davis County never stopped trying to enforce racial segregation in schooling. On October 29, 1969, about six months before my grandfather started his third term as sheriff, the US Supreme Court issued another decision about schools. *Alexander v. Holmes County Board of Education* required districts to "immediately terminate dual school systems based on race and operate only unitary school systems." Holdouts like Jeff Davis, places that allowed a few Black students in otherwise white schools while still operating separate Black schools, would finally have to comply with *Brown*. They would actually have to integrate instruction for all Black and white children.

Over at the *Headlight,* Ruth Parker still urged resistance to this "tyranny": "Wish somebody would put a strand of barb wire on the top of that fence Governor John Bell Williams of Mississippi is straddling. It is time for the people and officials of the South to stop letting the federal government spit in their faces, and rub it in." "The 'silent majority' is taking it like dumb animals led to the slaughter," she mourned. "They'd rather become a race of mulattoes than speak up for God and law, and their constitutional rights to send their children to schools of their own choosing."

But other local leaders were doing something to resist integration: they were working to organize a new private school. Interested parents and community members had started meeting in the fall of 1969 at the time of the *Alexander* decision, and at some point, ministers like Dr. F. W. Tripp of Prentiss Presbyterian and county officials like Chancery Clerk Guy Magee, Circuit Clerk James Daniel, and county attorney Donald Kruger got involved. On January 22, 1970, the State of Mississippi issued the new school a charter, and five days later, organizers held a meeting at the courthouse to provide information about what was originally called Jefferson Davis Academy. Sometime that spring, they got a $30,000 loan, and in

June, they purchased land. Building started immediately. At the end of the summer, community members pitched in with cleaning and painting. On September 14, Prentiss Christian School opened with 180 white students in grades one through nine with the idea that grades ten through twelve would be added later. As most white kids transferred to this and other segregation academies, the public schools became almost entirely Black.

I was too young to know what was going on, but I remember a lot of talk about the new private school. I remember my grandfather's badge and his white sedan with the magnetic JEFFERSON DAVIS COUNTY SHERIFF sign on the side and the detachable blue light and siren on the roof. I also remember the way both Black and white people deferred to him.

Across the rural South that spring and summer of 1970, public school teachers, principals, coaches, and other staff members were busy carrying books, equipment, furniture, and other supplies out of the schools they were leaving. If it was happening in Jeff Davis County, it would have been my grandfather's job as the head law enforcement official there to stop it, because stealing public property was illegal. But in 1970, just like in 1947, rule of law was whatever Oury Berry said it was. Given everything else I know about him, I do not think my grandfather intervened. He may even have helped. Because besides Dr. Tripp, my grandparents were also close to Guy Magee, the son of the former sheriff who had in 1940 prevented a lynching, and my grandmother's boss for years. Magee served as the secretary-treasurer of the board of the new school and some of his grandchildren attended. He was also the convener of those daily coffee breaks at which my grandparents, Dr. Tripp, and Donald Kruger, another Prentiss Christian board member and parent, gathered. And while many of the children of my grandparents' friends had moved away, like their own, my uncle Jim and my mom, Joan, the few who had stayed sent their kids to Prentiss Christian. No doubt if my mom had ever moved back to Prentiss, I would have gone to school there, too.

In the fall of 2020, when Gamblin took me to the site where Versie Johnson had died, what was there surprised me, and I dug into the property deeds at the Jeff Davis County chancery clerk's office just to make sure Gamblin had gotten it right. He had. The Lipseys sold a parcel of their land in 1970. Today, that lynching ground is still green and open, but it's not a farm. It's the football field at Prentiss Christian.

When Versie Johnson was alive, many Black people considered Jefferson Davis County a pretty good place for Black people to live. Compared to rural Kemper County in east-central Mississippi, where whites lynched twenty-four Black people between 1877 and 1950, and even Simpson County, immediately north of Jeff Davis, where whites lynched eight Black people, the county was not that violent. The Klan was never very active there either, not during the 1910s and 1920s, when membership soared nationwide, nor in the 1950s and 1960s, when Klan members bombed and burned Black homes, churches, and businesses and shot at and sometimes killed civil rights activists.

What Jeff Davis did have was a courageous group of Black residents who never stopped fighting for their rights. By operating underground through its first decade, the Prentiss NAACP branch survived the violence and economic reprisals that increased as the segregationist movement grew in the aftermath of *Brown*. But the chapter continued to operate even after county officials discovered its existence. In 1959, dairy farmer Wardell Gray became president, presiding over an organization still made up mainly of farm owners, teachers, preachers, and faculty and staff from the Prentiss Institute. NAACP members provided evidence for *United States v. James Daniel* and also another federal suit, *United States v. Board of Education of Jefferson Davis County*, which never came to trial because county school officials reinstated teachers like Mabel Armstrong, who had been fired in retaliation for voting rights activism, after the case was filed. Mitchell Gamblin was a longtime member of the Prentiss NAACP. Recently, Duane Johnson, grandson of funeral home founder Estus Johnson, has served as the organization's president.

Even this tradition of Black resistance could not save Jeff Davis County. Today, job loss, population decline, waning property values, and disinvestment have created a downward economic spiral from which it is difficult to imagine an exit. Of course, it is not just white supremacy that is killing the county. Other factors include changes in American politics and the global economy. But all these transformations are linked. In the United States, a new conservative politics has dismantled unions, an already weak social safety net, and a regulatory federal government that invested in public goods and replaced them with a weakened government, a "free" market, low tax rates, falling working-class wages, and inexpensive consumer goods. Many scholars call our current economic and political system neoliberalism, but historian Bryant Simon has more accurately described it as the system of cheap. According to Simon, the central idea of this way of thinking about and structuring society is "that the combination of less pay, less regulation, and less attention to the economic and racial inequities of the past" is "the best way to solve the nation's most pressing problems." "Cheap" would not have been possible without the votes of all those white southerners who switched from the Democratic to the Republican Party. And federal support for racial integration was the single most important factor in producing this shift.

In places where many voters had been Democrats since before the Civil War, this transformation did not happen overnight. My own grandparents, lifelong Democrats, made the leap in 1976 when they backed Ronald Reagan in his first run for the Republican presidential nomination. By November 1980 my grandfather was dead, but my grandmother voted for Reagan in an election in which the Republican swept the South, losing only Carter's home state of Georgia. Party realignment laid the groundwork for today's epidemic of inequality.

Clear-cutting the old longleaf pine forests turned parts of the Jeff Davis County countryside into a wasteland by the 1930s, but in the 1940s and 1950s the county's towns were thriving. In the era of cheap, almost everything has become a ruin. The main problem is the lack of jobs. In the past, the county had at least one chicken processing plant. Never a good place to work, that business is now closed. The North American Free Trade Agreement (NAFTA) killed off the last light industry, a plant in a city-owned building in Prentiss that ran twenty-four hours a day and employed about eight hundred people manufacturing wiring harnesses for Cadillac. For a few years, a Detroit-based cell phone refurbishing company provided jobs for a few hundred people, but that business closed after everyone started buying new phones. More recently, the city pinned its hopes on a CBD oil company that promised not just to sell CBD products but also to run a plant that would extract the oil from legally grown hemp. Large drug busts in the county in 2017 and 2018 proved that cannabis plants grew well in the area's hot and humid summers. But after less than a year, that company, too, closed.

Some Jeff Davis County residents still farm. The most recent study, the USDA's 2017 Census of Agriculture, found 355 farms in the county owned by 567 "producers," including 190 Black men and women. Many farmers raise chickens, for both meat and eggs, as well as cattle. They also grow hay, soybeans, and some corn. Most of the work is mechanized and does not require much labor, so there are few farm jobs. Landowners also sell some timber. Most stable and decent-paying white-collar jobs in the county are in public sector work, including the public schools and the county and city governments, as well as in health care, at Jefferson Davis Community Hospital, now a division of the nonprofit Forrest Health system. But these white-collar workers increasingly live outside the county and commute in from homes in more vibrant places like the college town of Hattiesburg.

Schools are also a problem. A county that cannot afford one school system somehow runs two. Money is not the most important measure of the quality of education, but in Prentiss, white and Black elementary school students are living a contemporary version of "separate but equal" because both groups attend class in old buildings in need of renovation. No doubt Jeff Davis County public schools and Prentiss Christian have some great teachers, but both institutions seem to struggle to provide the kinds of science labs and advanced classes that prepare kids for the modern economy. After the recent consolidation of the Prentiss and Bassfield high schools into the new Jeff Davis County High, public school students did get a new facility. In contrast, a parent of a Prentiss Christian student told me that the high school there operates on a meager budget. Tuition is very low, and the school holds fundraisers to pay for "extras," like a December 2019 firearm raffle, "15 Guns for 15 Days" to support athletic programs.

After school integration, Prentiss Normal and Industrial Institute functioned as a junior college, but unlike the Utica Institute, one of the other "Little Tuskegees," it did not become a public institution. In 1989, it closed for good, and the county has never had another college. With the exception of the original 1907 House, where the Johnsons lived and taught their first classes, and the Rosenwald Building, restored with grant funding, the campus is a wreck of falling-in structures and weed-choked grounds.

None of the county supervisors were willing to talk to me, but I sat down with the longtime Prentiss mayor Charlie Dumas. He attended Prentiss Christian, and yet he agreed that the county did not have the resources to adequately fund a public and a private school system. He also explained how hard it was simply to keep the town functioning. When he first became mayor in 1997, he got residents to pass a bond issue and double the millage rate to pave all the roads, buy new firefighting and maintenance equipment, and upgrade the water and sewer systems. Now, over twenty years later, streets, sidewalks, and buildings are again in bad repair and that equipment is worn-out. But with a declining population of around a thousand and around thirty vacant homes, he cannot raise taxes. Without state and federal grants worth in his estimation about $20 million over the past two decades, the town, which employs about twenty people full-time across all divisions, could not operate. Every summer, he spends most of the town's discretionary funds just to keep the yards mowed around the abandoned houses. The cost gets added to each property's tax bill, but the owners of many of these properties are unable to pay their taxes. It seems likely the county faces similar problems. Driving around the countryside, I encountered crumbling pavement, damaged bridges, and closed roads.

The population of Jeff Davis County is aging, with 24 percent of residents sixty-five or older. Almost all these people receive Social Security checks, and these federal deposits supply much of the money that flows through local banks. Some Black retirees are back after spending some or all of their working lives in places like Atlanta, Chicago, and Oakland. Living on Social Security and other fixed payments, they value the low cost of living. Yet they say the main thing that drew them "home" was the family land, property their parents and grandparents had worked so hard to secure.

White retirees, too, are deeply rooted in this place. Just before the pandemic, I took my mom along on one of my research trips. It had been about twenty years since she had seen her hometown, and the current state of the place made her cry. At lunch with a group of people she had gone to high school with, I got to see a side of white residents that they did not display when they talked to me in my role as a historian. One of them complained that "the only way to get a government check is to black your face." All these years later, he still could not recognize his Black neighbors as citizens with legitimate claims on public resources. Nor could he admit what is painfully clear. The entire place runs on government checks: Social Security and all those state and federal municipal grants plus Medicare, Medicaid, welfare, and WIC (Special Supplemental Nutrition Program for Women, Infants, and Children) payments; USDA agricultural subsidies; the salaries of public sector employees; and other transfers of state and federal funds. But in the era of cheap, they are never enough.

It may have been there earlier, but I first noticed the graffiti around Jeff Davis County in the summer of 2021. Sometimes the letters are white. Sometimes they are red or black. Whatever the color, the sentence scrawled on abandoned businesses—closed cafés, junk shops, and convenience stores; rusting warehouses and cotton gins; and abandoned garages and sawmills—is always the same: "You deserve to be here." But the truth is, no one should have to live in these ruins, not even the white people who have done so much to create them. No one.

UNWRITTEN HISTORY

History is how the secular world attends
to the dead.

—Saidiya Hartman, *Lose Your Mother*

This is the story of a lynching. Early one summer evening, as a crowd of angry white men lingered on the courthouse lawn, my grandfather decided to take his prisoner, a Black man accused of raping a white woman, out of the relative security of the jail and to a nearby farm. That plan could only have one outcome. In Mississippi then, it was the sheriff's job to be an executioner, but in that moment, Sheriff Oury Berry declared himself, as well as highway Patrol Officers Spencer Puckett and Andy Hopkins, judge and jury, too. He knew what he was doing.

But this is also the story of a lie. My grandfather, Hopkins, and Puckett killed Versie Johnson, but many other white people participated in the cover-up. The shortest possible list includes the witnesses at the Lipsey farm, along with F. A. and Ruth Parker of the *Headlight*; R. E. Tyrone, W. C. Williamson, L. W. King, J. P. Parish, T. B. Slater (the five members of the Board of Supervisors), and the clerk, Clifford Bass; District Attorney E. B. Williams; and justice of the peace C. V. Sutton. Most likely there were more, additional law enforcement officers and other local officials and business owners. All of these people knew what they were doing, too.

Beneath this local lie lay the bigger lies that served as the foundation of post-Reconstruction American life, that segregation and discriminatory voting requirements did not violate the Constitution. Lying was how the system worked, and most people knew that, too. For a time, the civil rights movement forced the lies into the open and broke them apart. And yet today, the radical promise of the Supreme Court's *Brown* decision remains only partially implemented. The Voting Rights Act lies in tatters. Few white people are even willing to talk about, much less support, the material reparations that might begin to address the harm caused by both slavery and segregation. And violence continues to deprive Black people of their futures.

In the last decade, Michael Brown, Eric Garner, Philando Castile, George Floyd, and Breonna Taylor, like Versie Johnson, have all been killed by law enforcement officials. Others, like Ahmaud Arbery, have been killed by vigilantes. And while the particulars are important both to the families of the people killed and to the process of trying to hold the perpetrators legally accountable, the details can obscure an important commonality. In all these cases, the killers, whether law enforcement officials or not, believed that they were acting as the hands of the law. But law enforcement officers do not have unlimited legal authority to act. They, too, can be guilty of breaking the law even when, in their own minds, they are enforcing it. In that sense, they, too, can become vigilantes. They can become lynchers.

Across American history, efforts to end this kind of vigilante violence, like the anti-lynching movement, have often had the unintended consequence of driving these acts underground. That can mean the perpetrators cover up what they do. But it can also mean that people who want to be the hands of the law, who want to feel like they personally hold the law's power, have an incentive to go into law enforcement work, where they can act with greater impunity.

Today, the lying continues. Rather than trying to stop vigilante behavior, many state laws encourage it. "Stand your ground" and "open carry" laws tempt citizens to act like law enforcement officers. More recently, state anti-abortion laws offer to pay rewards to citizens who police other citizens' reproductive health choices. Vigilantes are being transformed into heroes. But what many anti-lynching activists understood in the past remains true today. Citizenship is meaningless if a person's body is not safe. Protection from violence is the essential foundation of our democratic life. This, ultimately, is what my grandfather set out to kill on that day in 1947.

This is the story of a lynching and a lie—but it is also an attempt at reckoning with that past, both in its broadest and most intimate forms.

Much of what I remember about Oury Berry had nothing to do with his work as sheriff. After he finished his third term in 1973, he retired again, and this time it stuck. My grandmother Grace Berry tried to retire, too, but she soon went back to work for Guy Magee at the chancery clerk's office, though she did cut back to half days. Her schedule left them lots of time to spend with family, including me and their other grandchildren.

Back in 1952, after Oddie McInnis, a Black farm owner, died in debt, my grandparents bought forty acres from his widow, Linnie Mae McInnis, and her ten minor children for $1,050 minus the $361 the family still owed. After he retired, my grandfather spent hours most days out at the land that he and my grandmother called the Place.

He purchased a used trailer, cleaned it, added a screen porch, and made a camp where the grandkids could spend the night. He fenced off a section and planted a huge garden. He also built a dam to catch the water that seeped out of the ground from springs in the backwoods, and he stocked the pond that formed with catfish. Like many of their white and Black neighbors, my grandparents believed in owning land. A home in town might be convenient, but a family without acres of their own, a place to plant a garden and hunt, was poor. Land was the only reliable source of security.

On my solo summer visits, we spent our afternoons at the Place. Some days we fished. My grandfather baited the hooks, and we cast from the bank. If the catfish were big enough, we put them in a bucket. If we got three or four, we took them back to town, where my grandfather gutted, cleaned, and fried them for our supper. Other days we might pick peas or tomatoes and shuck fat silky ears so my grandmother could make the creamed corn I loved. If I was visiting when the blackberries ripened, I picked them in the bramble patches where the pasture met the woods. The prickles left scratches on my arms that were the same color as the juice that stained my fingers and my tongue. Back at the house in town, my grandmother and I made cobbler.

But my favorite thing to do at the Place was horseback riding. All through my childhood, my grandfather kept a series of ponies and horses there for the grandkids to ride: Sugar, a fat, blond pony who once dumped me in a splash of cow manure; Princess, a slight bay mare who also pulled a plow for the garden; Rex, a beautiful buckskin barrel racer and my first love; Cherokee, an Appaloosa who kicked me so hard with his back feet that he knocked me out; and Mack, a chestnut racking horse. Over the years, the other grandkids lost interest, preferring to drive the go-kart or shoot guns at the snapping turtles. But I never tired of cantering whatever horse was there on the wide, earthen dam around the end of the pond. Only when my grandfather died and left me Mack did I realize that for years he had kept those horses for me.

I was fifteen when that happened. It was seven years after my grandfather had retired as sheriff for the last time. He and my grandmother made a day trip to visit my uncle Jimmy and his family on the Gulf Coast. Back home that evening, relaxing in front of the television with his wife of forty-eight years, he slumped over in his recliner. Later we found out an aneurysm in his brain had burst while he was resting there. He died without waking up. Everyone said he would have wanted to go that way—quick, quiet, and easy. On him perhaps, but for all of us left behind, it was devastating.

For me, Oury Berry was not a sheriff. He was a great bear of a man I called Pa. Kind to me, like my father, but different, too. He never left the house without a hat, a straw or felt fedora to be exact. I never saw him wear what he called a ball cap. He liked his food hot and kept a bottle of small, pickled peppers on the kitchen table so he could sprinkle the juice on his eggs and meat. After he dared me to try it, I became the only other person in the family to like spicy food, too. We had an easy, warm relationship. He made me feel grounded, safe, and secure. He made me feel loved. And I in turn loved him. He taught me that if I kept my mind open to the traces of the past and learned to tell a good story, I could bring to life the history that was everywhere around us. And he was right. I wonder what he would make of this irony.

I wish I could reach through time and stop him there, before he put the key in the cell door and turned the bolt, before he placed Versie Johnson in handcuffs and led him out of the jail. I want my grandfather to know that even if he believed Mississippi "justice" meant a quick trial and a certain death sentence, that likely outcome did not absolve him. Neither did the fact that he might have to shoot people he surely knew and who might even have voted for him if they tried to storm the jail. It did not even matter that he understood more than most people that killing, and being killed, in that mobile electric chair was its own kind of torture. He had a model for acting otherwise. Previous Jeff Davis sheriff Gwinn Magee had protected his Black prisoners by sending them away to jails elsewhere. Sheriff Oury Berry did not make that choice.

As extreme as my own family's story might sound, we are not alone. Some Americans know it and many more do not, but many white people have ancestors who participated in lynchings. Other Americans have ancestors who were enslavers or bankers who financed slave markets or soldiers who fought in the Civil War for a country founded to protect the institution of slavery. More than a few are related to people who were members of the Ku Klux Klan or similar terrorist groups, or participants in the Citizens' Councils, or organizers of segregation academies. Still more have ancestors who committed acts of financial harm, from racist hiring practices, rent gouging, and redlining to restrictive real estate covenants, contract selling, and inequitable tax assessments. I do not pretend all these crimes are equal. I simply suggest that they are widespread, even ubiquitous. Most white people throughout US history have lived in systems that enabled them to deny the common humanity of people they did not think about as white. All too few have resisted. Too few, today, seek to reckon with this past.

Because of my grandfather's actions, Versie Johnson did not get to have a future. Nothing I can do will change the fact that his life was cut short. In these pages, I have tried instead to give him a history, to put his mattering on the record and place his story within our collective understanding of the flow of time. It is important to dig the facts out of the archives and the memories of people who were there. It is important to know the truth. In telling Versie Johnson's story and the broader history of Black flourishing in the Piney Woods of Mississippi, I have tried to offer a counternarrative to the denial of Black humanity at the heart of white supremacy. I have tried to write a history in which Versie Johnson can live.

But there is a huge part of Versie Johnson's history that I have not been able to uncover. His descendants must have memories of his life and his death. I have tried to find the children and grandchildren of his siblings. I have talked to current residents of Jeff Davis County, searched census records and obituaries, and sent letters to individuals and churches. But while I have uncovered more than I expected to learn about the man my grandfather killed, I have failed to find his family. Johnson is a common name, and in the mid-twentieth century, many Black people were on the move. It is also possible that some of my letters reached Versie Johnson's relatives, and they simply have no desire to talk to a stranger who writes out of the blue to ask uncomfortable questions about one of their own who died under suspicious circumstances so many decades ago. But my failure to find them does not mean Versie Johnson's surviving family members do not have their own stories. I hope one day they will tell them.

ACKNOWLEDGMENTS

Writing is a solitary endeavor, but researching and publishing this book required the knowledge, support, and hard work of so many people that my great fear is that I will leave someone out. In the fall of 2017, then UVA associate dean Francesca Fiorani laid the groundwork for this project by repeatedly urging me to apply for a Carnegie Fellowship even though I kept saying that as a single parent I did not have time. Winning this award made it possible to research this book, and I am grateful to the Carnegie Foundation for selecting me as a 2018–2019 fellow and to Greta Essig and Mary Gentile there for handling the details. My former agent, Geri Thoma, of Writers House always believed my writing should have a larger audience. In the COVID-19 spring of 2020, she rescued me from the deep funk of a canceled nationwide tour for my previous book by selling the proposal for this one. When Geri decided to retire at the end of 2020, I cried. But she turned me over to her colleague, the incredible Dan Conaway, whose wise advice and careful attention to the business end of publishing has made it possible for me to finish this book.

My amazing editor, Alex Littlefield, managed to read every page of this manuscript multiple times and offer every possible form of criticism, from line edits and multiple rounds of suggestions about signposting to comments about structure, narrative flow, and titles. When I started this book, I knew how to write a pretty sentence. Alex, as skilled at communicating with authors as he is at editing, not only taught me how to think about story, structure, and characters. He also made the process of revising feel like we were having a deeply meaningful and inspiring conversation. As importantly, he brought me along on the kind of journey through publishing house consolidations that often sinks books, and I feel so very fortunate to have landed with him at Little, Brown. Thanks are due here again to Dan Conaway, who worked out the details to make that happen. At Little, Brown, I am also deeply grateful to Tracy Sherrod for a round of careful editing that greatly improved this manuscript, to Bruce Nichols, for his support, and to my incredible publicist Lena Little. Copyeditor David Goehring had just the right touch and saved me from many errors. Jessica Vestuto at Houghton Mifflin Harcourt and Morgan Wu at Little, Brown offered helpful comments at different stages in the process. James Fenelon made the wonderful maps.

It is impossible to express how grateful I am to Cori Field, Brian Foster, Jennifer Greeson, Amy Halliday, Bruce Holsinger, Andrew Kahrl, Tom Klubock, Bryant Simon, and Liz Witner for taking the time to read some or all of this manuscript and for their enormously valuable feedback. Special thanks to Brian, who knows more about rural and small-town Black life in Mississippi than anyone else I know.

Friends and colleagues near and far have supported this work both indirectly and directly, including, in addition to those mentioned above, Sarah Betzer, Carl Bon Tempo, Anna Brickhouse, Kristin Celello, Sylvia Chong, Sheila Crane, Gina Drosos, Justine Hill Edwards, Kevin Everson, Marcie Cohen Ferris, Sonya Glasserkey, Lisa Goff, Emmet and Edith Gowin, Margaret Hall, Paul Halliday, Claudrena Harold, Matt Hedstrom, Will Hitchcock, David Holton, Jessica Hunt, Eric Hupe, Sanjay Jain, Carrie Janney, Richard Kraft, Tim and Virginia Michel, Sarah Milov, Franny Nudelman, Lisa Pearson, John Pepper, Kamalini Ramdas, Davin Rosborough, Sandhya Shukla, Mark Simpson-Vos, Liz Varon, Penny Von Eschen, Lauren Winner, and David Woody. I am also grateful to current and former UVA PhD students including Monica Blair, Cleo Boyd, Jon Cohen, Bart Elmore, Alison Kelley, Connor Kenaston, Cecilia Marquez,

Scott Matthews, Olivia Paschal, Joey Thompson, and Katie Wu and to former UVA undergraduates including Erin Bernhardt, Lauren Tilton, and Ruthie Yow. Special thanks to Liza Pittard and Olivia Paschal, who served as excellent research assistants on this project; Jimmy Burse, who tracked down photographs at MDAH; and Ayse Erginer and Emily Wallace at *Southern Cultures*.

Writers and scholars Ralph Eubanks, Bill Ferris, and Joe Crespino, who were all born in Mississippi and now live elsewhere, deserve a special thanks. Without Ralph, I would not have met Alvin Williams. Without Alvin, I would not have met Mitchell Gamblin. Thanks also to all the Mississippi-based historians and journalists who shared their knowledge with me, including Ted Ownby, Rebecca Tuuri, Jere Nash, Curtis Wilke, Jerry Mitchell, and Anna Wolfe. I am indebted to all the archivists at the Mississippi Department of Archives and History; the University of Mississippi Archives and Special Collections, including Lauren Rogers; and the McCain Library and Archives at the University of Southern Mississippi, including Lorraine Stuart and Jessica Clarke. I want to single out Jennifer Brannock at USM for special thanks for her research help. Rosalba Varallo Rechia at Princeton University Special Collections provided scans of relevant files from the John Doar Papers during the pandemic shutdown. Thanks to Kevin Kruse for pointing me in that direction. Sara Brewer helped me navigate the Justice Department files on Jefferson Davis County, Mississippi, at the National Archives at Atlanta. On Mississippi research trips, grad school friends Amy and Andy Forbes and cousins Robin and Sandy Sanderson and Judy and Frank Tolar provided hospitality beyond measure. In and near Prentiss, I am grateful to Janice and James Armstrong, Leon Griffith, Alvin Williams, Ruth Williams, and especially Mitchell Gamblin, who died on March 3, 2021, about six months after I talked to him. Finally, I want to thank genealogists Shelly Murphy, Nicka Sewell-Smith, and especially Sharon Leslie Morgan, whom I was able to hire as a consultant to check and extend my research, for sharing their knowledge of Black family history.

This was not an easy book to write. My family—my spouse, Bill Wylie, an artist, and my daughters, Sarah and Emma Hale, college students during the writing of this book—supported me with love, joy, laughter, delicious food and drink, a willingness to talk about this story, and a reminder that the world contains more than this painful past. Bill also served as a first reader, an in-house design department, and an unpaid photographer and research assistant on a trip to Mississippi. Without his unwavering faith in me and his boundless love and support, I would never have been able to complete this project. Sarah, who prefers Italian medieval and Renaissance art history to anything related to the United States, agreed in spite of that to travel with me to Mississippi twice and work there and at home as an unpaid research assistant after the pandemic canceled her study-abroad program. Emma, who loves the study of US history as much as I do, completed the circle by moving to Mississippi after she graduated to teach US history at a public high school. Without them and our pandemic pup, Lucy, this work would have been impossible.

A NOTE ON SOURCES

In addition to my own research, I have drawn on the scholarship of many historians who have come before me. For general information about Black history from Emancipation through the civil rights movement, I am indebted to all the work of W.E.B. Du Bois but especially *The Souls of Black Folk* (Chicago: McClurg, 1903) and *Black Reconstruction in America* (New York: Harcourt, Brace, 1935). Other essential sources on Black life in this period include Tera Hunter, *Bound in Wedlock: Slave and Free Black Marriage in the Nineteenth Century* (Cambridge, MA: Harvard University Press, 2019); Leon Litwack, *Trouble in Mind: Black Southerners in the Age of Jim Crow* (New York: Knopf, 1998), and *Been in the Storm So Long: The Aftermath of Slavery* (New York: Knopf, 1979); William H. Chafe, Raymond Gavins, and Robert Korstad, eds., *Remembering Jim Crow: African Americans Talk About Life in the Segregated South* (New York: New Press, 2001); Kidada E. Williams, *They Left Great Marks on Me: African American Testimonials of Racial Violence from Emancipation to World War I* (New York: New York University Press, 2012); Herbert G. Gutman, *The Black Family in Slavery and Freedom, 1750–1925* (New York: Pantheon, 1976); and Jacqueline Jones, *Labor of Love, Labor of Sorrow: Black Women, Work, and the Family, from Slavery to the Present* (New York: Basic Books, 1985). I am particularly indebted to Saidiya Hartman, *Wayward Lives, Beautiful Experiments: Intimate Histories of Social Upheaval* (New York: W. W. Norton, 2019), and to Sarah Haley, *No Mercy Here:*

Gender, Punishment, and the Making of Jim Crow Modernity (Chapel Hill: University of North Carolina Press, 2019), for their formal innovations in reconstructing the lives of Black working-class people out of the few surviving documents. Though she focuses on North Carolina, Glenda Gilmore's *Gender and Jim Crow* (Chapel Hill: University of North Carolina Press, 1996) has shaped my thinking about southern, middle-class Black people.

On the history of Mississippi, Neil McMillen's *Dark Journey: Black Mississippians in the Age of Jim Crow* (Urbana: University of Illinois Press, 1984) has been indispensable. I have also relied on William Sturkey, *Hattiesburg: An American City in Black and White* (Cambridge, MA: Belknap Press/Harvard University Press, 2019); Jason Morgan Ward, *Hanging Bridge: Racial Violence and America's Civil Rights Century* (New York: Oxford University Press, 2016); Charles Payne, *I've Got the Light of Freedom: The Organizing Tradition and the Mississippi Freedom Struggle* (Berkeley: University of California Press, 1995); John Dittmer, *Local People: The Struggle for Civil Rights in Mississippi* (Urbana: University of Illinois Press, 1995); Joseph Crespino, *In Search of Another Country: Mississippi and the Conservative Counterrevolution* (Princeton, NJ: Princeton University Press, 2007); Stephen Berrey, *The Jim Crow Routine: Everyday Performances of Race, Civil Rights, and Segregation in Mississippi* (Chapel Hill: University of North Carolina Press, 2015); and Patricia Michelle Boyett, *Right to Revolt: The Crusade for Racial Justice in Mississippi's Central Piney Woods* (Jackson: University Press of Mississippi, 2015).

To describe Mississippi farming practices as well as rural life more broadly, I have drawn on Pete Daniel, *Breaking the Land: The Transformation of Cotton, Tobacco, and Rice Cultures Since 1880* (Urbana: University of Illinois Press, 1985), and *Dispossession: Discrimination Against African American Farmers in the Age of Civil Rights* (Chapel Hill: University of North Carolina Press, 2013); and Jack Temple Kirby, *Rural Worlds Lost: The American South, 1920–1960* (Baton Rouge: Louisiana State University Press, 1987). On the understudied topic of interactions between white and Black small farmers, I have found Adrienne Monteith Petty, *Standing Their Ground: Small Farmers in North Carolina Since the Civil War* (New York: Oxford University Press, 2013), to be very helpful despite the fact that it is not about Mississippi. For the specific history of the Mississippi Piney Woods, I have relied on Noel Polk, ed., *Mississippi's Piney Woods: A Human Perspective* (Jackson: University Press of Mississippi, 1986); Nollie W. Hickman, *Mississippi Harvest: Lumbering in the Longleaf Pine Belt, 1840–1915* (Jackson: University Press of Mississippi, 1962); Lawrence S. Earley, *Looking for Longleaf: The Rise and Fall of an American Forest* (Chapel Hill: University of North Carolina Press, 2004); and James E. Fickle, *Mississippi Forests and Forestry* (Jackson: University Press of Mississippi, 2001).

I have done much of the research for this book in genealogical sources including census, draft registration, marriage, and other documents and cemetery records available on Ancestry.com, FamilySearch.org, and Findagrave.com. Mostly, with the exception of references to Versie Johnson's family, I have not cited those sources directly. But if I describe where someone lives, what they do, whether they are literate, how much they earn, whether they served in the military, or who their relatives are, then I have found this information in genealogical records.

Though the name is the same, Jefferson Davis County's newspaper the *Prentiss Headlight* has a completely different owner and editor than it did from the 1940s through the 1970s. Today, the paper covers the lives of both Black and white residents and does not condone or support white violence against Black people.

List of abbreviations:

MDAH: Mississippi Department of Archives and History

USM: McCain Library and Archives at the University of Southern Mississippi

NAACP Papers: the archives of the National Association for the Advancement of Colored People, held at the Library of Congress and available in a digital version at research libraries

NARA-A: National Archives and Records Administration, Atlanta, the location of records created by federal courts and agencies in Mississippi

NOTES

PROLOGUE: TWO TALES

xvii   *"trapped in them"*: James Baldwin, *Notes of a Native Son* [1955] (Boston: Beacon Press, 1984), 193.

xix   *communities rather than individuals:* Ida B. Wells-Barnett, *Southern Horrors: Lynch Law in All Its Phases* (New York: New York Age Print, 1892).

xix   *"Popular justification"*: James Elbert Cutler, *Lynch Law: An Investigation into the History of Lynching in the United States* (New York: Longmans, Green, 1905).

xix   *extended this understanding:* A revised version of the Dyer Act, the Emmett Till Anti-lynching Act, became law in 2022.

xix   *or upholding tradition:* Christopher Waldrep, "War of Words: The Controversy over the Definition of Lynching, 1899–1940," *Journal of Southern History* 66, no. 1 (February 2000): 75–100.

xx   *"told the sheriff"*: ="Negro Killed by Officers in Scuffle for Gun," *Prentiss Headlight*, August 7, 1947.

INTRODUCTION: SPLINTERS AND SILENCE

xxix   *steadily climbs:*US Census Bureau, American Community Survey, 2020 American Community Survey 5-Year Estimates, Tables S0601, S1902, S1701, generated by research assistant Olivia Paschal using Data.census.gov, https://data.census.gov/cedsci/. See also US Census Bureau QuickFacts, Jefferson Davis County, MS, for 2021, online at https://www.census.gov/quickfacts/fact/table/jeffersondaviscountymississippi/PST040221.

xxxii   *"altogether dangerous phase"*: NAACP, "Lynching Goes Underground: A Report on a New Technique," 1940, Folder 001527-013-0578, NAACP Papers.

xxxiii   *"racial terror lynchings"*: Equal Justice Initiative, *Lynching in America: Confronting the Legacy of Racial Terror*, report online at https://lynchinginamerica.eji.org/report/.

xxxvii   *each enslaved person:* For an argument for calculations based on another measure of what is owed, the value over time of forty acres and a mule, see William A. Darity and A. Kirsten Mullen, *From Here to Equality: Reparations for Black Americans in the Twenty-First Century* (Chapel Hill: University of North Carolina Press, 2020).

CHAPTER 1: IN THE PINES

4 *"land killers":* Edwin Ruffin, "Southern Agricultural Exhaustion and Its Remedy," *DeBow's Review* 14 (January 1954): 43.

6 *named Lucas:* Thomas M. Armstrong and Natalie R. Bell, *Autobiography of a Freedom Rider: My Life as a Foot Soldier for Civil Rights* (Deerfield Beach, FL: Health Communications, 2011), 16–18.

7 *land grants:* The Mississippi Agricultural and Mechanical College, Alcorn (a public HBCU), and the Mississippi Industrial Institute and College (later Mississippi University for Women) received a total of 67,019 acres, all of which were sold. Mississippi State also sold its acreage. The only school that did not sell its land grant acres in the state was the University of Mississippi. Roy V. Scott, "Land Grants for Higher Education in Mississippi: A Survey," *Agricultural History* 43, no. 3 (1969): 357–68, http://www.jstor.org/stable/4617692.

8 *electric light in 1940:* Harley W. Chaney, *A Short History of Bethany Baptist Church,* 1949, a manuscript commissioned by the church, MDAH.

8 *two of his brothers:* Likely Richard Lafayette Berry and Josh Lampkin Berry, whose wife was a Blount and probably the daughter of the store's founder.

9 *work in progress:* See "News, Views, and Comments," *Prentiss Headlight,* January 10, 1952, for early history of the town.

10 *Great Valley Road:* FamilySearch provides free and reliable information on paths and roads taken by migrants in the United States. On the Great Valley Road, see https://www.familysearch.org/en/wiki/Great_Valley_Road.

11 *named him German:* The 1800 and 1810 census records state German Berry was born in Chesterfield, South Carolina. It is likely the birth date of 1766 in the death record is wrong, and German was born later, in the early 1770s, or alternately, he was not born in North Carolina. The 1830 census record for German Berry, Simpson County, Mississippi, also suggests a later birth date than the death record.

12 *cotton production:* Charles F. Kovacik, "Cotton," *South Carolina Encyclopedia,* last updated May 10, 2019, https://www.scencyclopedia.org/sce/entries/cotton/.

12 *sold people:* On the internal slave trade, see Ira Berlin, *The Making of African America: The Four Great Migrations* (New York: Viking, 2010); and "The Domestic Slave Trade," *In Motion: The African American Migration Experience,* Schomburg Center for Research in Black Culture, New York Public Library, http://www.inmotionaame.org/migrations/topic.cfm@migration=3&topic=2.html. Recent research suggests that in many slave-exporting states, agriculture was flourishing. It was not so much "soil exhaustion" but a desire to make higher profits that made enslavers sell enslaved people.

12 *west to the Pearl:* On Mississippi migration routes, see https://www.familysearch.org/en/wiki/Category:Mississippi_Migration_Routes. On the Federal Road, see https://www.familysearch.org/en/wiki/Federal_Horse_Path. On the Three Chopped Way, see http://lewis-genealogy.org/genealogy/History/3_Chopped_Way.htm.

12 *new state of Mississippi:* By the 1820 census, German Berry had settled in Wayne County on the Alabama border, along the route of the Three Chopped Way on the

northern edge of the pine forest. John Berry, Jemima Shivers, and their families lived south of the Three Chopped Way along the Pearl River in Marion County in households that included only free persons. Their brother David Berry moved to a Mississippi River county south of Natchez called Wilkinson.

13   *become Jefferson Davis County:* For maps of land patents in Simpson and Jefferson Davis Counties, see Gregory A. Boyd, *Family Maps of Simpson County, Mississippi* (Norman, OK: Arphax Publishing, 2010), and *Family Maps of Jefferson Davis County, Mississippi* (Norman, OK: Arphax Publishing, 2010).

14   *until 1870:* I was unable to locate any of Versie Johnson's relatives in the Freedman's Bureau papers, which date back to 1865.

15   *Jack and Rachel Baggett:* 1870 census, Jack and Rachel Baggett in Lawrence County, MS.

15   *William Pickens Baggett:* 1870 census, William P. Baggett in T6N, R19W, Lawrence County, MS.

15   *two daughters, Anna and Clara:* 1860 slave census, Lawrence County, MS.

15   *Beat 1:* Beat 1 of Lawrence County, MS, encompasses the area surrounding Monticello, the county seat.

15   *Rachel, age sixty:* The 1880 census lists Rachel's birthday as January 1828 rather than 1820. In an era before birth certificates, these kinds of discrepancies were common.

15   *the second Middle Passage:* More than 1.2 million enslaved people underwent forced migration farther west into new colonies and territories; most were part of the domestic slave trade. About 30 to 40 percent of them migrated with the people who owned them. Some made the trip walking, chained together, on trips that could last up to eight weeks and up to six hundred miles. A smaller number were transported via railroad, and others via the Mississippi River or the Alabama River. See "The Domestic Slave Trade."

15   *a partial map:* Rachel Baggett, Lawrence County, MS, 1880 census.

16   *new boundary line:* It was possible the family moved short distances back and forth across the county line. It was also possible the census taker made mistakes in an area along the border.

16   *remains a mystery:* I hired Sharon Leslie Morgan, a specialist in Black genealogy, to check my research and locate information I may have missed. She found a Black family headed by Richmond Johnson, born in Mississippi in 1832, who acquired 160 acres in Lawrence County south of Monticello, the county seat, and just west of the Pearl River in 1876. He also had a son around 1876, a boy he named William. But in 1900, 1910, and 1920, a William Johnson the right age and married to a Black woman named Victoria and their children lived on land he owned in the same section of Lawrence County as Richmond Johnson. This William Johnson was likely Richmond's son. But he was not Versie's father.

CHAPTER 2: A GAMBLE

18   *more likely Ambrose Wood:* There are men named Ambrose Wood in the 1900 census but not a Wood Ambrose. Ambrose Woods, age fourteen and living with his parents in Russellville, Alabama, appeared in the 1900 census and then disappeared from future counts. A Black Ambrose Wood turned up in the same Alabama town, but he shows up again later, in the 1920 census. One of the newspaper articles about the

lynching calls the man who was killed Ambrose Wood as well as Wood Ambrose. See "Negro Lynched," New Orleans *Times-Democrat,* June 12, 1906. The AP wire might have gotten his name wrong and spread the incorrect version everywhere.

18 *lynched in Prentiss:* Newspaper reports on this lynching include "Negro Lynched"; "Mob Lynches Negro at Prentiss, Miss.," *Los Angeles Express,* June 12, 1906; "Shot to Death by a Mob," *Clarke County* [MS] *Times,* June 15, 1906; "A Week's News Condensed," *Richmond Planet,* June 16, 1906; [Untitled], *Hinds County* [MS] *Gazette,* June 15, 1906; "Shot to Death by a Mob," *Macon* [MS] *Beacon,* June 16, 1906; "Shot to Death by a Mob," *Lexington* [MS] *Advertiser,* June 14, 1906; "Negro Lynched at Prentiss," *Natchez* [MS] *Democrat,* June 12, 1906; and "Chips" (a column that contains a variety of news items), Chicago *Broad Ax,* June 23, 1906.

18 *large sawmills:* Nollie W. Hickman, *Mississippi Harvest: Lumbering in the Longleaf Pine Belt, 1840–1915* (Jackson: University Press of Mississippi, 1962), 243.

19 *50 cents a day:* T. M. Bushnell, *Soil Survey of Jefferson Davis County, Mississippi* (Washington, DC: Government Printing Office, 1916), USM.

19 *not a local:* No one with a name like this lived anywhere nearby in the 1900 census.

20 *John Williams:* The 1900 census shows a John Williams, white and sixteen, in Lawrence County (Jeff Davis County did not exist during that census). He would have been twenty-two at the time of Wood's lynching.

20 *"lost his money and temper":* "Negro Lynched."

21 *Constable T. E. Davidson and Marshal R. R. Berry:* On officers appointed by Governor Vardaman when the county was formed, see "News, Views, and Comments," *Prentiss Headlight,* January 10, 1952; and "Jefferson Davis. A New and Prosperous County," *Jeff Davis News* [a very short-lived local newspaper], April 4, 1940. Jeff Davis's first sheriff (appointed) was George Holloway.

21 *"a jury of the whole people":* Jackson *Clarion-Ledger,* March 22, 1889, quoted in Neil R. McMillen, *Dark Journey: Black Mississippians in the Age of Jim Crow* (Urbana: University of Illinois Press, 1989), 242.

22 *"men and women at heart":* Meridian *Star,* September 5, 1919, quoted in McMillen, *Dark Journey,* 239.

22 *"shouting murder":* J. F. H. Claiborne, "Rough Riding Down South, *Harper's,* June 1862.

22 *raping a young white woman:* Virgil Keene was my grandmother Grace's father, and he was almost lynched twice, the second time when his daughter and my grandmother's sister, my great-aunt Minnie, accused him of rape. But she, too, recanted.

22 *treatment of a dog:* The Beck-Tolnay lynching inventory (which will in the future be maintained online by the Library of Congress but was previously online as the CSDE [Connecticut State Department of Education] lynching database) lists this Mississippi case that grew out of an argument over a dog as a "possible lynching": on August 23, 1906, Ben Jack Moore, a white man, was "riddled with bullets" by five white men.

22 *two thousand Black people:* This figure is from Equal Justice Initiative, *Reconstruction in America: Racial Violence After the Civil War* (2020), https://eji.org/reports /reconstruction-in-america-overview/. It is almost certainly an undercount, as the report itself explains.

23 *through the 1890s:* Michael Greenberger, a University of North Carolina political science graduate student, shared with me his unpublished research on the politics of changing county boundaries and new county formation in the South in this period.

According to Greenberger, Lawrence and Covington Counties both elected at least a few Black officials in the 1880s. Jeff Davis County was likely formed because of political infighting between populist and elite Mississippi Democrats after disfranchisement. James K. Vardaman, the first Mississippi governor elected after the institution of political primaries (before the 1903 elections Democratic Party leaders chose the nominees), was not surprisingly also the first populist Mississippi governor. Jeff Davis was probably created to increase the number of counties that supported the Vardaman brand of Democratic Party politics. Because Black people had already been disfranchised by 1906, Vardaman and his allies did not worry that the new county was majority Black.

23   *political alliances that opposed them:* The best book on this topic is Jane Dailey, *Before Jim Crow: The Politics of Race in Postemancipation Virginia* (Chapel Hill: University of North Carolina Press, 2000). On Mississippi, see Stephen E. Cresswell, *Rednecks, Redeemers, and Race: Mississippi After Reconstruction, 1877–1917* (Jackson: University Press of Mississippi, 2006), and *Multiparty Politics in Mississippi, 1877–1902* (Jackson: University Press of Mississippi, 1995).

23   *379 Black people:* Numbers for 1883–1905 are from the Beck-Tolnay lynching inventory. In the years 1865 to 1971, lynchers in Mississippi murdered at least 673 Black people. Historian Terence Finnegan counted 572 lynching incidents in Mississippi between 1881 and 1940, the most for any state. His figure includes victims of all races. See Finnegan, *A Deed So Accursed: Lynching in Mississippi and South Carolina, 1881–1940* (Charlottesville: University of Virginia Press, 2013), 4.

23   *white "protective" leagues:* Gunnar Myrdal, *An American Dilemma: The Negro Problem and Modern Democracy,* vol. 1 [1944] (New York: Routledge, 2017), 449.

23   *Whitecaps:* William F. Holmes, "Whitecapping: Agrarian Violence in Mississippi, 1902–1906," *Journal of Southern History* 32, no. 2 (May 1969): 165–85; and Finnegan, *A Deed So Accursed,* 159–62.

24   *acted as a group:* Christopher Waldrep, "War of Words: The Controversy over the Definition of Lynching, 1899–1940," *Journal of Southern History* 66, no. 1 (February 2000): 75–100.

24   *as a rate:* On the difference between counting the number of lynchings versus calculating the rate of lynching based on the relationship between the number of Black people killed in a place and the number of Black people who live there, see Michael Ayers Trotti, "What Counts: Trends in Racial Violence in the Postbellum South," *Journal of American History* 100, no. 2 (September 2013): 375–400. Many counties with very high lynching rates have very few Black residents.

24   *656 lynchings:* Equal Justice Initiative, *Lynching in America,* https://lynchinginamerica.eji.org/explore.

25   *"wounding a white man":* "Chips."

25   *"dangling":* "Negro Lynched."

25   *first lynching:* In this period when white people bragged about lynchings and newspapers reported on them frequently, it is unlikely (but not impossible) that another lynching occurred in the three months between the March formation of Jefferson Davis County and Wood's lynching in June.

CHAPTER 3: A SEPARATE WORLD

26 *their own separate world:* Terence Finnegan, *A Deed So Accursed: Lynching in Missis-sippi and South Carolina, 1881–1940* (Charlottesville: University of Virginia Press, 2013).

27 *buying land and homesteading:* Mitchell Gamblin interviews, October 8 and 9, 2020, Prentiss, MS; and Thomas Armstrong and Natalie Bell, *Autobiography of a Freedom Rider: My Life as a Foot Soldier for Civil Rights* (Deerfield Beach, FL: Health Com-munications, 2011).

28 *names like Polk, Hall, Griffith, and Johnson:* Throughout this chapter, I draw on cen-sus records, military draft registration forms, land deeds, cemetery indexes, newspapers, and other public records as well as the WPA history of the county to fill in the histories of these Black families.

28 *own, separate spaces:* Charles Johnson, *Shadow of the Plantation* (Chicago: University of Chicago Press, 1934). A journalist found that substantial racial separation still existed in 1943 in the rural South, but that many rural Black folks encountered seg-regation rarely because they simply did not interact much with white people. Enoc Waters, "Waters Finds Rural Areas Lag Behind Cities in Race Militancy," *Chicago Defender,* May 15, 1943.

28 *six hundred Black farm owners:* Works Progress Administration, source materials for Jefferson Davis County, volume 33 of the Mississippi Statewide Historical Research Project, https://www.mlc.lib.ms.us/mlc-services/online-resources/wpa-county-files/. Census figures show the Black population of the county peaking in 1940 at 8,782.

29 *Pearl and Leaf depot:* Description of the town drawn from the first few issues of the *Prentiss Headlight.* The earliest issue I could find was published September 20, 1907. Longtime Prentiss mayor Charlie Dumas also shared an undated postcard of Prentiss from very early in the town's history and a panorama photograph of the town from 1921. The history of farming in the early years of the county is taken from T. M. Bushnell, *Soil Survey of Jefferson Davis County, Mississippi* (Washington, DC: Govern-ment Printing Office, 1916), USM.

30 *The oldest, Mt. Zion:* The history of Black schools in Jefferson Davis County is cov-ered in Works Progress Administration, source materials for Jefferson Davis County.

30 *a school close enough:* There is no official archive for the Prentiss Institute, but the alumni association runs a museum in the original building that they call the 1907 House. They also keep historical materials in a room in the Rosenwald Building, which was renovated in 2013 and serves as a community center. I have drawn my history of the school from these materials as well as interviews with alumni at the Rosenwald Building on the Prentiss Institute campus, January 29, 2019; a small col-lection of photographs, pamphlets, and other materials at the MDAH; a video made by alumna and former employee Mrs. Rosie Hooker; a typed two-page history of the school given to me by alumnus Leon Griffith; the National Register of Historic Places Registration Forms for the 1907 House and for the Prentiss Normal and In-dustrial Institute Historic District; a booklet about the school produced for the program celebrating the renovation of the Rosenwald Building in 2013; the 2015 reunion program; materials including a pamphlet produced for the school's Golden Jubilee in 1957 in the Prentiss Institute Vertical File at USM; and articles about the school in the *Prentiss Headlight* and other newspapers. The school is also described in Charles H. Wilson, *Education for Negroes in Mississippi Since 1910* (Boston:

Meador Publishing, 1947), 469–71; and "Prentiss Institute Grew Up from Private School Opened in Antebellum Home in 1907," *Jackson Daily News,* June 19, 1950. The *Prentiss Headlight* included a description of the school's history in an article about its fortieth anniversary. See "40th Commencement of Prentiss Institute," *Prentiss Headlight,* May 22, 1947.

30 *attended school in 1900:* On Black education in the South, see James D. Anderson, *The Education of Blacks in the South, 1860–1935* (Chapel Hill: University of North Carolina Press, 1988), and Neil McMillen, *Dark Journey: Black Mississippians in the Age of Jim Crow* (Urbana: University of Illinois Press, 1989), 72–108.

30 *"ruining our Negroes":* Vardaman is quoted in Ray Stannard Baker, *Following the Color Line: An Account of Negro Citizenship in the American Democracy* (New York: Doubleday, Page, 1908), 247.

31 *J. E. and Bertha stood out:* In 1900, there were four hundred Black college and professional school graduates across the entire South, according to James D. Anderson, *The Education of Blacks in the South.*

32 *Booker T. Washington:* Booker T. Washington, *Up from Slavery: An Autobiography* [1901] (New York: Modern Library, 1999); Louis R. Harlan, *Booker T. Washington: The Making of a Black Leader, 1856–1901* (New York: Oxford University Press, 1972), and *Booker T. Washington: The Wizard of Tuskegee, 1901–1915* (New York: Oxford University Press, 1983); and Robert J. Norrell, *Up from History: The Life of Booker T. Washington* (Cambridge, MA: Belknap Press/Harvard University Press, 2009).

33 *ruined cabins:* On the existence of the ruins of enslaved people's cabins on the original campus, see Wilson, *Education for Negroes in Mississippi Since 1910,* 469. The Magee house, the original building at the Prentiss Institute, is now called the 1907 House. It was restored and turned into a museum with a grant from the MDAH in the 1970s and listed on the National Register of Historic Places in 1979. The entire campus was listed in 2016.

34 *a rooster to pay tuition:* Rosie Hawthorne Hooker interview, 2012, DVD, given to me by Leon Griffith in Prentiss. She graduated in 1939 and later worked as a secretary and in the administration at the Prentiss Institute.

34 *sixteenth-section lands:* The US Land Ordinance of 1785 written by Thomas Jefferson established the practice of setting aside the 16th section (640 acres / one square mile) of every 36-section township to be held in trust to support public education.

35 *Mississippi Baptist Seminary:* For the history of the organization, see William P. Davis, "The Long Step," an article collected by the Mississippi Sovereignty Commission, SCR ID# 9-25-0-11-2-1-1, at Mississippi Sovereignty Commission Online, MDAH.

35 *seven different kinds:* They were: elementary, high school, junior college, teacher's college, vo-tech school, seminary, and agricultural school. Enrollment peaked at about eight hundred in the post–World War II era.

35 *"school carriers":* Minutes of the Board of Supervisors, Jefferson Davis County, Mississippi, Term: November 1944, ledger 11, p. 83.

35 *special property tax levies:* In 1922, Jeff Davis officials provided $1,200 of the school's annual operating budget of about $14,000, which covered programs for about 360 students. "Negro School Ends Successful Session," *Jackson Daily News,* June 4, 1922; and "P. I. Grew Up from Private School Opened in Antebellum Home in 1907," *Jackson Daily News,* June 18, 1950.

36 *"'Uncle' Joshua Johnson":* The 2016 National Register of Historic Places Registration Form for the Prentiss Institute quotes this story published in the *Hattiesburg American* in 1928 at length.

36 *"Gwinter git one":* The National Register form includes this dialect quote, too, and attributes it to that same story in the Hattiesburg paper.

36 *"a bloodless educational revolution":* "Prentiss Institute Graduates Follow in Footsteps of Founders," *Columbian-Progress,* May 13, 1971.

38 *so-called mulatto children:* The category "mulatto" existed in the US census from 1850 to 1890 and in 1910 and 1920. But because so much of the 1890 census was lost, there is a thirty-year gap in this information for much of southern Mississippi between the 1880 and 1910 censuses.

38 *close to white people:* This seeming contradiction occurred in other parts of the rural South, too. See Adrienne Monteith Petty, *Standing Their Ground: Small Farmers in North Carolina Since the Civil War* (New York: Oxford University Press, 2013); and Mark Schultz, *The Rural Face of White Supremacy: Beyond Jim Crow* (Urbana: University of Illinois Press, 2007).

38 *Estus's father:* Multiple conversations with Ruth Williams in Prentiss, MS, in 2019; and Johnson family history, http://www.beyondesignllc.com/EstusJohnson.htm.

41 *burial insurance:* Suzanne E. Smith, *To Serve the Living: Funeral Directors and the African American Way of Death* (Cambridge, MA: Belknap Press/Harvard University Press, 2010).

42 *boll weevil:* [Untitled notice], *Prentiss Headlight,* September 27, 1907.

43 *long boundary line:* Land deeds in the chancery clerk's office confirm that the Berry and Johnson properties shared a boundary.

43 *Central Johnson who answered:* Mitchell Gamblin interviews, Prentiss, MS, October 8 and 9, 2020.

CHAPTER 4: BLACK BOY

44 *had a future:* I draw here on other kinds of sources, too, on records related to his family members and on the work of historians referenced in the Note on Sources.

46 *his family's cabin:* Census records for this family include the following: 1910 census, Bill and Lizzy Johnson in Lincoln County; 1920 census, Bill and Lizzie Johnson in Lincoln County; 1930 census, William and Elizabeth with Gertrude and Bursie [Versie], and grandson Mack in Rankin County; 1940 census, Lizzie and Vernon [Versie] in Jefferson Davis County; and 1950 census, Lizzie living with Eula Mae and her family. Lizzie and Bill were married in Lincoln County on December 23, 1898.

47 *Around thirty-five:* It's hard to calculate Lizzie Cooper Johnson's age. She does not appear with her family in the 1880 census, so she was born after the information was collected on June 7, 1880. In the 1900 census, she is listed as nineteen with a birthday in June 1880. The 1910 census (her information was collected on April 22 or 23) did not record birthdays, but she is listed as twenty-seven, which would, given her June birthday, make the year of her birth 1882. Virginous (Versie) Johnson's birth certificate lists her age at her last birthday (June 1915) as thirty-eight, making her birth year 1877. In the 1920 census (information collected in January), she is

listed as thirty-eight as well, making her birth year 1881. In all likelihood, the early information is closer to correct and she was probably born in June 1880.

47 *the name on the birth certificate:* Census workers in 1910 and 1920 did not find a single Black man living in Mississippi with the name Virginous.

48 *about five years older:* Versie's birth and death certificates are the only documents I have that provide information about Versie's father before the 1910 census, as I have been unable to locate him with any certainty before he married Lizzie. Versie's death certificate lists his father's name as Willie and his birthplace as Rankin County. His sister Gertrude Johnson provided the information.

48 *they had Ella:* Bill Johnson appears in official records as Willie and Bill. Because the relevant parts of the 1890 census do not survive, it is difficult to track Bill and Lizzie Johnson in this period.

48 *grandmother Rachel Baggett:* She appears in the 1870, 1880, and 1900 censuses, and her name is sometimes spelled Rachael.

48 *survived slavery:* In the first census after Emancipation, Rachel and her husband and Lizzie's grandfather Jack Baggett lived with two of their children, Lizzie's mother, Clara, born in 1855, and another daughter, identified only as A., born in 1852. Rachel probably had other children before freedom, but it is unclear whether they survived. A twenty-two-year-old Black man named Benj Baggett living next door to Rachel and Jack in 1870 might have been a married son.

49 *Norfield sawmill:* Interview with Thomas Lynwood Moak, Lincoln County Oral History Project, Lincoln-Lawrence-Franklin Regional Libraries, https://www.llf.lib.ms.us/oral-history-thomas-l-moak-march-5-1987.

49 *been a prisoner:* David Oshinsky, *Parchman Farm and the Ordeal of Jim Crow Justice* (New York: Free Press, 1996); Douglas A. Blackmon, *Slavery by Another Name: The Re-enslavement of Black Americans from the Civil War to World War II* (New York: Doubleday, 2009); Talitha LeFlouria, *Chained in Silence: Black Women and Convict Labor in the New South* (Chapel Hill: University of North Carolina Press, 2015); and Sarah Haley, *No Mercy Here: Gender, Punishment, and the Making of Jim Crow Modernity* (Chapel Hill: University of North Carolina Press, 2019).

49 *Bill and Willie and William:* These are very common names among Black men born in Mississippi around 1874 or 1875.

52 *had a community:* I have not been able to figure out what church the Johnsons attended, though it is very likely that they had one.

53 *what he knew firsthand:* Richard Wright, *Uncle Tom's Children* (1938), in *Richard Wright: Early Works,* edited by Arnold Rampersad (New York: Library of America, 1991), 221–441, and *Black Boy (American Hunger)* (1945), in *Richard Wright: Later Works,* edited by Arnold Rampersad (New York: Library of America, 1991), 1–365. Wright also lived in Elaine, Arkansas, in approximately the fall of 1916 and early 1917. His family had to flee after Silas Hoskins, the husband of his mother's younger sister Maggie, was murdered by white men who wanted to take over his profitable business, a saloon. Two years later, in 1919, white people in and around Elaine murdered hundreds of Black people. The exact account is unknown, but this tragedy was one of the deadliest racial conflicts in US history. "Elaine Massacre of 1919," *Encyclopedia of Arkansas,* https://encyclopediaofarkansas.net/entries/elaine-massacre-of-1919-1102/.

53 *"wear no drawers":* Richard Wright, "Big Boy Leaves Home," in *Richard Wright: Early Works,* 239.

53 *"Dis train":* Wright, "Big Boy Leaves Home," 240, 241.

54 *"Hell naw!":* Wright, "Big Boy Leaves Home," 245, 256.

57 *James Cooper, married Carrie:* In the 1920 census, Lizzie's father, Jim Cooper, has a one-month-old son with his new twenty-one-year-old wife, Carrie. In the 1930 census, Jim and Carrie live with five children.

57 *Ella's child:* Ella is listed in the 1920 census as Ella Johnson even though the Johnson surname is not repeated after the head of household (her father, Bill Johnson) for any of the other family members. In effect, she is listed as Ella Johnson Johnson. It is possible the white census taker listed her this way to make it clear she has a child, a son listed then as Mack Frelix, and yet is single and lives with her parents.

57 *domestic service:* In the 1940 census, there is a Cora Johnson the right age and born in Mississippi who works as a cook in a white family's home in Memphis.

58 *with his first wife:* In the 1920 and 1930 censuses, Reggie is married to Mattie Knight. If the couple had children, they did not survive long enough to be listed in the census.

58 *a criminal record:* "Caught Bunch of Gamblers," Jackson *Clarion-Ledger,* March 6, 1929; [Untitled], Jackson *Clarion-Ledger,* November 15, 1929; and "Liquor Raids Are Made at Prentiss," Jackson *Clarion-Ledger,* June 28, 1933. It is possible he was arrested at other times, too, but the arrest was not mentioned in the Jackson paper.

60 *to try to help:* Mitchell Gamblin described white residents of Jeff Davis County getting Black residents who worked for them off when they committed crimes.

60 *at $460: The Economic Situation of Negroes in the US* (Washington, DC: US Department of Labor, 1961). This figure includes part- and full-time workers fourteen and older. The median wage for full-time workers in this category was $639.

60 *the most racist places:* Interview with Curtis Wilkie, longtime Mississippi political activist, January 26, 2021.

60 *World War II draft:* Versey [Versie] Johnson, World War II draft registration form. His employer is listed as "Mr. Alton White," proving he was white. A Black man would not have been listed as "Mr."

61 *brother-in-law Reggie Knight:* Reggie Knight, World War II draft registration form.

62 *No records survive:* Email from Witt Fortenberry, chancery clerk, Simpson County, MS, December 21, 2020.

CHAPTER 5: THE LAW

66 *drinking got worse:* "Seriously Hurt by Sliding Lumber," Jackson *Clarion-Ledger,* July 25, 1926.

66 *decent cotton crop:* "Cotton Blooms Are Coming In," Jackson *Clarion-Ledger,* June 3, 1925, described H. J. Berry having fifty acres of thick cotton.

68 *unlimited local authority:* Toby Moore, "Race and the County Sheriff in the American South," *International Social Science Review* 72, nos. 1–2 (1997): 50–61.

68 *"above reproach":* "Oury Berry Announces for Sheriff and Tax Collector," *Prentiss Headlight,* January 28, 1943.

69 *all his life:* After my grandmother died, my mom gave me my grandfather's CMTC badge.

69 *in the military:* A photo of Oury Berry at CMTC bears the mark of an Alabama photography studio, making it clear that he served at Camp McClellan rather than at the CMTC camp in western Florida. Approximately twenty-five camps operated

across the country between 1921 and 1940, and CMTC participants were sent to one of the camps closest to where they lived.

70 *into the middle class:* My grandfather kept a folder of correspondence about his pension. Multiple times across his lifetime, he wrote authorities and collected evidence from doctors to support continuing and also at times increasing his payments.

70 *earned in rural Mississippi:* Enoc P. Waters, "War Bound to Improve Mississippi Since State Cannot Be Any Worse," *Chicago Defender,* March 6, 1943.

71 *a builder and a farmer:* "Oury Berry Announces for Sheriff and Tax Collector."

71 *housed their dairy:* John Sanford is listed as living on First Street with his wife and children in the 1930 census. The 1940 census was made after Sanford died, and it lists his widow and kids living in the country in a house they owned, on a farm they owned, a residence they had been in since at least 1935. Flora Etta Sanford's last name is listed as Sanfford or Sandford, but it is clearly the same person, as the children are the same.

72 *Sweet Beulah and First Street:* See *Jefferson Davis County Land Deed Record,* vol. 47, p.1, for the deed of sale transferring this land from Pickens Brady's son T. Brady Jr. to Guy Oury Berry. See also *JDC Land Assessment Roll,* 1944–1945, 121, 189.

72 *the Lipsey farm:* On the Lipsey land in this area, see *JDC Land Assessment Roll,* 1944–1945, 121, 189. On the history of the Lipsey businesses, see *Lipsey Gin-Tech,* https://www.lipseygintech.com/who-we-are.

72 *"friends and neighbors":* V. O. Key, *Southern Politics* (New York: Knopf, 1949).

73 *"arm in a sling":* "Jeff Davis Folks," Jackson *Clarion-Ledger,* March 21, 1943.

73 *someone in the military:* During the war years, the weekly *Prentiss Headlight* printed news about local people serving in the military and sometimes also their photos or excerpts of their letters. Though they received less coverage than white residents, the paper sometimes mentioned Black Jeff Davis County residents serving in the military, too.

74 *from California to Georgia:* The *Prentiss Headlight* often printed news about where locals had gone and what exactly they had done after they completed their missions and the information could be shared.

74 *often violent discrimination:* Phillip McGuire, *Taps for a Jim Crow Army: Letters from Black Soldiers in World War II* (Lexington: University Press of Kentucky, 1993); Thomas A. Guglielmo, "'Red Cross, Double Cross': Race and America's World War II–Era Blood Donor Service," *Journal of American History* 97, no. 1 (June 2010): 63 –90; and Thomas A. Guglielmo, *Divisions: A New History of Racism and Resistance in America's World War II Military* (New York: Oxford University Press, 2021).

74 *earned good wages:* Ira Katznelson, *When Affirmative Action Was White: An Untold History of Racial Inequality in Twentieth-Century America* (New York: W. W. Norton, 2005), 103–8.

74 *"Going among strangers":* Pete Daniel, "Going Among Strangers: Southern Reactions to World War II," *Journal of American History* 77, no. 3 (December 1990): 886–911.

75 *they acted intentionally:* Studs Terkel, *The Good War: An Oral History of World War II* (New York: Pantheon, 1984), 152–53; McGuire, *Taps for a Jim Crow Army;* and Neil R. McMillen, "Fighting for What We Didn't Have: How Mississippi Black Veterans Remember World War II," in Neil R. McMillen, ed., *Remaking Dixie: The Impact of World War II on the American South* (Jackson: University Press of Mississippi, 1997).

75 *between forty-five and seventy-five lynchings:* Figures are from Daniel, "Going Among Strangers."

75   *shot by white police:* Thomas Sancton, "The Race Riots," *New Republic* 109, no. 1 (July 5, 1943): 9–13.

75   *"like rabbits":* Terkel, *The Good War,* 152–53.

76   *"We hang ' em":* Terkel, *The Good War,* 370–71.

76   *Camp Van Dorn:* Lucius M. Lampton, "Camp Van Dorn," in Center for the Study of Southern Culture, *Mississippi Encyclopedia,* https://mississippiencyclopedia.org /entries/camp-van-dorn/.

76   *"like wild animals":* John Vernon, "Jim Crow, Meet Lieutenant Robinson: A 1944 Court Martial," *Prologue: The Journal of the National Archives* (Spring 2008): 36.

76   *"complicity of their countrymen":* James Baldwin, *Notes of a Native Son* [1955] (Boston: Beacon Press, 1984), 101.

76   *less than a week:* Jason Morgan Ward, *Hanging Bridge: Racial Violence and America's Civil Rights Century* (New York: Oxford University Press, 2016).

76   *"gettin' uppity":* Victor Bernstein, "Mississippi Laments Lynchings—but Doing Something About Them Is Another Matter," *PM Magazine,* October 28, 1942, 2–4.

77   *"in their place":* Bernstein, "Mississippi Laments Lynchings."

77   *"mad that way":* Bernstein, "Mississippi Laments Lynchings." See also Enoc P. Waters, "Ignorance and War Hysteria Found Underlying Causes of 2 Lynchings," *Chicago Defender,* March 13, 1943.

77   *"declare war on":* "Declare War on the Home Front This Year," *Prentiss Headlight,* January 14, 1943.

78   *"the negro believe":* Theodore G. Bilbo, Washington, DC, June 14, 1943, to Harry J. Lockman, Forest Hills, New York, Box 1076, Folder 2, Bilbo Collection, University of Southern Mississippi Special Collections.

78   *rape white women:* Rankin represented Mississippi's first district. As the leading House sponsor of the G.I. Bill, he demanded a decentralized administration of benefits that enabled states and localities that wanted to do so to discriminate against Black veterans.

78   *put them to work:* "The Race Problem in Jeff Davis County," *Prentiss Headlight,* July 12, 1943.

78   *"swung by the neck":* "Jeff Davis Folks," Jackson *Clarion-Ledger,* March 21, 1943.

78   *"merely tolerated":* "Lynching and Liberty," *The Crisis* 47, no. 7 (July 1940): 209. In 1940, Roy Wilkins edited the editorial page for this magazine published by the NAACP.

78   *"The lynching spirit":* Victor Bernstein, "A Belligerent Program for Limited Objectives: An Editorial," *Baltimore Afro-American,* September 19, 1942.

78   *"Improve Mississippi":* Waters, "War Bound to Improve Mississippi."

78   *"the race problem":* "The Race Problem in Jeff Davis County."

79   *"The Southern colored man":* The entire speech was reprinted in the *Baltimore Afro-American,* July 11, 1942.

79   *"put in your pipe":* Victor Bernstein, "No Belief in Democracy," *Baltimore Afro-American,* September 19, 1942.

80   *"pattern of illegality":* Gunnar Myrdal, *An American Dilemma: The Negro Problem and Modern Democracy,* vol. 1 [1944] (New York: Routledge, 2017), 450.

80   *"harnessed to the practice":* Gunnar Myrdal, *An American Dilemma: The Negro Problem and Modern Democracy,* vol. 2 [1944] (New York: Routledge, 2017), 533.

81   *any southern state:* Neil R. McMillen, *Dark Journey: Black Mississippians in the Age of Jim Crow* (Urbana: University of Illinois Press, 1989).

81   *attempting to escape:* Silvan Niedermeier, *The Color of the Third Degree: Racism, Police Torture, and Civil Rights in the American South, 1930–1955* (Chapel Hill: University of North Carolina Press, 2019).

81   *on white crime:* Michael J. Klarman, "Is the Supreme Court Sometimes Irrelevant? Race and the Southern Criminal Justice System in the 1940s," *Journal of American History* 89, no. 1 (June 2002): 119–53.

83   *1,770 to 864: Prentiss Headlight,* August 26, 1942.

83   *lords of the county:* The few women who served as sheriff in Mississippi in the mid-twentieth century were appointed to fill their husbands' terms. No Black men were elected sheriff in the South until after the 1965 Voting Rights Act.

84   *every poll tax paid: Minutes of the Board of Supervisors, Jefferson Davis County,* August 1947 term, vol. 12, p. 25.

85   *Black business district:* Interviews with Mitchell Gamblin, Prentiss, MS, October 8 and 9, 2020, and Leon Griffith, Prentiss, MS, January 30, 2019.

86   *their own company:* Thomas M. Armstrong and Natalie R. Bell, *Autobiography of a Freedom Rider: My Life as a Foot Soldier for Civil Rights* (Deerfield Beach, FL: Health Communications, 2011), 26.

86   *"we wouldn't obey":* Paul Exposé, "To the Colored People of Jeff Davis County," *Prentiss Headlight,* January 6, 1944. Paul Exposé, transcribed incorrectly as Paul Espose, is listed in the 1940 census, SD 6, ED 33-3, Sheet 1A, Jefferson Davis County, Beat 1. He is a fifty-eight-year-old widower and owns a farm worth $800, on Expose Road, a little less than nine miles southwest of Prentiss. The road was probably named after him or his relatives. His great-niece wrote a memoir: Bevelyn Charlene Exposé, *On the Land of My Father: A Farm Upbringing in Segregated Mississippi* (Jefferson, NC: McFarland, 2014).

87   *"uproar down here":* Richard Wright, "The Ethics of Living Jim Crow," in Arnold Rampersad, ed., *Richard Wright: Early Works* (New York: Library of America, 1991), 237.

87   *registered voters:* See *Darby v. Daniel* (1958), a Jeff Davis County case that originated out of efforts there in the mid-1950s to disfranchise Black residents who had actually managed to register to vote.

88   *actually see:* Steven V. Lawson, *Black Ballots: Voting Rights in the South, 1944–1969* (New York: Columbia University Press, 1976); and Alexander Keyssar, *The Right to Vote: The Contested History of Democracy in the United States* (New York: Basic Books, 2009).

88   *"such rot":* "Those Responsible Will Pay Some Day!" *Prentiss Headlight,* April 6, 1944.

89   *"Black coffee":* "Convicted Slayer Pays with His Life," *Prentiss Headlight,* May 11, 1944.

CHAPTER 6: GONE UNDERGROUND

91   *the blowtorches:* Newspaper articles on the Windham murder include "State Grocer Is Ambushed: Duck Hill Merchant Shot While Eating Supper in Store," Jackson *Clarion-Ledger,* January 1, 1937; "Grocer in Mississippi Is Killed by Bandit," *Atlanta Constitution,* January 1, 1937; "Two Negroes Held: Brothers Detained in Ambush Slaying of Grocer," *Birmingham News,* January 2, 1937; "Winona Murder Suspect Cries," Jackson *Clarion- Ledger,* January 4, 1937; "Two More Negroes Held in Mur-

der," Jackson *Clarion-Ledger,* January 8, 1937; "3 More Murder Suspects Freed," Jackson *Clarion-Ledger,* January 15, 1937; "Negro Is Sought as State Slayer," Jackson *Clarion-Ledger,* January 20, 1937; "Seventh Arrest Made in Murder," Jackson *Clarion-Ledger,* January 24, 1937; and "Negro Is Held [on] Murder Charge at Duck Hill," *Greenwood Commonwealth,* April 6, 1937.

92   *cents a pound:* Pete Daniel, *Breaking the Land: The Transformation of Cotton, Tobacco, and Rice Cultures Since 1880* (Urbana: University of Illinois Press, 1985).

92   *particularly fraught:* On the extent of debt, see Federal Writers' Project of the Works Progress Administration, *Mississippi: A Guide to the Magnolia State* (New York: Viking, 1938), 8–10; and Jack Temple Kirby, *Rural Worlds Lost: The American South, 1920–1960* (Baton Rouge: Louisiana State University Press, 1987).

93   *"Negro dogs":* Tyler D. Parry and Charlton W. Yingling, "Slave Hounds and Abolition in the Americas," *Past & Present* 246, no. 1 (February 2020): 69–108.

94   *hellhounds of the blues:* Adam Gussow, *Seems Like Murder Here: Southern Violence and the Blues Tradition* (Chicago: University of Chicago Press, 2002).

94   *"tell the sheriff":* "Winona Murder Suspect Cries."

94   *extract confessions:* Chairman George W. Wickersham, *National Committee on Law Observance and Enforcement Report on Lawlessness in Law Enforcement* (Washington, DC: Government Printing Office, 1931); and Silvan Niedermeier, *The Color of the Third Degree: Racism, Police Torture, and Civil Rights in the American South, 1930–1955* (Chapel Hill: University of North Carolina Press, 2019).

95   *his report:* Howard Kester, Nashville, May 8, 1937, to Walter White, New York City, and fake letter from Ira E. Chapman, Memphis attorney, May 3, 1937, in Folder 001527-013-0754, NAACP Papers.

96   *euphemism for lynching:* My account here is taken from Kester's report. NAACP, "Lynchings by Blow-torch," in Folder 001527-013-0754, NAACP Papers.

96   *famously mob-proof jail:* "Hinds Citizens Will Dedicate New Courthouse Tuesday," Jackson *Clarion-Ledger,* December 14, 1930.

96   *"the forms of the law":* [Untitled editorial], *Greenwood Commonwealth,* April 14, 1937.

96   *guilt or innocence:* Michael J. Klarman, "Is the Supreme Court Sometimes Irrelevant? Race and Southern Criminal Justice in the 1940s," *Journal of American History* 89, no. 1 (June 2002): 119–53.

97   *an hour and a half:* "Mob Is Burning Negroes at the Stake," *Greenwood Commonwealth,* April 13, 1937; "Lynchers Torture, Burn Two Negroes," *New York Times,* April 14, 1937; "2 Negroes Slain by Mob; Officers Will Investigate," Jackson *Clarion-Ledger,* April 14, 1937; "Mob Lynches Two Negroes, Beats a Third at Duck Hill," Greenville *Delta Democrat-Times,* April 14, 1937; "Punishment of Lynchers Demanded," *Biloxi Daily Herald,* April 14, 1937; "Governor Silent on Mob Action in Montgomery," Jackson *Clarion-Ledger,* April 15, 1937.

97   *"Let's get them":* "2 Negroes Slain by Mob."

97   *"and orderly":* "2 Negroes Slain by Mob."

97   *without a fight:* "Races: Lynch and Anti-lynch," *Time,* April 26, 1937, offers one description of what happened.

97   *mob action:* Arthur F. Raper, *The Tragedy of Lynching* (Chapel Hill: University of North Carolina Press, 1933).

98   *turned up mysteriously:* NAACP, "Lynchings by Blow-torch."

98   *see the lynching:* Ralph Matthews, "Eye-Witness Tells Story," *Baltimore Afro-American,* April 24, 1937.

98 *in the head:* NAACP, "Lynchings by Blow-torch."

99 *"1937 style":* The *Afro-American* published the photograph above the article: Matthews, "Eye-Witness Tells Story." On the circulation of the photographs, see Amy Louis Wood, "'Somebody Do Something!' Lynching Photographs, Historical Memory, and the Possibility of Sympathetic Spectatorship," *European Journal of American Studies* 14, no. 4 (December 23, 2019). The white Memphis paper, firmly antilynching, put the photograph on the front page.

100 *ever held accountable:* On good versus bad lynchings, see the book by Piney Woods journalist and editor James Street, *Look Away: A Dixie Notebook* (New York: Viking, 1936), 62; and "Kennedy, Craigen, Study, 1942–1944," NAACP Papers Part 17: National Staff Files, 1940–1955; Series: Group II, Series A, General Office File.

100 *denounced the bill:* William M. Colmer, "Congressional Sidelights," *Prentiss Headlight,* April 22, 1937.

100 *undercover reporting:* Robert L. Zangrando, *The NAACP Crusade Against Lynching, 1909–1950* (Philadelphia: Temple University Press, 1980).

100 *"sectional issue":* "Races: Lynch and Anti-lynch"; and George C. Rable, "The South and the Politics of Antilynching Legislation, 1920–1940," *Journal of Southern History* 51, no. 2 (May 1985): 201–20.

100 *killing it, too:* Zangrando, *The NAACP Crusade Against Lynching.*

101 *"politically equal":* Zangrando, *The NAACP Crusade Against Lynching,* 150.

101 *"Mississippi courts":* White is quoted in Neil McMillen, *Dark Journey: Black Mississippians in the Age of Jim Crow* (Urbana: University of Illinois Press, 1990), 251.

101 *federal anti-lynching law:* In 2022, Congress passed and President Biden signed the Emmett Till Antilynching Act.

101 *actually condemn them:* Zangrando, *The NAACP Crusade Against Lynching,* 214–15.

101 Prentiss Headlight *complied:* "Anti-lynching Laws," *Prentiss Headlight,* April 22, 1937.

102 *"human torture":* The Raleigh *News & Observer* is quoted in "Southern Paper, For Anti-lynch Bill, Says Mobs Would Fear G-Men," *Pittsburgh Courier,* April 24, 1937.

102 *in 1938:* "Six (?) Lynchings," *Baltimore Afro-American,* September 17, 1938; "Mob Changes into 'Posse,'" *Baltimore Afro-American,* September 24, 1938; "New Tactics May Get by 'Lynch Law,'" *Indiana Catholic and Record,* August 5, 1938; Roy Wilkins, New York, September 7, 1938, to Howard Kester, Nashville, in Folder 001527-021-0605, NAACP Papers; and McMillen, *Dark Journey,* 251–52.

102 *"dangerous phase":* NAACP, "Lynching Goes Underground: A Report on a New Technique," 1940, Folder 001527-013-0578, NAACP Papers.

104 *for cash:* Lawrence S. Earley, *Looking for Longleaf: The Fall and Rise of an American Forest* (Chapel Hill: University of North Carolina Press, 2004), 151.

104 *dead wood:* The Hercules Powder Company opened a plant in Hattiesburg, Mississippi, in 1923. In addition to producing other chemicals, the company invented a steam process to extract turpentine from wood pieces including ground-up stumps. See William Sturkey, *Hattiesburg: An American City in Black and White* (Cambridge, MA: Belknap Press/Harvard University Press, 2019); and Haskel Burns, "A Look Back—and Ahead—at the Hercules Plant," *Hattiesburg American,* July 4, 2015, https://www.hattiesburgamerican.com/story/news/local/hattiesburg/2015/07/04/look-back-hercules/29721429/.

105 *"a girl":* "'Guilty as Charged'—Negroes Sentenced to Hang Feb. 23rd," *Prentiss Headlight,* January 18, 1940. For another account of what happened, see "Prentiss Negroes to Hang," Jackson *Clarion-Ledger,* January 14, 1940.

105 *join them:* "'Guilty as Charged'"; "Prentiss Negroes to Hang."

105 *Moore's Ford:* Laura Wexler, *Fire in the Canebreak: The Last Mass Lynching in America* (New York: Scribner, 2003).

105 *restaurants nearby:* "Suspect in Jeff Davis Slaying Brought to City as Mob Threatens," Jackson *Clarion-Ledger,* January 6, 1940.

106 *"be careful":* "'Guilty as Charged.'"

106 *former marshal:* "Prentiss Loses Noble Citizen," *Prentiss Headlight,* January 4, 1940.

106 *"joined in":* "Bank of Blountville Robbed by Ray Hamilton and Companion," *Prentiss Headlight,* April 4, 1935.

106 *the bad guys:* "Former Railroad Town Boasts a Rich History," clipping from unlabeled paper, January 15, 2005, "Prentiss MS" vertical file, USM.

106 *"enforce the law:"* "Bank of Blountville Robbed."

107 *multiple times:* "'Guilty as Charged.'" See also "Prentiss Negroes to Hang"; and "Prentiss Loses Noble Citizen."

107 *"any shooting":* "Suspect in Jeff Davis Slaying Brought to City."

107 *left in the car:* "Suspect in Jeff Davis Slaying Brought to City."

107 *two occasions:* "Wounded Killer in Hiding," Jackson *Clarion-Ledger,* January 5, 1940; "Suspect in Jeff Davis Slaying Brought to City"; and [Untitled], *Delta Democrat-Times,* January 4, 1940.

107 *"of my office":* "Negro Taken to Jackson for Safekeeping," *McComb Daily Journal,* January 5, 1940.

108 *"no other trouble":* "Suspect in Jeff Davis Slaying Brought to City."

108 *three holes:* "Prentiss Negroes to Hang."

108 *"to interfere":* "Three Guard Companies on Duty at Trial," *Biloxi Daily Herald,* January 9, 1940.

109 *"this county seat":* "Three Guard Companies on Duty at Trial."

109 *"undisclosed":* "Prentiss Trial Ordered Friday; Motion Denied," Jackson *Clarion-Ledger,* January 10, 1940.

109 *jail in Jackson:* "Prentiss Trial Ordered Friday"; and "Three Guard Companies on Duty at Trial."

110 *death sentences:* "Supreme Court Overrules Error Suggestion," *Prentiss Headlight,* January 19, 1940; and "Cleveland Holloway Executed for Murder," *Prentiss Headlight,* February 1, 1940.

110 *"town and country":* "'Guilty as Charged.'"

111 *"ought to be hung":* "Prentiss Negroes to Hang."

111 *"No move":* "Jerome Franklin and Hilton Fortenberry Go on Trial Friday for Murder of Officer," *Prentiss Headlight,* January 11, 1940.

112 *his home county:* "Wounded Killer in Hiding"; "Mob Possibility Justified Sending Troops to Prentiss," Jackson *Clarion-Ledger,* January 10, 1940; "Prentiss Trial Ordered Friday"; "S. Gwinn Magee, Sr., Former Sheriff, Dies Suddenly," *Prentiss Headlight,* August 5, 1948. The obituary of Magee's son, Guy Magee, also gives details of Gwinn Magee's career. See Marky Aden, "Guy Magee, Ex-Chancery Clerk," Jackson *Clarion-Ledger,* May 26, 1994.

112 *to hang:* "Prentiss Negroes to Hang."

112 *denied every claim:* Franklin v. State, 196 So. 787 (Miss. 1940), decision of Mississippi Supreme Court filed June 10, 1940.

113 *mobile electric chair:* "Portable Electric Chair Recommended," *Biloxi Daily Herald,*

March 1, 1940; and "Fight to Abolish the Gallows Finally Won in the Legislature," Jackson *Clarion-Ledger,* April 5, 1940.

113 *on display:* "Mississippi Hires Executioner," *Hattiesburg American,* July 2, 1940; "Electric Chair Late; Negroes Get Reprieves," *Hattiesburg American,* July 17, 1940; and "Electric Chair Will Be Exhibited Here Thursday," Jackson *Clarion-Ledger,* September 17, 1940.

113 *condemned men:* "Roberts Becomes Governor Today," Jackson *Clarion-Ledger,* July 14, 1940. "Jeff Davis Pair Will Die on Gallows Friday," Jackson *Clarion-Ledger,* October 8, 1940.

113 *life in prison:* "Negro's Sentence Reduced to Life," Jackson *Clarion-Ledger,* October 9, 1940; "Quick Death in New Chair: Two Slayers Executed; One Hanged at Prentiss; One 'Burns' at Lucedale," *Hattiesburg American,* October 11, 1940. On Black men with powerful white supporters receiving pardons even in cases of rape, see Lisa Dorr, *White Women, Rape, and the Power of Race in Virginia, 1900–1960* (Chapel Hill: University of North Carolina Press, 2004).

114 *"safer place":* "Quick Death in New Chair." The *Prentiss Headlight* admitted this mass meeting occurred only a decade later, when Governor Johnson's son, also named Paul Johnson, ran for governor. See "News, Views and Comments," *Prentiss Headlight,* August 23, 1951, which quotes the resolutions, suggesting that the Parkers saved papers from the meeting.

114 *would live:* "Negro's Sentence Reduced to Life"; "Quick Death in New Chair."

114 *"knotted noose":* "Two More Must Decide Between the Chair and Noose: Executions Held Friday Offered as Comparisons," Jackson *Clarion-Ledger,* October 12, 1940.

115 *"entitled to see it":* "Two More Must Decide Between the Chair and Noose."

115 *Sebe Dale:* "Judge Dale Dies," *Columbian Progress,* October 11, 1979.

115 *"has ever occurred":* "Two More Must Decide Between the Chair and Noose"; and "Guard Escorts Jeff Davis Negro to Noose," Jackson *Clarion-Ledger,* October 11, 1940.

CHAPTER 7: A LIE

117 *Democratic primary:* "Negro Killed by Officers in Scuffle for Gun," *Prentiss Headlight,* August 7, 1947.

118 *did nothing:* FOIA requests for any FBI records on Versie Johnson's killing turned up nothing. On the FBI's investigations into other lynchings in 1942 and 1947, see Jason Morgan Ward, *Hanging Bridge: Racial Violence and America's Civil Rights Century* (New York: Oxford University Press, 2016); and Rebecca West, "Opera in Greenville," *New Yorker,* June 14, 1947.

120 *concentration camp:* Gamblin's service in the military is documented at National Archives at College Park, College Park, MD; *Electronic Army Serial Number Merged File, 1938–1946;* NAID: *1263923;* Record Group Title: *Records of the National Archives and Records Administration, 1789–ca. 2007;* Record Group: *64;* Box Number: *15463;* Reel: 370.

120 *main source:* "Rape Suspect Slain at Scene of His Crime," *Chicago Daily Tribune,* August 2, 1947; and "Negro Rape Suspect Shot Near Prentiss," Jackson *Clarion-Ledger,* August 2, 1947.

121   *one to two miles:* The *Headlight* says two miles and the *Clarion-Ledger* says three, but on a map the distance is about a mile.

121   *"Berry said":* "Rape Suspect Slain at Scene of His Crime."

122   *nearby Lipsey farm:* Mitchell Gamblin did not remember Thompson's first name. Several white men with the last name of Thompson living in or near Prentiss appear in the 1940 census.

122   *the rape myth:* Ida B. Wells, one of the first anti-lynching activists, countered the rape myth by arguing that white women willingly had sex with Black men. See *Southern Horror: Lynch Law in All Its Phases* (1892), reprinted in Jacqueline Jones Royster, ed., *Southern Horrors and Other Writings: The Anti-lynching Campaign of Ida B. Wells, 1892–1900* (Boston: Bedford Books, 1997).

123   *"get a confession":* Hartzog is mentioned by name in several papers including "Rape Suspect Slain at Scene of His Crime." The Associated Negro Press picked up the story with Hartzog's name, and many Black newspapers included it. See "Report Mob Forming Before Police Slew Rape Suspect," *Atlanta Daily World,* August 9, 1947.

123   *"out of curiosity":* "Negro Rape Suspect Shot Near Prentiss."

123   *sheriff's office:* The *Prentiss Headlight* included a notice that Miss Mollie Hartzog had gone to work at the Post Office and had been replaced at the sheriff's office by Mrs. Huling Parker. See [Untitled], *Prentiss Headlight,* October 2, 1947. See also her obituary: John Meyers, "Mollie H. Brinson, Ex-Postmistress," Jackson *Clarion-Ledger,* July 23, 1994. Her brother reports here that she worked for the Jefferson Davis County sheriff's office from 1946 to 1954. These dates are wrong.

123   *"sniff Johnson's shoes":* "Negro Rape Suspect Shot Near Prentiss."

123   *fifty dollars: Minutes of the Board of Supervisors, Jefferson Davis County,* vol. 12, September term, p. 25.

124   *corroborating evidence:* Richard H. Lipscomb, "Admissibility in Criminal Prosecution of Evidence of Tracking by Bloodhounds Indicating Guilt of Accused," *Washington and Lee* 9, no. 2 (January 1952): 248–54.

125   *murder suspects:* See quotes from resolutions written at mass meeting held in 1940 in "News, Views, and Comments," *Prentiss Headlight,* August 23, 1951.

126   *job he held:* Toby Moore, "Race and the County Sheriff in the American South," *International Social Science Review* 72 (1997): 50–61; and Anthony Gregory, "Policing Jim Crow America: Enforcers' Agency and Structural Transformations," *Law and History Review* (2021): 1–32.

126   *Howard Wash:* "Mississippi Mob Lynches a Slayer," *New York Times,* October 18, 1942; and Ward, *Hanging Bridge.*

127   *"honest ones":* "Sheriff Makes Public Statement to the People," *Prentiss Headlight,* February 27, 1947.

127   *"by rumor":* "To the People of Jefferson Davis County," *Prentiss Headlight,* June 5, 1947 (date printed wrong on paper and corrected by hand on front page).

128   *concrete ditch:* "News, Views, and Comments," *Prentiss Headlight,* September 24, 1944.

129   *managed the situation:* In thinking about what it means to focus on doing the job even when that work involves killing other human beings, I have drawn on Hannah Arendt, *Eichmann in Jerusalem: A Report on the Banality of Evil* [1964] (New York: Penguin Classics, 2006).

130   *how many:* "Trial of Police for Slaying to Be 'Whitewash,'" Norfolk *New Journal and Guide,* August 9, 1947; "Trial of Police to Be 'Mere Formality' Says District Atty.,"

Atlanta Daily World, August 12, 1947; and "Dismiss Charges Against Officers," *Biloxi Daily Herald,* August 7, 1947.

131 *"at close range":* "Local Chapter AVC and State NAACP Send Telegrams to Attorney General," *Jackson Advocate,* August 9, 1947. This article incorrectly states that Versie Johnson was a veteran.

131 *"FBI investigation":* "CRC Urge Federal Prosecution in Prentiss Case," *Jackson Advocate,* August 16, 1947. The CRC statement was also reported in "Clark Told FBI Should Act at Once," Norfolk *New Journal and Guide,* August 16, 1947.

131 *state's police force:* Justin Mark Randolph, "Civil Rights Arrested: Black Freedom Movements and Mass Incarceration in Rural Mississippi, 1938–1980" (PhD dissertation, Yale University, 2020).

132 *"murder people":* Mitchell Gamblin interviews, Prentiss, MS, October 8 and 9, 2020.

CHAPTER 8: THE COST

133 *"insufficient" evidence:* "Dismiss Charges Against Officers," *Biloxi Daily Herald,* August 7, 1947. See also "Prentiss Trial Proves? Mere Formality," *Jackson Advocate,* August 16, 1947.

133 *"for the entire year":* Minutes of the Board of Supervisors, Jefferson Davis County, vol. 12, p. 40.

134 *to enjoy it:* Jeff Wiltse, *Contested Waters: A Social History of Pools in America* (Chapel Hill: University of North Carolina Press, 2010). On the filled-in pool as a metaphor for how white supremacy hurts all Americans, see Heather McGhee, *The Sum of Us: What Racism Costs Everyone and How We Can Prosper Together* (New York: One World, 2021).

134 *"immediate program":* To Secure These Rights: The Report of President Harry S. Truman's Committee on Civil Rights (New York: Simon and Schuster, 1947), 139, 87.

135 *rejected democracy:* On an earlier version of this cycle, see W.E.B. Du Bois, *Black Reconstruction in America* (New York: Harcourt, Brace, 1935).

135 *sometimes protested:* Terence Finnegan, *A Deed So Accursed: Lynchings in Mississippi and South Carolina, 1881–1940* (Charlottesville: University of Virginia Press, 2013).

136 *to Versie Johnson:* Minutes of the Board of Supervisors, Jefferson Davis County, vol. 12, p. 25. Louise Anderson, Stanley Arnold, and Elaine Bullock, *Cemeteries of Jeff Davis County* (Sherwood, AR: S. W. Arnold, 1989), includes a list of all graves found there in 1988.

136 *Eula Mae Knight:* Lizzie and Versie (called Vernon) Johnson are listed as living with Reggie Knight in the 1940 census, which mistakenly lists Reggie's wife Eula Mae Knight's first name as Velma. Alternatively, Velma might have been Eula Mae's nickname. In the 1950 census made three years after Versie died, Johnson is still living with Eula Mae Knight and her family, and this time her name is entered correctly. I have found many examples of white census takers copying Black people's names wrong in this part of Mississippi.

138 *pragmatic approach:* Neil R. McMillen, *Dark Journey: Black Mississippians in the Age of Jim Crow* (Urbana: University of Illinois Press, 1990), 278, 308–12; and Becca Walton, "Bertha LeBranche Johnson," in Center for the Study of Southern Culture, *Mississippi Encyclopedia,* July 11, 2017, https://mississippiencyclopedia.org/entries /bertha-lebranche-johnson/.

138 *quiet appeals:* See "Report of Rev. H. D. Darby," October 14, 1958, SCR ID# 4-2-0-3-1-1-1; and Zack J. Van Landingham, "Memorandum: Garrett Eugene Gray; Henry Cullen Watts, Applicants, Supt. of School, Prentiss, MS," February 17, 1959, SCR ID# 2-52-0-10-1-1-1, both in Mississippi Sovereignty Commission Online, MDAH, for descriptions of Bertha Johnson as having a restraining influence on would-be activists in the county and as "absolutely all right (meaning anti-integration)" and anti-NAACP, though readers of these documents should account for the fact that these reports were collected by a spy agency that cultivated informants. The first report is said to come from Bertha's son, A. L. Johnson, then dean of the Prentiss Institute, which his mother was then running. He seemed to be trying to distance the Prentiss Institute from an NAACP voting rights lawsuit. The second report cites Percy Greene, an increasingly conservative Black journalist and editor of the *Jackson Advocate,* who in 1959 was giving information to the Mississippi Sovereignty Commission (MSC). According to Greene, Bertha Johnson was on the correct side, but A. L. Johnson was "playing both sides against the middle." An undated article in the MSC files praising "Uncle Toms," defined as Black people "who fail to go out on radicalism" and "make it a point to get along with white people," calls J. E. Johnson an Uncle Tom. See "Editorial— Uncle Tom," *Mid-South Informer,* SCR ID# 1-57-0-10-1-1-1, Mississippi Sovereignty Commission Online, MDAH.

138 *"the general improvement":* McMillen, *Dark Journey,* quotes, 278. On uplift, see Kevin Gaines, *Uplifting the Race: Black Leadership, Politics, and Culture in the Twentieth Century* (Chapel Hill: University of North Carolina Press, 1996).

138 *at least 667:* This list of Black men who served in World War II appears in a document in the Prentiss Institute Museum in the Rosenwald Building on the former campus in Prentiss.

139 *at Black churches:* Oak Grove is mentioned in the Prentiss NAACP minutes. "NAACP, Prentiss, Mississippi," Memorandum from Zack J. Van Landingham, March 13, 1959, SCR ID# 2-52-0-12-1-1-1, Mississippi Sovereignty Commission Online, MDAH, mentions the names of voting activists from the Mt. Zion community. On NAACP meetings at Mt. Zion Church, see Alvin Williams interview, Prentiss, MS, June 18, 2021.

139 *white retaliation:* The NAACP files at the Library of Congress have only membership numbers on this branch, in folders marked "Nationwide Membership Campaign" and "membership quotas and apportionment," in Branch Files, 1940 –1955, NAACP, LOC. Many thanks to Patrick Kerwin, manuscript reference librarian at the Library of Congress, for scanning these non-digitized files for me. All other information, including the names of members, comes from the minutes of meetings held between 1948 and 1954, turned over to the Mississippi Sovereignty Commission, February 9, 1959, by Jeff Davis County circuit clerk James Daniel, who got them from an unnamed Black informant. These minutes are very vague about activities, probably intentionally, although they do include lists of members. The Sovereignty Commission put the names of everyone listed in these minutes into its index of people to watch. See Minutes of the Prentiss NAACP, SCR ID# 2-52-0-8-1-1-1, Mississippi Sovereignty Commission Online, MDAH.

139 *Wardell Gray's parents:* Mary Otis Gray's divorced mother, Annie Johnson, owned land in Jeff Davis County in the 1920 census, when Will and Mary Gray lived with

her. By 1950, Will and Mary Gray lived on a farm they owned along with their son Wardell, back from the war and married. Wardell's father had worked as a foreman for the Illinois Central Railroad and his mother had run a boardinghouse in Sumrall, and they used the money they made to buy land in Jeff Davis County. See "A Concurrent Resolution Mourning the Passing of Decorated World War II Veteran, Respected Civil Rights Activist and Prentiss, Mississippi, Civic Leader and Businessman Wardell Gray, and Extending the Condolences of the Legislature to His Surviving Family," Mississippi Senate Concurrent Resolution No. 534, Regular Session 2018.

139 *Ernest Lockhart:* Thomas M. Armstrong and Natalie R. Bell, *Autobiography of a Freedom Rider: My Life as a Foot Soldier for Civil Rights* (Deerfield Beach, FL: Health Communications, 2011), 23.

140 *two extraordinary petitions:* "Citizens and Taxpayers of Jefferson Davis County," *Prentiss Headlight,* April 19, 1951.

140 *NAACP members:* The Prentiss NAACP meeting minutes make clear that the chapter focused on education.

141 *sold that property:* My grandparents made $12,000, a nice profit on a house and land they paid $1,600 for in 1942 and in 1947 sold a railroad right of way on for $1,000. Property deeds in the chancery clerk's office, Prentiss, Mississippi, provide the dates and terms of these purchases and sales.

141 *in the courthouse:* They paid $7,500 for the house and two city lots. Property deeds in the chancery clerk's office, Prentiss, Mississippi, provide the dates and terms of these purchases and sales.

141 *"open for inspection":* "G. O. Berry Announces for Sheriff and Tax Collector," *Prentiss Headlight,* February 8, 1951. See also "To the People of Jefferson Davis County," *Prentiss Headlight,* May 10, 1951.

142 *Shelby L. Mikell Sr.:* The *Prentiss Headlight* printed the vote tallies for the Democratic primaries by the Jeff Davis County precinct on the front page of the paper on August 9, 1951, and September 6, 1951.

142 *the primaries, too:* T. B. Wilson, Mississippi Progressive Voters League, Jackson, Mississippi, August 21, 1947, to Thurgood Marshall, New York, New York, Folder 001517-009-0001, NAACP Papers; and Ruby Hurley, Memorandum, May 7, 1951, to Gloster B. Current, Walter White, Thurgood Marshall, Roy Wilkins, and Lucille Black, Folder 001493-015-0300, NAACP Papers.

142 *always been Black:* In the 1950 census, the Black population of Jeff Davis County was 8,610, almost 56 percent of the total population.

143 *"103 Negro voters":* "There Is Only One Issue in This Race," *Prentiss Headlight,* August 23, 1951.

143 *"NOT HAPPEN HERE":* "Another Warning to the People," *Prentiss Headlight,* August 23, 1951.

143 *"bloc voting":* "News, Views, and Comments," *Prentiss Headlight,* August 30, 1951. See also the precinct results in large type in the next week's paper: "Official Tabulation," *Prentiss Headlight,* September 6, 1951.

143 *his own dad:* My mother told me this story about Curtis Chance.

143 *his father died:* H. J. Berry's obituary, *Prentiss Headlight,* January 10, 1952.

144 *"a political court":* Purser Hewitt, "State Seeks Answer to Adverse Ruling on School Segregation," Jackson *Clarion-Ledger,* May 18, 1954; and Al Kuettner, "South's Segregationists to Fight to Bitter End Against Court's Decision," and Una Franklin,

"Mississippi Congressmen Have Varied Reactions to Segregation Decision," both in Greenville *Delta Democrat-Times,* May 18, 1954.

144 *the segregationist movement:* Michael Klarman, *From Jim Crow to Civil Rights: The Supreme Court and the Struggle for Racial Equality* (New York: Oxford University Press, 2004).

144 *"the old Brady place":* The title to this farm is in the author's possession.

144 *movement's handbook:* Thomas Brady, *Black Monday* (Greenwood, MS: Association of Citizens' Councils, 1955); and William P. Hustwit, "Thomas P. Brady," in Center for the Study of Southern Culture, *Mississippi Encyclopedia,* April 13, 2018, https://mississippiencyclopedia.org/entries/thomas-p-brady/.

144 *at the courthouse:* Notice about Citizens' Council meeting at the courthouse, *Prentiss Headlight,* July 11, 1955. For estimate of membership, see Numan V. Bartley, *The New South, 1945–1960* (Baton Rouge: Louisiana State University Press, 1995), 199. On the Citizens' Councils, see Neil R. McMillen, *The Citizens' Council: Organized Resistance to the Second Reconstruction, 1954–64* (Urbana: University of Illinois Press, 1971); and Clive Webb, ed., *Massive Resistance: Southern Opposition to the Second Reconstruction* (New York: Oxford University Press, 2005).

145 *acts of terrorism:* NAACP, *M Is for Mississippi and Murder* (New York: NAACP, 1955), Folder 001459-013-0469, NAACP Papers; John Dittmer, *Local People: The Struggle for Civil Rights in Mississippi* (Urbana: University of Illinois Press, 1995), 1–69; and Gene Roberts and Hank Klibanoff, *The Race Beat: The Press, the Civil Rights Struggle, and the Awakening of a Nation* (New York: Knopf, 2006), 75–85.

145 *"from his teeth":* NAACP, *M Is for Mississippi and Murder,* 4.

145 *"blood all over him":* NAACP, *M Is for Mississippi and Murder,* 5.

146 *an NAACP plot:* NAACP, *M Is for Mississippi and Murder,* 6.

146 *approximately 3,923:* C. R. Darden, Jackson, MS, September 29, 1956, to Gloster B. Current, NAACP, New York, NY; "Memorandum from Gloster B. Current to Mr. Wilkins RE Dr. F. H. Dunn," October 9, 1956; and "Unofficial Figures, Table 34, Mississippi Registration Statistics," which includes population in Jefferson Davis County over twenty-one in 1950, all in Folder 001471-002-0055, NAACP Papers. These documents contain two estimates from two men working in the Jackson NAACP office. C. R. Darden said the county "had 1300 [Black voters] registered and now there are about 50." Medgar Evers said the figures were "1100 reduced to 60." In public documents, the NAACP usually said almost 1,300 reduced to around 100. The estimate of the white Jefferson Davis County population over twenty-one in 1950 was 3,847, making Black residents of voting age the majority.

146 *to register successfully:* Larkin Davis served as circuit clerk from 1944 until 1952. When he ran for reelection in 1947, no one ran against him, suggesting that white voters had not noticed any increase in Black voting at that point.

147 *a moderating influence:* "Report of Rev. H. D. Darby," Mississippi Sovereignty Commission. James Featherston, "Good Neighborliness, Prentiss' Proudest Boast," Jackson *Clarion-Ledger/Jackson Daily News,* January 16, 1955, called the Prentiss Institute a public and private school in 1955, but he also argued incorrectly that the county had merged its Black high schools into the Prentiss Institute. In 1954, Jefferson Davis County opened its first public Black high school, Carver High in Bassfield. This school had been in the planning stages since at least 1952. See "Notice for Bids," *Prentiss Headlight,* May 29, 1952.

147 *after her husband:* The Black elementary school in Prentiss was also called J. E. Johnson, and it is still open.

147 *member of the NAACP:* Prentiss NAACP Minutes. Between 1941 and 1943, before he was a member, A. L. Johnson wrote the national NAACP for advice and collected money for the organization at meetings of the Sixth Educational District Teachers' Association, the Mississippi Association of Teachers in Colored Schools, and the Committee of One Hundred. See Johnson letters in Folder 001512-009-0183, NAACP Papers.

147 *a "beehive":* For the Prentiss Institute as a "hot bed [*sic*] of NAACP activity," see "NAACP, Jefferson Davis County, Prentiss, MS, Integration Organization," Memorandum from Zack J. Van Landingham, December 15, 1958, SCR ID# 2-52-0-4-1-1-1, Mississippi Sovereignty Commission Online, MDAH. For the Prentiss Institute as a "beehive for NAACP activities," see Albert Jones, Director, Mississippi Sovereignty Commission, February 20, 1963, to Governor Ross Barnett, Jackson, MS, SCR ID# 2-52-0-32-1-1-1, Mississippi Sovereignty Commission Online, MDAH.

147 *across the state:* NAACP, "All Because We Wanted to Vote" [sponsored message], *Washington Post,* July 26, 1957, copy in Folder 001471-002-0055, NAACP Papers.

147 *Daniel's satisfaction:* Affidavits from rejected Jefferson Davis County voters are in Folder 001475-027-0130, NAACP Papers.

147 *100 in 1956:* NAACP flyer and advertisement, "Why Reverend H. B. [*sic*] Darby Went to Court," Folder 001471-002-0055, NAACP Papers.

147 *to cast ballots:* The NAACP cites Governor James P. Coleman in a speech before the House Judiciary Committee on February 6, 1957, as the source of these statistics in "Why Reverend H. B. [*sic*] Darby Went to Court."

147 *allow any:* "Negroes Claim Can't Vote in 31 Counties," *Jackson Daily News,* December 9, 1958, clipping in Folder 001471-002-0055, NAACP Papers.

148 *voting rights case:* "Negroes Test Ballot Laws: Jeff Davis Minister Seeking Injunction," *Jackson Daily News,* March 17, 1958.

148 *courage to fight:* C. R. Darden, Jackson, MS, September 29, 1956, to Gloster B. Current, NAACP, New York, NY; "Memorandum from Gloster B. Current to Mr. Wilkins RE Dr. F. H. Dunn," October 9, 1956, both in Folder 001471-002-0055, NAACP Papers.

148 *in another county:* "NAACP to Appeal Its Loss over State Voter Law," *Laurel Leader-Call,* November 7, 1958, clipping in SCR ID# 2-5-1-59-1-1-1; "Report of Rev. H. D. Darby," October 14, 1958, SCR ID# 4-2-0-3-1-1-1; and "NAACP, Jefferson Davis County, Prentiss, MS, Integration Organization," Memorandum from Zack J. Van Landingham, December 15, 1958, SCR ID# 2-52-0-4-1-1-1, all in Mississippi Sovereignty Commission Online, MDAH; and Armstrong and Bell, *Autobiography of a Freedom Rider,* 34–35.

148 *favor of Daniel:* For the text of the *Darby v. Daniel* decision, see "Darby v. Daniel," *Justia US Law,* https://law.justia.com/cases/federal/district-courts/FSupp/168/170/1981875/.

148 *not to appeal:* I could not find a record in the NAACP files specifically referencing why they decided not to appeal, but in general, the legal team was brutally strategic about their use of resources. The following reports demonstrate state-level Mississippi NAACP officials, including Medgar Evers, pressing onward with a strategy of

engaging the new US Civil Rights Commission: "NAACP, Prentiss, Mississippi," Memorandum from Zack J. Van Landingham, February 11, 1959, SCR ID# 2-52-0-9-1-1-1; "NAACP, Prentiss, Mississippi," Memorandum from Zack J. Van Landingham, February 18, 1959, SCR ID# 2-52-0-11-1-1-1; and "NAACP, Prentiss, Mississippi," Memorandum from Zack J. Van Landingham, March 13, 1959, SCR ID# 2-52-0-12-1-1-1, all in Mississippi Sovereignty Commission Online, MDAH.

149 *"at Prentiss":* "NAACP, Prentiss, Mississippi," Memorandum from Zack J. Van Landingham, February 18, 1959, SCR ID# 2-52-0-11-1-1-1.

149 *1948 to 1954:* Minutes of Prentiss NAACP chapter, 1948–1954, SCR ID# 2-25-0-8-1-1-1; and James W. Daniel, Circuit Court, Jefferson Davis County, February 7, 1959, to Zack J. Van Landingham, State Sovereignty Commission, Jackson, SCR ID# 2-52-0-7-1-1-1, both in Mississippi Sovereignty Commission Online, MDAH.

149 *voting application:* Armstrong says Daniel was in touch with the Mississippi Sovereignty Commission in 1956 and that he rejected all applications from suspected NAACP members. I can find no evidence in the MSC files that Daniel was talking to MSC officials before 1958, but Armstrong may have other sources. See Armstrong and Bell, *Autobiography of a Freedom Rider,* 32–33.

149 United States v. James Daniel: Hearing transcripts, copies of rejected voter registration forms, names of witnesses, affidavits, and other materials are in the two boxes of records for *United States v. James Daniel, Circuit Court Clerk and Registrar, Jefferson Davis County, Mississippi; and State of Mississippi* 1961 Case No. 1655 at NARA-A.

149 *to retaliate:* "Roster of Jeff Davis County Negroes Who Are Complainants in Federal Case," *Prentiss Headlight,* December 21, 1961.

149 *it had raised:* On the civil rights movement in the Piney Woods area more broadly, see William Sturkey, *Hattiesburg: An American City in Black and White* (Cambridge, MA: Belknap Press/Harvard University Press, 2019), 234–309; and Patricia Michelle Boyett, *Right to Revolt: The Crusade for Racial Justice in Mississippi's Central Piney Woods* (Jackson: University Press of Mississippi, 2015).

151 *"left the vicinity":* Virgil Downing, "Report on Church Burning in Adams County," July 20, 1964, SCR ID# 2-63-1-119-1-1-1, Mississippi Sovereignty Commission Online, MDAH. In an undated clipping, the *Prentiss Headlight* described bombings of Black churches in Mississippi as "put-up jobs planned by demons hell-bent on passing so-called civil rights legislation."

151 *at last apply:* Photographs of voter registration in Prentiss, Mississippi, in August 1965 and accompanying captions about the work of federal registrars there appear in Winfred Moncrief Photograph Collection, MDAH, https://da.mdah.ms.gov/moncrief/image.php?display=search&keyword=Voter%20registrationMississippiPrentiss.

152 *now also gone:* The Twenty-Fourth Amendment to the Constitution, ratified in 1964, outlawed the poll tax for federal elections. In 1966, a panel of federal judges declared Mississippi's poll tax, the last surviving state poll tax, unconstitutional.

152 *Magnolia Motel rooms:* Moncrief photograph of Joe Ella Moore is online at https://da.mdah.ms.gov/moncrief/image.php?display=item&item=339.

152 *suddenly resigned:* Kermit Hathorn, Prentiss, April 20, 1970, to Willie Fortenberry, President, Jefferson Davis County Board of Supervisors, *Minutes of the Board of Su-*

pervisors, vol. 26, p. 734. His stated reasons were somewhat unclear: "ill health in the family, and better economic conditions available."

152 *a special election: Minutes of the Board of Supervisors, Jefferson Davis County,* ledger 26, April 6, 1970, 734–37, including documents with dates April 20 to April 24, 1970. To make up for the fact that the sheriff got paid through fees, fines, and tax collections that varied over the year, on May 4, 1970, the board also appointed Oury Berry county patrol officer at a salary of $200 a month until the new elected sheriff began his duties. *Minutes of the Board of Supervisors, Jefferson Davis County,* ledger 26, May 4, 1970, 20. These ledgers are kept in the Jefferson Davis County chancery clerk's office in Prentiss.

152 *on the ballot:* Interestingly, Spencer Puckett, one of the state police officers who had helped my grandfather shoot Versie Johnson, also ran for sheriff in this special election.

152 *Wardell Gray:* Hon. Bennie G. Thompson, "Honoring Wardell Gray," *Congressional Record,* January 16, 2018, E43.

153 *published photographs: Prentiss Headlight,* May 28, 1970.

153 *"rub it in":* Mrs. F. A. Parker, "News, Views, and Comments," *Prentiss Headlight,* January 29, 1970. After F. A. Parker died in 1958, Ruth Parker ran the paper herself, serving as editor and publisher. She sold the paper around the time she published this article.

153 *got involved:* All these men served as board members of Prentiss Christian and all of them likely had children or grandchildren who attended.

154 *Jefferson Davis Academy:* Notice about meeting on the Jefferson Davis Academy on January 27, 1970, at 7 p.m. at the courthouse in *Prentiss Headlight,* January 22, 1970; and Holly Cochran, "Prentiss Christian School Celebrates 50 Years," *Prentiss Headlight,* February 28, 2020, https://www.prentissheadlight.com/2020/02/28/prentiss-christian-school-celebrates-50-years/. See also the notice about the January opening of a private school called Tri-County Christian Academy, *Prentiss Headlight,* January 15, 1970. This school was originally in the settlement of Old Hebron in northwestern Jeff Davis County near the border with Lawrence and Simpson Counties, but it soon moved to Hebron in Lawrence County.

154 *almost entirely Black:* White kids from low-income families often received scholarships to attend segregation academies.

155 *not that violent:* My figures here are from the Equal Justice Initiative, *Lynching in America: Confronting the Legacy of Racial Terror: County Data Supplement,* February 7, 2020, and the interactive map online at https://lynchinginamerica.eji.org/explore/mississippi. Covington County, an older county that gave up some of its territory to make Jeff Davis, had zero lynchings, allowing as always for the fact that some might be discovered with further research. It is one of four Mississippi counties in which there were no reported lynchings.

155 *became president:* "A Concurrent Resolution."

155 *case was filed:* "Jefferson Davis County, Mississippi," Box 24, John Doar Papers, Seeley G. Mudd Manuscript Library, Special Collections, Princeton University, Princeton, NJ. One of the teachers got a job elsewhere before he could be reinstated.

155 *organization's president:* In June 2021, I met Duane Johnson at Mitchell Gamblin's memorial service.

156 *"most pressing problems":* Bryant Simon, *The Hamlet Fire: A Tragic Story of Cheap Food, Cheap Government, and Cheap Lives* (New York: New Press, 2017), 15.

157 *for Cadillac:* Charlie Dumas interview, June 21, 2021, Prentiss, MS.

157 *humid summers:* Therese Apel, "Drug Agents Find $70M in Marijuana in Jefferson Davis County," Jackson *Clarion-Ledger,* September 11, 2018, https://www.clarionledger.com/story/news/local/2018/09/11/drug-agents-find-50-million-marijuana-jefferson-davis-county/1262947002/; and Jessica Bowman, "Possibly Largest Pot Bust in Mississippi History," *WLBT 3 Jackson,* August 18, 2017, https://www.wlbt.com/story/36163836/possibly-largest-pot-bust-in-mississippi-history/.

157 *567 "producers":* "Jefferson Davis County, Mississippi County Profile," *USDA Census of Agriculture,* 2017, https://www.nass.usda.gov/Publications/AgCensus/2017/Online_Resources/County_Profiles/Mississippi/cp28065.pdf.

158 *"15 Guns":* A raffle flyer listing which gun would be given away which day and a statement of the rules were posted online at the Prentiss Christian School website before the December 2019 event, where I downloaded them.

158 *Charlie Dumas:* Interview with Charlie Dumas, Prentiss City Hall, Prentiss, MS, June 21, 2021.

158 *declining population:* The 2020 census counted 976 people in Prentiss. For the first time in the town's history, more Black people lived there than white people.

159 *sixty-five or older:* US Census Bureau QuickFacts, Jefferson Davis County, MS, estimates for 2021 based on 2020 census numbers, https://www.census.gov/quickfacts/fact/table/jeffersondaviscountymississippi/PST040221.

159 *working lives:* Group interview with alumni of Prentiss Normal and Industrial Institute, March 26, 2019, Prentiss, MS. I am grateful to alumna Janice Armstrong for setting up this interview as well as a tour of the Rosenwald Building and the 1907 House.

159 *"black your face":* Lunch on December 4, 2019, at Big Boy Buffet, a short-lived restaurant in Prentiss, MS.

EPILOGUE: UNWRITTEN HISTORY

160 Lose Your Mother: Saidiya Hartman, *Lose Your Mother* (New York: Farrar, Straus and Giroux, 2007), 18.

162 *to half days:* When Sheriff Grubbs, who served from 1960 to 1964, had trouble finding an office manager, my grandmother worked for him for a while beginning in April 1961. Working as my grandfather's office manager launched Grace Berry's own career as a county worker, as a staff person in the sheriff and tax collector's office, and in the chancery clerk's office.

162 *still owed:* Dates for this transaction, which included all surface rights and half the mineral rights (the other half had already been sold), are from the deeds registered on June 17 and 21, 1952, Jeff Davis chancery clerk's office, Prentiss, MS.

ILLUSTRATION CREDITS

1. Grace Elizabeth Hale and Oury Berry
Author's collection

1. Postcard of Prentiss, Mississippi

Author's collection

2. Timber workers near a steam skidder

Steam skidder photograph, M134 Goodyear Yellow Pine Company Photographs Collection, Historical Manuscripts, The University of Southern Mississippi

2. The Prentiss Institute class of 1938

Courtesy of the Archives and Records Services Division, Mississippi Department of Archives and History

3. The Prentiss Institute's Rosenwald Building

Courtesy of the Archives and Records Services Division, Mississippi Department of Archives and History

3. The Magee family

Courtesy of the Archives and Records Services Division, Mississippi Department of Archives and History

4. Versie Johnson's birth certificate

Author's collection

4. Versie Johnson's World War II draft registration card

Author's collection

5. Versie Johnson's death certificate

Author's collection

5. Postcard of the Jefferson Davis County Courthouse

Louisiana-Mississippi News Co. of McComb, MS / E. C. Kropp Co. of Milwaukee, WI. From the collection of Keith Vincent.

6. Oury Berry and Grace Keene Berry

Author's collection

6. Oury Berry and officers outside the Jefferson Davis County Jail

Author's collection

7. Oury Berry's Jefferson Davis County sheriff's badge

Author's collection

7. Prentiss Christian School football field

Photograph by William Wylie

8. Federal examiner C. A. Phillips and Joe Ella Moore

Courtesy of the Archives and Records Services Division, Mississippi Department of Archives and History

8. Downtown Prentiss, Mississippi

Photograph by William Wylie

INDEX

activism, 151–153, 155–156. *See also* civil
   rights movement; voting rights
   before and after Johnson's lynching,
     137–141
   anti-lynching, xix, 101–102, 135–136
African Methodist Episcopal (AME)
   Church, 148–149
aging population, 159
agriculture
   Black landowners and, 6–7
   cotton, 11–12, 42, 50–51, 92
   decline of, 156–157
   federal price control and, 146
   federal relief programs and, 92, 93,
     103–104
   in the Piney woods, 3–4
   renting in, 40–41
   sharecropping, 16, 40
Alabama Dry Dock and Shipbuilding
   Company, 73
alcohol, 66
   bootlegging, 77
   law enforcement control and, 68, 128
   legislation as control method, 68
   whiskey tax in sheriffs' income and,
     84–85
Alcorn college, 30–31, 32
*Alexander v. Holmes County Board of Edu-
   cation,* 153
Ambrose, Wood. *See* Wood, Ambrose

*An American Dilemma: The Negro Problem
   and Modern Democracy* (Myrdal),
   79–81
Anders, Odell, 151
anti-abortion laws, 162
Arbery, Ahmaud, 161
Armstrong, D. D., 73
Armstrong, Mabel Walker, 149, 155
Association of Southern Women for the
   Prevention of Lynching, 101

Baggett, Jack, 15–16, 48
Baggett, Rachel, 15–16, 48
Baggett, William Pickens, 15
Baldwin, James, xvii
Baltimore Afro-American (newspaper), 98,
   99, 102, 118
Bank of Blountville, 30, 106–107
Barnes, Hannah, 38
Barnes, John E., 147
Barnes, Willie, 105–106, 107,
   110
Bass, Clifford, 160
Berry, Abner Wilkes, 14
Berry, Albert Gallatin, 14
Berry, Arlene, 73
Berry, David, 11–14
Berry, Edith Ann Polk, 13–14
Berry, Effie, 72
Berry, German, 11–14

Berry, Grace, xxii–xxv, xxx
    marriage of, 70
    move of to Prentiss, 141
    office management by, 84
    opposition of to running for sheriff, 65
    as registrar, 61
    retirement of, 162
Berry, Guy Oury, 121
    author's childhood experiences of,
        xxii–xxv, 162–164
    barber shop of, 70–71
    birth of, 17
    bonus received by, 133
    campaigns of for sheriff, 65–69, 72–73,
        141–143, 152–153
    childhood of, 53–54, 66
    complicity of, 160–165
    death of, 163
    election of as sheriff, 82–83
    executions under, 88–89
    father's reputation and, 65–67
    as fire marshall, 150
    first version on told to the author,
        xvii–xviii
    on Hartzog's statement, 118, 122–123
    information controlled by, 123–124
    on Johnson, 117–118
    Johnson story problems, 123–124
    manslaughter charges against, 133
    marriage of, 70
    military experience of, 69–70
    mob's ultimatum and, 125–129
    move of to Prentiss, 141
    newspaper versions of Johnson lynch-
        ing, xviii–xxi
    participation of in Johnson's death,
        130–132
    public addressed by, 127–128
    reputation of, 65–66, 72–73
    reputation protection by, 128–129
    retirement of, 162–164
    Sanford Dairy and, 71–72, 141
    second term of as sheriff, 141–143
    second version on told to the author,
        xviii–xxi
    in segregationism, 149–151
    white supremacy supported by,
        134–135
Berry, Henry (Harry), 13–14
Berry, Henry Jackson, 14, 20, 65–66, 104, 143
Berry, Jemima, 11–14
Berry, Jimmy, 70
Berry, Joan, 70, 83, 118
Berry, John, 11–14
Berry, John (2nd), 11–14
Berry, John L., 38–39, 41
Berry, Lula Brady, 66, 143
Berry, Martha, 38
Berry, Prentiss Webb, 38–39
Berry, P. W. "Prent," 8, 9, 14, 38, 40–41,
    58, 65
Berry, Richard Talley, 38
Berry, R. R., 21
Berry, Susannah, 11–14
Berry, W. S., 59, 61
Berry, Zilla Huckaby, 13–14
Berry's Barber Shop, 70–71
Bethea, Rainey, 114
"Big Boy Leaves Home" (Wright), 53–55
Bilbo, Theodore, 77–78, 101
Black Boy (Wright), 53
Black Monday (Brady), 144
"Black Monday" speeches (Brady), 144
Black people
    activism by, 137–141
    assault and rape of, 37–39
    autonomy of, 27–29, 36
    burial insurance for, 41–43
    common last names among, 16, 28, 45
    communities built by, xxviii, 5–6,
        26–29, 36
    dealings with white people and, 31–33,
        39–41, 59–60, 85–86, 113–114
    effects of employment on, 18–19
    independence of, 30–37
    invisibility of in records, xxxi–xxxiii,
        14–16, 44–46
    landownership by, 27, 28
    migration from the South by, 87
    occupations of, 18–19, 150
    separate world of, 26–43
    World War II and, 73–79
    Wright on, 52–55
boll weevil, 42
bootlegging, 77
    Franklin and Fortenberry in, 104–115

Oury on, 82–83
as white men's prerogative, 96, 105
Bourn, Henry, 72
Bozeman, J. S., 29
Brady, Pickens, 72
Brady, Thomas, 72
Brady, Thomas Pickens, 144
Broom, "Uncle" Dock, 89
Brown, Michael, 161
Brown v. Board of Education, xxx, xxxiv, 143–144, 161
Brown v. Mississippi, 81, 96–97, 111
Bruce, Blanche K., 28
Bryant, Roy, 145–146
burial insurance, 41–43
Burroughs, Fred, 106
Butterfield Lumber Company, 49

Camp Claiborne, 76
Camp McCain, 77–78
Camp Shelby, 73
Camp Shenando, 75
Camp Van Dorn, 73
cannabis, 157
Carnegie Corporation, 80
Carolina Sandhills, 11
Castile, Philando, 161
Cathy, Truett, xxii
CBD oil, 157
Census of Agriculture, 157
Chance, Curtis, 128, 143
cheap, system of, 156–159
Chicago Daily Tribune (newspaper), 120
Chicago Defender (newspaper), 78
Chicago Tribune (newspaper), 121
Chickasaw, 13
Chick-fil-A, xxii
childbirth, 46–47
Choctaws, 3–4, 5, 6, 13, 17
Christian, "Uncle" Jim, 98
church bombings, 135, 150–151, 155
"Citizens and Taxpayers of Jefferson Davis County," petitions to, 140
Citizens' Councils, 144–145, 147–150
citizenship rights, 27–28, 159, 161–162
education and, 32
Vardaman on, 30

white men as hands of the law and, 103–104
Civilian Military Training Camp, 69
civil rights. *See also* citizenship rights; voting rights
backlash against, 27–29, 150–151
criminal procedures and, 81–82
fight against, xxxiv–xxxv
history of, xxxii–xxxiv
investigations on, xxxi
law enforcement abuse of, 94–95
vigilantism used against, 21–25
white *vs.* Black, 127–129
who gets them?, xxxv
Civil Rights Committee, 134
Civil Rights Congress, 118, 131
civil rights movement, xxx, xxxiii, xxxiv
fight against, xxxiv–xxxv
voting rights and, 138–141
white backlash against, 134–135
Clarion-Ledger (newspaper), 21, 78, 94, 108, 120, 123
Colmer, William, 100
Committee of Onne Hundred, 138
Congress of Racial Equality (CORE), 150
conservatism, 156–159
Cook, R. C., 41–42
Cooper, Carrie, 57
Cooper, Clara Baggett, 15, 47, 48, 57
Cooper, James, 15, 48, 57
Cooper, Lizzie, 16
Cooper, Minnie, 57
cotton gin, 11–12, 29, 72
cotton production, 11–12, 42, 50–51
federal price control and, 146
in World War I, 92
Courts, Gus, 145, 146
COVID-19 pandemic, 119–120, 159
criminal justice system, 81–82, 96–97, 125–127. *See also* law enforcement
all-white juries in, 109–110
confessions in, 111
The Crisis (magazine), 78
Curtis, Hugh, 97
Cutler, James Elbert, xix

Dale, Fred, 57–58
Dale, Joe, 106, 149

Dale, Nona, 57–58
Dale, Sebe, 113, 114–115
Daniel, James, 147, 148–149, 153
Darby, H. D., 148–149
Darby v. Daniel, xxix, 148–149
Davidson, T. E., 21
Davis, Larkin, 146
deforestation, xxvii, 4–5, 9, 17, 156–157
Delphia, 37–38, 40
Democratic Party, 67, 156
demographics, xxix, 67–68, 159
Detroit race riot, 78
D'Lo, Mississippi, 60–62, 116
dogs, tracking with, 93–94, 123–124, 133
Dorroh, Shorty, 98, 99
Dorsey, George, 105
Dorsey, Mae Murray, 105
Down Home Cookin' (Parker), xxx
Downing, Virgil, 150–151
Du Bois, W.E.B., 52
Duckett, Alfred, 76
Duck Hill lynchings, 90–100
    effects of, 101–103
    newspaper coverage of, 116
Dumas, Charlie, 158
Dyer Anti-Lynching Bill, xix, 100–101

Earle, Willie, 118
Eastland, James O., 144
economic decline, 156–159
economic independence, 27–28
education. *See also* schools
    in Johnson's family, 51–52
    Mississippi spending on, 77
    rates of for Black children, 30
    Vardaman on, 30
EJI. *See* Equal Justice Initiative (EJI)
electric chair, 112–113
entertainment, 53–55
entitlement, xxxvi, xxxvii
Equal Justice Initiative (EJI), xxxi, 20, 24
"The Ethics of Living Jim Crow" (Wright), 87
Ethridge, Mark, 79
Eubanks, Ralph, 119
Evers, Medgar, xxiii, 148
executions, 88–89
    of Fortenberry, 113–115
    legal *vs.* lynching, 96–97, 99

methods in, 112–113
    viewing of, 114–115
Exposé, Paul, 86

family histories
    author's, 10–14
    Berry family reputation and, 65–66
    Black, 14–16
    documentation of, 10, 14–16, 44–46
    racial mixing in, 37–39
    sharecropping life and, 50–51
    violence in Black, 26–29
    white, 10–14
    white supremacy and, xxxvii, xxxviii,
        xxxi
FBI, xxviii, 118, 126, 131–132, 149, 150
federal government
    citizenship rights and, 27–28
    cotton price controls and, 146
    Dyer Anti-Lynching Bill, xv, 100–101
    entitlement programs, 159
    Gavagan-Wagner anti-lynching bill,
        100–101
    integration actions by, 134–135
    Johnson lynching and, 118
    Native American removals by, 4, 13
    relief programs, 92, 93, 103–104
    Southern Homestead Act (1866), 6
    Voting Rights Act (1965), xxx
    voting rights enforcement by, 151–153
Federal Road, 12
Fifteenth Amendment, 30, 152
Florida, Claude Neal lynching in, 95–96
Floyd, George, 161
Forrest Health, 157
Fort Benning, 75–76
Fort Dix, 75
Fortenberry, Hilton, 106–115
Fourteenth Amendment, 30
Foxworth, O. J., 107
Franklin, Jerome, 105–114, 125
"friends and neighbors" voting, 72–73

Gamblin, Mitchell, xxxii, 119–122,
        124–125, 132, 145, 155
gambling, 18–19, 20, 86
    Johnson charged with, 62
    Knight and, 58–59

Garner, Eric, 161
Gavagan-Wagner anti-lynching bill, 100–101
G.I. Bill, 35
Godbolt, A. J., 139
"going among strangers" in World War II, 74–75
graffiti, 159
Gray, A. D., 139
Gray, Mary Otis, 139
Gray, Wardell, 139, 149, 152–153, 155
Gray, Will, 139
Great Depression, 42–43, 85, 92, 103–104
Great Valley Road, 10–11
Great Wagon Road, 12
Green, Ernest, 76, 118
Green Grove Missionary Baptist Church, 41
Greggs, James, 75
gun laws, 161–162

Hall, Felix, 75–76
Hartzog, Essie, 139
Hartzog, Ford, 140
Hartzog, Isaac, 139
Hartzog, Mary, 139
Hartzog, Virginia, 118, 122–123, 125
Hartzogg, Alice, 38, 39
Hartzogg, Bill, 38
Hartzogg, Charlotte, 38, 39
Hathorn, Kermit, 152
Hawthorn, Dudley, 147
health care, 46–47, 157
Herrin, George, 40
history
    centrality of white violence in, xxxi–xxxv
    exposing lies in, xxxvi
    inner lives of people and, 55–56
    lies in telling, 160–165
    as personal and intimate, xxxvi–xxxvii
    as progress, xxxv–xxxvi
    reckoning with the past and, 162–165
Holland, J. C., 73
Holloway, Cleveland, 110
Holloway, Genora, 147
homesteading, 6–7

Hopkins, Andy, xx, 117–118, 128–129, 130, 132, 160
    manslaughter charges against, 133

income inequality, 137
Indian Removal Act (1830), 13
Ingalls Shipyard, 73
integration, xxii

Jackson Advocate (newspaper), 118, 131
Jackson Army Air Base, 73, 76
Jefferson Davis Academy, 153–154
Jefferson Davis Community Hospital, 157
Jefferson Davis County, Mississippi, xxi–xxiii, 155–156
    Black communities in, xxxi, xxxviii, 5–6, 26–29
    creation of, 5
    decline in, 156–159
    demographics of, xxix
    disfranchisement in, 67–68
    economic decline in, 29
    first lynchings in, 20–25
    graffiti in, 159
    Great Depression and, 103–104
    history of, xxxi
    invisibility of Black people in, xxxi–xxxiii
    landscape of, xxvii–xxix
    lynchings in, 23–25, 27
Jett, Henrietta, 46–47
J. H. Williams and Sons, 30
Jim Crow
    activism against, 137–141
    all-white juries and, 109–110
    Black *vs.* white versions on, xxxi–xxxiii
    business models under, 42–43
    defiance of, 75–78, 85–88
    documentation of lives under, 56–57
    government-sanctioned lying in, 27–28
    risk of talking to white people under, 31
    underground violence supporting, xxxi–xxxv
J. J. Newman Lumber Company, 8, 9, 27
Johnson, A. L., 147
Johnson, Bertha LaBranche, 28, 30–31, 138, 146–147
Johnson, Central, 43, 120, 131, 132

Johnson, Charles, 28
Johnson, Cora, 51–52
Johnson, Delphia, 38–39, 40
Johnson, Doretha, 39
Johnson, Duane, 155
Johnson, Ella, 47, 51–52
Johnson, Estus, 28, 38, 39–43
Johnson, Frankie Weathers, 42–43
Johnson, Gertrude, 50, 51, 52, 56, 58, 59,
    136–137
    death certificate information from, 62
Johnson, Jesse, 47, 52
Johnson, Jonas Edward, 28, 138
    founding of Prentiss Institute by, 29–34
Johnson, Joshua, 36
Johnson, Lizzie Cooper, 16, 45, 136–137
    marriage and life of, 48–52
    move to Prentiss, 58
    move to Rankin County, 57
    Versie's birth and, 46–48
Johnson, Lyndon, 151
Johnson, Mack, 57
Johnson, Margurette, 36
Johnson, Paul, 77, 113, 142–143
Johnson, Rosie Hawthorne, 34, 39–43
Johnson, Sandy, 37–38
Johnson, Versie, xxxviii, 165
    arrests of, 61–62
    birth of, 17, 46–48
    Black witnesses on, 118–120
    body of picked up, 43
    Census on, 52, 56–57
    childhood of, 55
    costs of killing, 133–135
    cover-up of truth about, 160–165
    cross drawn by, 121, 124
    death certificate of, 62, 131
    Duck Hill lynchings and, 90–91
    education of, 36–37
    effects of lynching of, 133–159
    escape attempt by, xvi, 120, 124, 130, 132
    first version told to the author,
        xvii–xviii
    genealogy of, 14–16
    Hartzog on, 118–122–123
    impact of lynching of, xxxii, 29
    impact on family of lynching of,
        136–137

lynching of, 130–131, 132
    mob's ultimatum on, 125–129
    move to D'Lo, 60–62, 116
    move to Prentiss, 29
    move to Rankin County, 57
    move to Simpson County, 60–62
    newspapers on, xviii–xxi
    official records on, 44–46, 52, 56–57,
        117–132
    physical description of, 61
    rape accusation against, 117, 120–122,
        124–125
    schooling of, 51–52, 57
    Thompson on, 121–122
    timeline problems in story on, 123–124
    versions of name of, 44–46
    Wood's murder compared with, 21–22
    wounds to, 131
Johnson, William, 16, 45
    death of, 58
    marriage and life of, 48–52
    move to Rankin County, 57
    Versie's birth and, 46–48
Johnson Funeral Home and Burial Associa-
    tion, xxvii, 42, 131, 133
Johnson School. See Prentiss Institute
Jonesboro, Mississippi, xxii
Justice Department, US, xxxii, 149

Keene, Grace. See Berry, Grace
Keene, Virgil, 22
Kemper County, Mississippi, 155
Kester, Howard "Buck," 95–96, 100,
    102–103
Key, V. O., 72–73
King, L. W., 160
KKK. See Ku Klux Klan (KKK)
Knight, Eula Mae, 45–46, 50, 52, 57–60,
    136–137
Knight, Reggie, 45–46, 58–60, 61
Knight, Reggie, Jr., 45–46
Knight, Velma, 45–46
Kruger, Donald, 149, 153, 154
Ku Klux Klan (KKK), xxii, 23, 27, 144,
    155, 164–165

Labor Battalion, 326th, 58
landownership, 27

Black, 6–7, 27, 28
by Estus Johnson, 43
Great Depression and, 104
NAACP membership and, 139–140
Native American removals and, 13
Lang, Charlie, 76, 118
law enforcement. *See also* Berry, Guy Oury
abuse of power by, 94–95
assumption of guilt by, 49
authority of, 68, 83–85, 127–129
Black voting rights and, 138–141
dogs in, 93–94, 123–124, 133
in Duck Hill lynchings, 93–100
executions and, 88–89
FBI ties to, 131–132
"forms of the law" and, 96–97
killings by, 161
in lynchings, 97, 130–132, 160–165
in maintaining white supremacy, 67–68
Myrdal on, 80–81
new structures for, 110
options of against mob threats,
125–129
personal politics and, 72–73
pressure on to solve crimes, 95–96
schools stripped of equipment and, 154
sheriffs' salaries and, 84–85
suspicions of toward Johnson, 59
torture by, 94–95, 96
White Citizens' Councils and, 144–145
white men as the hands of, 21–22,
75–78, 103–104, 106–107,
145–146
white supremacy supported by,
134–135
during World War II, 75–78
Lee, George W., 145, 146
Lee Park, xxii
legislation
anti-lynching, xix, 100–102
in covering up violence, 161–162
Dyer Anti-Lynching Bill, xix
Indian Removal Act (1830), 13
Southern Homestead Act (1866), 6
Voting Rights Act (1965), xxx
lies, 160–165
government-sanctioned, 28
history in exposing, xxxvi–xxxvii

law enforcement and, 97, 102
Myrdal on, 80
segregation covered by, 87–88
in vigilantism, 25
Life magazine, 99
Lincoln County, Mississippi, 16
Lipsey, W. T., 72
Lipsey farm, 72, 117–118, 155. *See also*
Johnson, Versie
literacy tests, 77, 147–148
Lockhart, Ernest, 139
Lockhart, Lorraine, xxv
Lucas, Ira Warren, 6
Lucas, Mississippi, 6
lynchings
accountability for, 99–100
activism against, xix, 135–136
of Ambrose Wood, 18–25
Black people's versions of, xxi,
118–122, 124–125
Citizens' Councils and, 145–146
definitions of, xix, 23–24
Duck Hill, 90–100
euphemisms for, 96
executions *vs.*, 96–97, 99
of Franklin, 105–114
investigations of, 95–96, 118, 130–131
in Jefferson Davis County, 20–25, 27
justifications of, 99
law enforcement in, 94–95, 97
as lay enforcement, 76–77
legislation against, xix, 100–102
monument to victims of, xxxiii, 25
of Neal, 95–96
negative publicity from, 90–91,
126–127
numbers of, 23–24, 27, 155
pattern for, 21–22
photographs of, 98–99
rape accusations as cover for, 120–122
reckoning with the past and, 164–165
souvenirs from, 98–99
underground/hidden, xxxii–xxxiii,
90–91, 101–103, 132
versions of stories on, xvii–xxi
during World War II, 75–78

Magee, Fred, 110, 114–115

Magee, Guy, 153, 154
Magee, Gwinn, 164
Magee, H. L. "Fate," 69
Magee, S. Gwinn, 104–105, 106,
    108–109, 112, 113, 125
Magee, Tobias, 33
Magee Courier (newspaper), 61–62
Magee Plantation, 33
Malcolm, Dorothy Dorsey, 105
Malcolm, Roger, 105
maps, viii–ix
Marine Corps, 74
Marshall, Thurgood, 88
Maston, Bud. *See* Wood, Ambrose
Mathison, W. H., 59
Mattison, W. H., 106
McDaniels, Robert "Bootjack," 96–100,
    116
Mchener, Earl Cory, 100
McInnis, J. R., 82, 83
McInnis, Linnie Mae, 162
McInnis, Oddie, 162
McNeal, Lloyd, 76
Memphis Press-Scimitar (newspaper), 99
Meridian Star (newspaper), 21–22
Middle Passage, 26
Middle Passage, second, 15–16
Mikell, Shelby L., Sr., 142, 149
Milan, J. W., 145–146
Mississippi Baptist Seminary, 35
Mississippi Department of Archives and
    History, xxix
Mississippi Federation of Colored Women's
    Clubs, 138
Mississippi Highway Patrol, 131–132
Mississippi Sovereignty Commission, 147,
    150–151
Mississippi State
    alcohol outlawed in, 66
    changes in in shaping residents' lives,
        16–17
    constitution of ratified, 67
    Duck Hill lynchings in, 90–100
    execution methods in, 112–113
    law enforcement authority in, 67–68
    map of south-central, xxiii
    migration into, 10–11
    number of lynchings in, 23, 24

old-growth woods in, 3–5
schooling in, 30
segregationist terrorism in, 145–146
sheriff positions in, 83–85
underground lynchings in, 102–103
viewing of executions in, 114–115
Mississippi State Penitentiary, 62
Mississippi Summer Project, 150
Moore, Joe Ella, 152
Moore's Ford, Georgia, 105
Moore v. Dempsey, 81
Morgan, Sharon, 45–46
Mosson, Rosie, 39
Mr. Carmel, Mississippi, 142
Mt. Carmel school, 30
Mt. Zion school, 30
mulattos, 38
Myrdal, Gunnar, 79–81, 85

NAACP. *See* National Association for the
    Advancement of Colored People
    (NAACP)
NAFTA. *See* North American Free Trade
    Agreement (NAFTA)
Natchez, Mississippi, church bombings
    around, 150–151
National Association for the Advancement
    of Colored People (NAACP)
    after World War II, 139–140
    anti-lynching legislation and, 100–102
    church bombings and, 151
    Darby v. Daniel and, xxix
    on Duck Hill, 100
    Jim Crow cases by, 87–88
    on Johnson lynching, 118
    on lynching, xxxii–xxxiii, 78
    lynching definition by, xix
    lynching investigations by, 95–96
    members of in Mississippi, 138,
        139–140
    Prentiss branch of, 139–140, 147,
        149155
    Prentiss Institute and, 147, 149
    Till lynching and, 145–146
    on underground lynchings, 102–103
    voting rights and, 146, 148–149
    voting roll purges and, 147–148
National Guard, 99, 109

National Memorial for Peace and Justice, xxxiii, 25

Native Americans
  Choctaw, 3–4, 5, 6, 13, 17
  land patents and, 13
  in Piney Woods, 3–4, 17
  removal of, 5, 6

Neal, Claude, 95–96

Negro dogs, 93–94

neoliberalism, 156–159

New Deal, 28, 103–104

News & Observer (newspaper), 102

newspapers
  on Ambrose lynching, 24–25
  on Duck Hill, 116
  on Jim Crow, 87
on Johnson, 117–118, 120–121
  on Johnson lynching, 44–45
  lynching condemned in, 101
  lynching photographs in, 98–99
  negative publicity in, 90–91, 126–127
  truth of white violence hidden by, xviii–xxi, xxxii–xxxiii, 78–79, 111–112, 117–118
  on white men's justice, 21–22

1907 House, xxxi

North American Free Trade Agreement (NAFTA), 157

"open carry" laws, 161–162

Packer, J. J., 38

Palace Drugs, 30

Parchman Farm. *See* Mississippi State Penitentiary

Parish, J. P., 160

Parker, F. A.
  Berry communication with, 128–129
  complicity of, 160
  on Eleanor Roosevelt, 88
  on the race problem, 78–79
  truth of white violence hidden by, 111–112
  on voting rights, 142–143
  on war on the home front, 77
  on the whiskey tax, 84–85
  Work or Fight order by, 82

Parker, Ruth, xxx

Berry communication with, 128–129
complicity of, 160
on Eleanor Roosevelt, 88
on the race problem, 78–79
on school integration, 153
truth of white violence hidden by, 111–112
on voting rights, 142–143
on war on the home front, 77
on the whiskey tax, 84–85

patronage, 39–41, 59–60, 113–114

Pearl and Leaf Rivers Railroad, 8, 29

Pearl Harbor attack, 71

Phillips, L. R., 89

Piney Woods, xxxviii
  author's family settled in, 12–14
  Black communities in, 5–6
  as Black refuge, xxxviii
  changes in in shaping residents' lives, 16–17
  deforestation of, xxviii, 4–5, 9, 17, 156–157
  first Black death in, 6
  as paradise, 3–4
  rural life in, 7–8
  timber companies and, 7, 8–10, 18–19
  white men's justice in, 21–22
  World War II lynchings in, 76–77

Piney Woods Farm School, xxvii

Pittsburgh Courier (newspaper), 118

political participation, 27–28. *See also* civil rights; voting rights

politics, personal nature of, 72–73

Polk, A. H., 106

Polk, Fred "Doc," 105, 107, 110

Polk, Hance, 105–106, 107, 110, 111

Polk, P. J., 139

Polk, Susie, 139

Polk, Z. P., 69

poll taxes, 27, 67, 87, 138, 143, 145, 152

Powell, D. F., 140

Prentiss, Mississippi, xxiii–xxiv
  author's research trips to, xxix–xxxii
  bank robbery in, 106–107
  Black Quarters in, 9, 29
  Black schools in, 30–37
  commerce and segregation in, 85–86

Prentiss, Mississippi, continued
  decline of, 156–159
  effects of World War II in, 73–75
  founding of, 8–10
  integration in, 134–135
  landscape of, xxviii–xxix
  Magnolia Motel, 151, 152
  map of, viii
  NAACP in, 139–140, 147, 149, 155
  networks of families around, 58
  public pool in, 134, 135
  thwarted lynchings of 1940 in, 90–91
  Wood lynching in, 18–25
Prentiss Christian School, 154–155, 157–158
Prentiss Headlight (newspaper), xviii–xxi, 88
  on bank robbery manhunt, 106–107
  Black residents in, xxxi
  on bloodhounds, 123
  on bootleggers in World War II, 77
  building of, xxviii
  campaign ads in, 82
  on Duck Hill, 116
  on Franklin and Fortenberry, 111–112
  on idle Black people, 78, 86
  on Johnson, 117–118, 120, 123
  on Johnson's lynching, 44–45
  lynching condemned in, 101
  on lynching statistics, 27
  owners of, xxx
  petitions in, 140
  on Phillips execution, 89
  public address from Berry in, 127–128
  on the race problem, 78–79
  on school integration, 153
  sheriff campaigns in, 68, 141, 153
  on voting rights, 142–143, 149
Prentiss Institute, xxxi, 28, 119, 146–147
  coffins stored at, 42
  NAACP at, 147, 149, 155
  origins of, 29–37
  voter purges and, 148
Prentiss Methodist Church, 70
Prentiss Normal and Industrial Institute, 158
Prentiss Wholesale Company, 70
prisons, 62, 107–109
Prohibition, 66, 68

protective leagues, 23
Puckett, Spencer, xx, 117–118, 128–129, 130, 132, 160
  manslaughter charges against, 133

railroads, 7, 8–10, 19
rambling, 19
Randolph, A. Philip, 78
Rankin, John F., 78
rape, 101
  accusations of, 22, 31
  Bilbo on increase in, 77–78
  of Black people, 37–39
  Johnson accused of, 117, 120–122, 124–125, 131
  Keene accused of, 22
  likelihood of conviction of, 126–127
  "proof" of, 124–125
  protection of white women in, 122
  relationships *vs.*, 121–122
Reagan, Ronald, 156
Reconstruction, 22, 80
Red Cross, 74
redemption, 23, 80
religion, xxx, 41
  Berry and, 129
  church bombings and, 135, 150–151, 155
  Oury Berry and, 70, 71
  in Prentiss, 9
reparations, xxxvii
Republican Party, 23, 67, 156
Revels, Hiram, 28
Roosevelt, Eleanor, 79, 88
Roosevelt, Theodore, 32
Ruffin, Edwin, 4
rural life, 50–55

Sanford, Flora Etta, 71
Sanford, J. C., 71
Sanford, John, 106, 107
Sanford, John C., 58–59, 104–105
Sanford Dairy, 71–72, 83
schools. *See also* Prentiss Institute
  Black, xxvii, xxxi, xxxiv, 28, 30–37
  equipment stripped from, 154
  fees for, 34, 35
  integration of, 134–135

private, 153–155
property taxes and, 35
public *vs.* private, 34–35
segregation in, 143–144, 153–154, 157–158
unequal funding of, 140
second Middle Passage, 15–16
segregation, xxii, xxxiv–xxxv, 28
activism against, 137–141
alcohol sales and, 68
in bootlegging, 105–106
burial insurance and, 41–43
church bombings and, 150–151, 155
commerce and, 85–86
defiance of, 75–78, 85–88
economic threats to support, 146–147
federal action to end, 134–135
lies in covering up, 161
residential, 38
segregationist movement supporting, 143–146
separate but equal, 134
Supreme Court on, xxx, 143–144, 153
ways around, 153–155
World War II and, 74–79
Seventy-Six Association, 23
sharecroppers, 16, 28, 39
Estus Johnson, 40–43
in the Great Depression, 92
Johnson's family, 48–51
Negro dogs for tracking, 93–94
payment of, 91–92
rhythm of life for, 50–51
Shivers, Jemima, 12–14
Shivers, John, 12–13
shooting the dozens, 53–54
Simpson County, Mississippi, 155
Slater, T. B., 160
slave patrols, 93–94
slavery, 5–6, 26
author's ancestors and, 12
cotton production and, 12
Emancipation and, 6
expansion of in Mississippi, 13
genealogy records and, 14–16
names and, 38
Piney Woods and, 5–6
reckoning with the past and, 164–165

second Middle Passage in, 15–16
slave schedules, 14
slave trade, 15–16, 26
Smith, Lamar, 145
Smith v. Allwright, 87–88, 138, 142
Society of the White Rose, 23
South Carolina, 10, 11–12
Southern Homestead Act (1866), 6
"Southern way of life," xxxii–xxxiii
"stand your ground" laws, 161–162
Strickland, Vance, 108
Student Nonviolent Coordinating Committee (SNCC), 150
Supreme Court, US
on criminal procedures, 81, 96–97
on segregation, xxx, 143–144, 153
on voting rights, xxix, 87–88, 138, 149
Sutton, C. V., 130–131, 160
system of cheap, 156–159

taxation, 84–85
poll taxes, 27, 67, 87, 138, 143, 145, 152
property, schools and, 35
Taylor, Breonna, 161
Terrell, R., 139
terrorism, 145–146
Thompson (Johnson accuser), 121–122, 124, 125
Three Chopped Way, 6, 12, 13
Till, Emmett, 145–146
timber industry, 4–5
Black workers in, 49
deforestation, economic decline, and, xxviii, 4–5, 9, 17, 156–157
effects of on workers' lives, 18–19
land ownership and, 27
mechanization of, 9
railroads and, 7, 8–10
Time magazine, 99, 100
torture, 90–91, 98, 111
by law enforcement, 94–95, 96
negative publicity from, 126–127
To Secure These Rights, 134, 143
Townes, Roosevelt "Red," 95–100, 116
Travis, Dempsey, 75
Treaty of Dancing Rabbit Creek, 13
Tripp, F. W., 153, 154
Truman, Harry S., 134, 142–143

Tuskegee Institute, 31, 32
Tyrone, John, 58–59
Tyrone, Leon, 31, 33, 34
Tyrone, R. E., 160

Uncle Tom's Children (Wright), 53
unemployment, 156–157
United States v. Board of Education of Jefferson Davis County, 155
United States v. James Daniel, 149, 155
uplift model of advancement, 138–139
US Census, 14
    on Bill Cooper, 49
    on Johnson, 52, 56–57, 60–62
US Department of Agriculture, 157
US Department of Justice, 118
Utica Institute, 158

Vardaman, James K., 30
vigilantism
    church bombings and, 135, 150–151, 155
    Franklin and, 107–108
    history of, 21–24
    law enforcement's cooperation with, 94–95
    lies in covering up, 161–165
    lying to cover truth of, 25, 28, 97, 102, 144–146, 161
    pattern of violence in, 23–25
    rape accusations and, 121–122
    reckoning with the past and, 164–165
    segregationist movement and, 144–146, 150–151
    threats of against Johnson, 125–129
    underground/hidden, xxxii–xxxiii, 90–91, 102–103, 161–162
voter registration, 145, 146, 147–150
    federal intervention in, 151–152
    purges of, 147–150
voting rights, 138–141
    backlash against, 27–28
    Darby v. Daniel on, xxv, xxix–xxxii
    demographics and, 67–68
    federal enforcement of, 151–153
    forced reregistration and, 147–150
    lies in covering up denial of, 161

    Mississippi disfranchisement and, 67–68
    poll taxes and, 27, 67, 87, 138, 143, 145, 152
    in primaries, 142–143
    in Reconstruction, 22
    segregationist movement and, 145–146
    sheriff elections and, 142–143
    socioeconomic class and, 150
    Supreme Court on, 87–88
    vigilantism used against, 22–24
Voting Rights Act (1965), xxx, 149, 151, 161

Walker, William, 76
Walton, B. G., 110
Wash, Howard, 76, 118, 126
Washington, Booker T., 31, 32
Watkins mill, 18–19
Well, Ida B., xix
whiskey tax, 84–85
White, Alton, 60–61
White, Ambrose, 152–153
White, Hugh, 109, 142–143
White, Walter, 78, 87, 95–96, 101
White, Willie, 153
Whitecaps, 23
White Citizens' Councils, 144–145, 147–150
white privilege, xxxvi, xxxvii
white supremacy. *See also* voting rights
    Black lives erased in, xxxiii–xxxiv
    class and ability to challenge, 150
    denial of Black humanity in, 165
    documentation of Black lives and, 56–57
    economic decline and, 156
    genealogies and, 14–16
    law enforcement in maintaining, 67–68, 79–82
    lengths taken to preserve, 134–135
    lynchings in supporting, 20–21
    newspapers in hiding the truth of, xx–xxi
    pattern of illegality in, 79–82
    placing yourself within, xxxvi–xxxvii
    rape accusations in, 122
    redemption and, 23
    service in World War II and, 74–79

Whitney, Eli, 11
Williams, Alvin, 119
Williams, E. B., 133, 160
Williams, John, 20
Williams, John Bell, 153
Williamson, W. D., 160
Windham, George S., 91–93
Women's Army Corps (WACS), 74
Wood, Ambrose, 18–25, 29, 106, 112
Woods, David, 75
worker safety, 18–19, 66
Works Progress Administration (WPA), xxix, 28, 110, 113

World War I, 27, 41, 58, 92
World War II, 35, 45, 60–61, 71
    effects of service in, 73–75, 138–139
    Johnson in, 116
    lynchings during, 75–78
    racial conflict in, 75–79
WPA. *See* Works Progress Administration (WPA)
Wright, Edgar, 93–97
Wright, Richard, 52–55, 87